THE HISTORY OF INDIA

THE HISTORY OF INDIA

HENRY MORRIS

GYAN

Published by

GYAN

Gyan Publishing House
5, Ansari Road
Daryaganj, New Delhi-110002
Phone: 011-47034999, 9811692060
E-mail: books@gyanbooks.com

Distribution Network
gyanbooks.com
India, USA, Canada, UK, Australia

ISBN: 978-93-6920-452-6 (PB)

First Published, 1864

2nd Impression 2025

Printed at: Gyan Press, Delhi.

THE HISTORY OF INDIA
Author: HENRY MORRIS

THE

HISTORY OF INDIA.

BY

HENRY MORRIS;

OF THE MADRAS CIVIL SERVICE.

"Spectemur agendo." "Try us by our actions.'

SEVENTH EDITION

Sixty-first Thousand.

MADRAS:

Printed and Published for the Madras School Book Society,

D SOLD AT THE DEPOSITORY, COLLEGE OF FORT SAINT GEO

1870

CONTENTS.

CHAPTER I.

THE COUNTRY, CHARACTER, AND ANCIENT HISTORY OF THE HINDUS.

To A. D. 77.

Pages.

The boundaries of India—Natural features of the country—Description of Hindostan—Basins of the Indus and the Ganges—The Great Desert—Central India—The Deckan—Rivers of Southern India—Vegetable productions of India—Agricultural and mineral productions—Commerce of India—Early civilisation of the Hindus—Stationary character of their institutions—The code of Menu—State of Hindu society in Menu's time—The mode of government—The revenue—Principal changes since the time of Menu—Village communities—Character of the Hindus—Ancient History of India—Origin of the Hindus—The kingdom of Oude—Rama—War of "the Mahabharata"—Hindu states on the Ganges—Kingdom of Magada—Chandragupta—Vikramarka—King Bhoj—History of Southern India—Kingdoms of Pandya and Chola—Smaller states—Salivahana—Uncertainty of the Hindu chronology,.. 1—1

CHAPTER II.

INDIA UNDER THE EARLY MUSSULMAN DYNASTIES.

FROM B. C. 328 TO A. D. 1556.

Expedition of the Persians—of the Greeks—Seleucus—The kingdom of Bactria—The Mahomedan invasion--Mahmud

Pages.

of Ghazni—His last expedition—The siege of Somnat —Mahomed Ghori—Kutb-ud-dien—The Slave Kings—The House of Khilji—The Toghlak dynasty—Mahomed Toghlak; his mad acts—Feroze Shah; his good reign—Tamerlane—The slaughter at Delhi—Anarchy in India—Baber—The first battle of Paniput—Baber's character —The Rajputs—Battle of Sikri, and Baber's victory—Humayun—Shir Shah dethrones him—Shir Shah's useful reign—Humayun recovers the throne—His flight into Persia—His return, restoration, and death............ 12—23

CHAPTER III.

THE GREAT MOGULS.

FROM A. D. 1556 TO A. D. 1744.

Akber—The prime minister, Behram—Akber's long and noble reign—His useful measures—Jehangir—Nur Jehan—Rebellions at the close of the reign—Shah Jehan —His treatment of his sons—Their characters—The Emperor's illness—Struggle between his sons for power —Aurangzib and Morad fight against Dara—Dara's defeat—Aurangzib defeats Shuja—Aurangzib's triumph—Shah Jehan's death—The Mahrattas—Their rise—Their mode of warfare—Sevaji—An example of his treachery and cunning—Wars with the Mahrattas—The Emperor enters the Deckan—His impolitic treatment of the Rajputs—Rebellions—Aurangzib's death—Decay of the Empire—Invasion by Nadir Shah—Massacre at Delhi—Dissolution of the Empire—Rise of independent powers —A new people come to conquer and to rule—State of India under the Mahomedans............................ 24—35

Pages.

CHAPTER IV.

EARLY EUROPEAN SETTLEMENTS IN INDIA.

To A. D. 1744.

Intercourse between India and Europe—The age of maritime adventure—Bartholomew Diaz rounds the Cape of Good Hope—Discovery of America—The first voyage round the Cape to India performed by Vasco de Gama—Cabral's voyage, and contest with the Zamorin—Vasco de Gama's second expedition—Early Portuguese settlements—Alphonso Albuquerque captures Goa and other towns—The Portuguese empire in the East—The Dutch trade with India—The English take a part in the same commerce—The East India Company—Contests between the three rival nations—The massacre of Amboyna—The second East India Company—Union of the two Companies—The settlements at Madras—Bombay—Fort St. David—and Calcutta—The French settlements in India, 36—45

CHAPTER V.

THE RISE OF ENGLISH POWER IN INDIA.

From A. D. 1744 to A. D. 1753.

War between England and France—The French in India—Dupleix—The English in India—Sepoy corps—Labourdonnais takes Madras—Siege of Fort St. David—Petty war in Tanjore—Peace in Europe: but the war continued in India—State of affairs in Southern India—Nazir Jung and Mirzapha Jung—Anwar-ud-dien and Chunda Sahib—Struggle for the thrones at Hyderabad and Arcot—The French take one side, and the English the other—M. Bussy—The French victorious—Salabut Jung made Nizam—Dupleix' triumph and delight—Ma-

Pages.

homed Ali besieged at Trichinopoly—Robert Clive takes Arcot—Gallant defence of that city—Victory at Arnee —Defeat of Rajah Sahib near Madras—Lawrence relieves Trichinopoly—Surrender of the French garrison at Seringham—Chunda Sahib murdered—Lawrence defeats the French at Bahoor—Clive takes Covelong and Chingleput—Returns to England........................ 46—57

CHAPTER VI.

THE BLACK HOLE AND SPEEDY RETRIBUTION.

FROM A. D. 1753 TO A. D. 1757.

Continuation of the war—Truce between the French and English—Clive's return—Gheriah destroyed—Surajah Dowlah—Capture of Calcutta—The Black Hole—Approach of the avenger—Calcutta retaken—The Nabob's army beaten—Peace with the Nabob—Chandernagore taken—Inconsistent behaviour of Surajah Dowlah—Conspiracy against him—Meer Jaffier—The English engage in the plot,—which is nearly defeated by Omichund—His avarice and cunning—He is disgracefully outwitted—The English march towards Moorshedabad—The battle of Plassey—The victory—The English reach the capital —Meer Jaffier is made Nabob—Disappointment and death of Omichund—Murder of Surajah Dowlah,...... 58—70

CHAPTER VII.

CONQUEST OF THE CARNATIC, AND THE TREACHERY OE MEER JAFFIER IN BENGAL.

FROM A. D. 1756 TO A. D. 1760.

Temporary quiet in the Carnatic—Renewal of hostilities —Troops sent to Tinnevelly and Nellore—The French at-

Pages.

tack Trichinopoly,—which is relieved by Capt. Calliaud—Arrival of a French army—Count de Lally—his character—Capture of Fort St. David—Recall of Bussy—Lally invades Tanjore—Siege of Fort St. George—Colonel Coote arrives from England—Captures Wandewash and Carangoly—The battle of Wandewash—The French defeated—they are besieged in Pondicherry—Colonel Forde defeats them in the Northern Circars—Pondicherry taken—Fate of Lally—Shah Alam invades Bahar—Flees before Clive—Meer Jaffer's ingratitude—The Dutch help him—Defeat of the Dutch expedition—Clive leaves Bengal,.. 71—80

CHAPTER VIII.

CHANGES, WARS, AND TROUBLES IN BENGAL.

FROM A. D. 1760 TO A. D. 1767.

Shah Alum invades Bahar again—Ramnarrain is defeated—Siege of Patna—Battle near Patna—Pursuit of the enemy—Death of Meeran—Return of the troops—Deposition of Meer Jaffier—Meer Cossim—The Emperor defeated—Meer Cossim's character—Condition of Bengal—Murder of Ramnarrian—Disputes with the Nabob—The English take Patna—It is retaken by Meer Cossim—Meer Jaffier restored—Battle of Geriah—Monghir captured—Meer Cossim's rage—The English advance—The massacre at Patna—The Nabob flees to Oude—The Emperor, Suja Dowlah, and Meer Cossim against the English—they are defeated—Mutiny among the sepoys—Battle of Buxar—Clive's return—The English receive the sovereignty of Bengal—Reformations in the civil service and the army—Clive suppresses a formidable mutiny—Leaves India for the last time—His character, 81—92

Pages.

CHAPTER IX.

THE FIRST WAR WITH HYDER ALI.

FROM A. D. 1767 TO A. D. 1769.

Rise of a new enemy in Southern India—The kingdom of Mysore—The adventures and progress of Hyder Ali —Hyder Ali usurps the throne of Mysore—Extension of his dominions—Alliance against Hyder with the Mahrattas and the Nizam—Treachery of the Mahrattas—Advance to Mysore—Defection of the Nizam—Colonel Smith's retreat—The battle of Changumma—The battle of Trinomalee—Defeat and repentance of the Nizam—Tippoo's foray at Madras—Gallant defence of Amboor —Captain Calvert's spirited message—Defeat of Hyder near Amboor—Hyder retires to the Western Coast—Invasion of Mysore—Capture of forts below the Ghauts —Supersession of Colonel Smith—Hyder's return and partial success—Reappointment of Colonel Smith—Peace concluded with Hyder,.................................. 93—100

CHAPTER X.

CHANGES IN THE GOVERNMENT OF INDIA, AND WAR WITH THE MAHRATTAS.

FROM A. D. 1767 TO A. D. 1780.

State of Bengal—Discontent in England—Changes effected by Warren Hastings—The Company stand forth as dewan—Tranquillity and good government in Bengal—The Regulating Act—Feuds in the Council Chamber—Treaty with Suja Dowlah—Expulsion of the Rohillas—Arrangements regarding Corah and Allahabad—Death of Suja Dowlah, and treaty with his successor—Intrigues of Nuncomar—His trial and execution—Mr. Hast-

Pages.

ings acquires a majority in the Council—State of affairs at Bombay—Dissensions among the Mahrattas—Capture of Tanna—Alliance with Ragoba—Interference of the Government of Bengal—Treaty of Poorundher—Mahrattas prepare for war—Operations against the Mahrattas—The march from Bombay—The retreat—Halt of the Bengal corps—Colonel Goddard's march to Surat—His successes—Captain Popham takes Lahar—The capture of Gwalior—Peace concluded with the Mahrattas,......101—110

CHAPTER XI.

INVASION OF THE CARNATIC BY HYDER ALI.

FROM A. D. 1780 TO A. D. 1784.

Hyder's invasion—Carelessness at Madras—Colonel Baillie's defeat—Sir Hector Munro retreats—Panic at Madras—Hastings sends reinforcements—Sir Eyre Coote's arrival from Calcutta—Wandewash relieved—Repulse at Chillambrum—Battle of Porto Novo—Hyder defeated—Colonel Pearse's march from Bengal—Second battle—The victory of Sholingur—Vellore relieved—War with the Dutch,—whose settlements are taken—Hyder approaches Madras again—Sir E. Coote resigns his command—Col. Brathwaite's defeat—Mysoreans repulsed at Tellicherry—Tippoo sent to the Western Coast—is defeated at Paniani—Hyder's death—Tippoo returns—General Mathews invades Mysore—Takes Bednore—His foolish security—Tippoo appears again—Retakes Bednore—His faithlessness—Siege of Mangalore—Colonel Fullarton's march—Peace with Tippoo Sultan,............111—125

Pages.

CHAPTER XII.

THE LAST DAYS OF HASTINGS IN BENGAL, AND WAR WITH TIPPOO SULTAN.

FROM A.D. 1781 TO A. D. 1792.

Gaining supplies for the war—Cheyte Sing—Hastings goes to Benares—The Rajah taken prisoner—Hastings in danger—Cheyte Sing defeated—Hastings at Chunar—Leaves India—Various opinions about his character—Changes in the Government of India—Mr. Fox's Bill—Pitt's Bill—Lord Cornwallis—Rumours of war—Tippoo's cruelty towards the Nairs—His war against Travancore—Is repulsed—Invasion Travancore—War with the English—Marching and counter-marching—Lord Cornwallis arrives at Madras—Bangalore taken—Advance on Seringapatam—Retreat—Operations on the Western Coast—Lord Cornwallis at Bangalore—Nundidroog taken—Second advance on the capital—The siege of Seringapatam—Peace—the terms of it—Tippoo's sons surrendered as hostages,......126—138

CHAPTER XIII.

THE FALL OF SERINGAPATAM.

FROM A. D. 1792 TO A. D. 1799.

The English assume temporary charge of the Carnatic—Capture of the French settlements—French intrigues—French officers take service in native states—Revenue systems—Sir John Shore—His peace policy—The Mahrattas attack the Nizam—The English keep aloof—Temporary withdrawal of the Nizam's subsidiary force—Death of Mahomed Ali—Disputed succession in Oude—Lord Mornington's arrival in India—Change of poli-

Pages.

cy—Negotiations with the Nizam—Tippoo prepares for war—Lord Mornington proceeds to Madras—Assembling of the English forces—The Nizam's troops join the army—A short campaign—Advance of the English—Tippoo is beaten at Seedasoor and Malvelly—The siege of Seringapatam—The assault—The triumph—The death of Tippoo—Partition of the conquered country—Restoration of the Rajah—Colonel Wellesley's government of Mysore—Present aspect of Seringapatam,..................139—149

CHAPTER XIV.

WAR WITH THE MAHRATTAS.

FROM A. D. 1799 TO A. D. 1803.

Arrangements with the Nizam—The English take possession of the Carnatic—Threatened invasion of Zeman Shah—Vizier Ali—Insurrection at Benares—Murder of Mr. Cherry—Mr. Davis's gallantry—Arrangements with regard to Oude—Disputes among the Mahrattas—Scindia and Holkar—Treaty of Bassein—War against Scindia and the Rajah of Berar—General Wellesley advances on Poona—Marches after the enemy—Description of the Mahratta encampment—The battle of Assaye—General Lake—Capture of Alighur—The battle of Delhi—Surrender of the French officers—Release of Shah Alum, the Emperor—The battle of Laswaree—Suspicious behaviour of Scindia—The battle of Argaum—Capture of Gawilghur—Conclusion of peace,........................150—162

CHAPTER XV.

ANOTHER WAR WITH THE MAHRATTAS.

FROM A. D. 1804 TO A. D. 1806.

Holkar's suspicious behaviour during the war—His insolent message to General Lake—General Lake's army

Pages.

set in motion—Pursuit after Holkar—Return of the English army—Colonel Monson's disastrous retreat—Defence of Delhi—The English army, in two divisions, pursues Holkar—The cavalry defeat him near Furruckabad—The infantry at Deeg—Favourable operations in the west—Capture of Deeg—Siege of Bhurtpore—Every assault repulsed—Ameer Khan—Rajah of Bhurtpore yields—Alliance between Holkar and Scindia—Marquis Cornwallis returns to India—His death—Sir George Barlow becomes Governor General—Fresh treaty with Scindia—Holkar flees to the Punjab—Pursuit after him—A treaty of peace concluded—The English abandon their allies, ... 163—175

CHAPTER XVI.

THE ADMINISTRATIONS OF SIR GEORGE BARLOW AND LORD MINTO.

FROM A. D. 1806 TO A. D. 1813.

Profound peace throughout British India—Mutiny at Vellore—Massacre of the European soldiers who were stationed there—The cavalry come from Arcot—Suppression of the mutiny—Causes of the disturbance—Treatment of the mutineers—Suppression of the mutiny in other places—Lord Minto is appointed Governor General—Sir George Barlow becomes Governor of Madras—Departure from the peace policy—Occurrences at Poona and Hyderabad—Embassies to Persia and Cabul—Unpopularity of Sir George Barlow—The Tent Contract—Disgraceful mutiny at Madras—Affair at Seringapatam—Return to duty—Restoration of peace and quiet—Expeditions against Java, Bourbon, and the Isle of France—Signs of approaching warfare—Disputes with the Goorkhas—Quarrels with the Burmese—Departure of Lord Minto.......................................176—185

Pages.

CHAPTER XVII.

THE WAR WITH NEPAUL.

FROM A. D. 1813 TO A. D. 1817.

Arrival of the Earl of Moira—The Goorkhas—They attack a small party of English on the frontiers—Commencement of the Goorkha war—Arrangements for an invasion of Nepaul—Description of the country—Operations of the second division—Siege of Kalunga—Advance on Jytak—Failure of the third and fourth divisions—Success of the first division—Nalagurh abandoned—Temporary cessation of hostilities—Ramgerh abandoned—Attack on the heights of Maloun—Capture of Almora—The Nepaulese ask for peace—The terms of peace—Renewal of war—Sir D. Ochterlony turns the Chiriaghati Pass—Battle of Makwanpur—Capture of Hariharpur—Conclusion of peace—Intrigues among the Mahrattas—The Pindarees—Description of their warfare—Foray into the Company's territories—Defeat of a Pindaree expedition—Preparations for extensive warfare............186—199

CHAPTER XVIII.

TWO TREACHEROUS ALLIES.

FROM A. D. 1815 TO A. D. 1817.

Relations with the Peishwa—Intrigues of Trimbakji—Disputes between the Peishwa and the Guicowar—Murder of Gangudhar Shastri—Imprisonment and escape of Trimbakji—He raises insurgent troops—Duplicity of the Peishwa—Decided conduct of the Resident at Poona—Rewards offered for Trimbakji's capture—New treaty

Pages.

with the Peishwa—The Peishwa's plots—Description of Poona—Attack on the Residency—Battle of Kirkee—Arrival of reinforcements—Flight of the Peishwa—Affairs at Nagpore—Appa Sahib made Regent—Alliance with the English—Appa Sahib becomes Rajah—Plots against his allies—Description of Nagpore—Battle of Seetabuldee—Capt. Fitzgerald's gallant charge, and victory of the English—Negotiations with the Rajah—Arrival of reinforcements—Battle of Nagpore—Siege and surrender of Nagpore—Battle of Jubbulpore—Restoration of Appa Sahib,..200—211

CHAPTER XIX.

CONCLUSION OF THE PINDAREE WAR.

FROM A. D. 1817 TO A. D. 1819.

Scindia—Jeswunt Row Holkar succeeded by his son—Scindia is intimidated—Majority of Holkar's chieftains declare for war—Murder of Toolsee Bhye—Battle of Mahidpore—Holkar's dominions subdued—Extirpation of the Pindarees—Kareem Khan surrenders—The end of Cheetoo—Pursuit after the Peishwa—Advance of the Peishwa on Poona—Gallant action at Corregaum—The Peishwa's flight continued—Bapur Gokla—Cavalry action at Ashtee—Surrender of the Peishwa—A residence assigned him at Bithoor—Restoration of the Rajah of Sattara—Trimbakji taken prisoner—Capture of Talnere—Execution of the warder—The Rajah of Nagpore—Renews his intrigues—Is taken prisoner—Is sent to Allahabad—Escapes—Flees to the Mahadeo Hills—Capture of Aseerghur—Appa Sahib flees again—Takes refuge in the Punjab—A new Rajah at Nagpore—Conclusion of the war,.......................................212—223

Pages.

CHAPTER XX.

THE EXPEDITION TO BURMAH.

FROM A. D. 1823 TO A. D. 1826.

Lord Amherst the new Governor General—Disputes with the Burmese—Dissensions about Shapooree—Affairs in Cachar—Declaration of war—Plan of the campaign—Capture of Rangoon—Attacks on stockades—Capture of Kemendine—Position of the English—Repulse of the enemy from the Great Pagoda—Fall of Martaban and other places on the coast—Advance of Maha Bandoola—Total defeat of the Burmese—Conflagration at Rangoon—Advance into the interior—The water column repulsed at Donabew—Backward movement of the land column—Capture of Donabew—Death of Maha Bandoola—The stay at Prome—Conquest of Arracan—Negotiations—A truce—Defeat of the enemy—Capture of Melloon—Battle of Pagahm—The English draw near Ava—Conclusion of peace—Disturbances at Bhurtpore—Dethronement of the youthful Rajah—Usurpation of Doorjun Saul—Government take the part of the Rajah—Siege and capture of Bhurtpore,................224—237

CHAPTER XXI.

WAR IN THE HIGHLANDS OF AFFGHANISTAN.

FROM A. D. 1828 TO A. D. 1842.

Administration of Lord William Bentinck—Conquest of Coorg—Suppression of Suttee—Changes in the Company's Charter—Apprehensions of Russian invasion—Revolutions in Affghanistan—Embassy to DostMahomed

Pages.

—Persian invasion of Herat—Siege of Herat—Declaration of war against Dost Mahomed—Tripartite Treaty—Invasion of Affghanistan—Installation of Shah Sujah at Candahar—Capture of Ghazni—Advance to Cabul—Return of the invading army—Return and surrender of Dost Mahomed—Delusive tranquillity in Affghanistan—Desertion and defeat of discontented chiefs—Insurrection at Cabul—Murder of Sir William Macnaghten—Disastrous retreat from Cabul—Arrival of Lord Ellenborough—Gallant defence of Jellalabad—Advance of Generals Pollock and Nott—Release of the English prisoners—Withdrawal of the troops to India,.... ....238—252

CHAPTER XXII.

OCCURRENCES IN SCINDE AND GWALIOR,

FROM A. D. 1842 TO A. D. 1844.

The Ameers of Scinde—Ill-feeling against the English Government—Infraction of treaties—A new treaty offered for their acceptance—Attack on the Residency—The battle of Meeanee—Surrender of Hydrabad, the capital of Scinde—The battle of Hydrabad or Dubba—Final subjugation of the Ameers—Conquest and pacification of the country—State of affairs at Gwalior—The Maharajah dies childless—Adoption and installation of a relative—Mama Sahib appointed Regent—Intrigues at the Maharajah's Court—Dada Khasjee Walla appointed in Mama Sahib's stead—The English Resident leaves the Court—State of the Mahratta army—Advance of the English troops—Failure of negotiations—The battles of Maharajpore and Punniar—Treaty with the Maharajah—Return of Lord Ellenborough to Calcutta—He is recalled by the Court of Directors......253—263

Pages.

CHAPTER XXIII.

FIRST CONTEST IN THE PUNJAB.

FROM A D. 1844 TO A. D. 1847.

Arrival of Sir Henry Hardinge—The Sikhs—Death of Runjeet Sing—State of the Punjab—Position of the Sikh Government—Power of the army—Invasion of British India—Advance of English troops—The battle of Moodkee—The Sikh's entrenched camp—The battle of Ferozeshah—A night on the battle field—The victory—The Sikhs return—Sir Harry Smith sent to Loodiana—The battle of Aliwal—Preparations for the final struggle—The battle of Sobraon—The English army cross the Sutlej—The advance to Lahore—Goolab Sing negotiates—Interview between the Maharajah and the Governor General—Treaty with the Maharajah—Conclusion of the war—Close of Lord Hardinge's administration, ...264—273

CHAPTER XXIV.

CONQUEST OF THE PUNJAB AND PEGU.

FROM A D. 1848 TO 1853.

Commencement of Lord Dalhousie's administration—Moolraj—His treacherous conduct—Is removed—Messrs. Agnew and Anderson sent to instal the new governor—Insurrection at Moultan—Murder of the British officers—Shere Sing sent to Moultan—Mr. Edwardes—His admirable conduct—Defeats Moolraj's forces—Appears before Moultan—General Whish arrives at Moultan—General insurrection in the Punjab—Shere Sing's defection—Siege of Moultan raised—The English army enters

Pages.

the Punjab—The action at Ramnuggur—The battle of Chillianwalla—The fall of Moultan—Sensation in England—The battle of Gujerat—Conquest of the Punjab—Conduct of the Governor of Rangoon—Commodore Lambert's mission—War with Burmah—Capture of Burmese forts—Character of the Burmese war—Advance to Prome—Subjugation of Pegu—Lord Dalhousie's policy ....274—284

CHAPTER XXV.

CONCLUSION OF LORD DALHOUSIE'S ADMINISTRATION.

FROM A. D. 1854 TO A. D. 1857.

Fresh treaty with the Nizam—State of affairs at Nagpore—Death of the Rajah without issue or relations—Nagpore placed in charge of English officers—The Sonthal insurrection—Restoration of tranquillity—The condition of Oude—Disturbances in that country—Assembling of English troops—Former treaty violated by the Nabob—The annexation of Oude—The province placed in charge of English officers—Departure of Lord Dalhousie—Social improvements during his administration—Changes in the Company's Charter—Arrival of Lord Canning as Governor General—Growth of English power in India—Benefits of English rule..................285—291

HISTORY OF INDIA.

CHAPTER I.

THE COUNTRY, THE CHARACTER, AND THE ANCIENT HISTORY OF THE HINDUS.

To A. D. 77.

The Boundaries of India—Natural Features of the Country—Description of Hindostan—Basins of the Indus and the Ganges—the Great Desert—Central India—the Deckan—Rivers of Southern India—Vegetable Productions of the Land—Agricultural and Mineral Productions—Commerce of India—Early Civilisation of the Hindus—Stationary character of their Institutions—the Code of Menu—State of Hindu Society in Menu's time—the Mode of Government—the Revenue—Principal Changes since the time of Menu—Village Communities—Character of the Hindus—Ancient History of India—Origin of the Hindus—Kingdom of Oude—Rama—War of "the Muhabharata"—Hindu States on the Ganges—Kingdom of Magada—Chandragupta—Vikramarka—King Bhoj—History of Southern India—Kingdoms of Pandya and Chola—Smaller States—Salivahana—Uncertainty of Hindu Chronology.

INDIA is situated in the south of Asia. It is bounded almost on three sides by the ocean, to which it has given a name; and it is separated on

CHAP. I.

the north from the table land of Central Asia by the Himalayas, a range in which the loftiest mountains in the world are found.

The natural features of India

India is divided into two large portions by the Vindhya mountains. The northern division is called Hindostan, a name which is sometimes applied to the whole country; the other portion is named the Deckan, or, as the original word signifies, Southern India.

Description of Hindostan.

Hindostan consists of two extensive plains, watered by the Indus and the Ganges, a large desert tract on the east of the Indus, and a table-land which is bounded on the south by the Vindhya mountains. The valley of the Indus includes the Punjab, or the country of five rivers, uniting in the larger stream already named, and Scinde, which forms the border land between India and Beloochistan.

Plain of the Indus.

Valley of the Ganges.

The plain through which the Ganges flows is the most fertile region in the land. It is the first country where the Hindus are known to have resided; it contains many of their sacred towns and their favourite river; and it is now the locality of the capital and of the richest provinces of British India.

The Great Desert and Central India.

The Great Desert is situated to the east of Scinde; and the table-land of Central India, extending, as we have already stated, along the north of the Vindhya mountains, enjoys a more pleasant climate than the hot plains by which it is surrounded.

Description of the Deckan.

The Deckan consists of an extensive plateau, which is on all sides enclosed by hills of various heights,

The mountains on the east and west of this tract are called the Eastern and Western Ghauts. The latter range runs parallel to the western coast of the peninsula, and is, in many parts, of great height: the former range follows the direction of the eastern coast from the river Kishna to the latitude of Madras, where it bends towards the west, and joins the Western Ghauts at the Neilgherries, in which those mountains attain their highest elevation. From the Kishna northwards a range of hills extends along the eastern coast as far as Cuttack. These hills are of an irregular and broken form, similar to the Eastern Ghauts.

Low lands of the Deckan.

The low country which lies between the mountains and the sea is generally rich and fertile. On the western coast this tract is narrow and rugged; but that upon the east forms the extensive countries known as the Carnatic and the Northern Circars.

Rivers of Southern India.

Many large rivers flow through the Deckan, generally in an eastern direction. The principal are the Godavery, the Kishna, the Pennar, and the Cauvery. The Nerbudda and the Tapti, in the north, flow from east to west, and fall into the Gulf of Cambay.

Vegetable productions of the country.

The vegetable productions of India are very numerous and useful. The cocoa, palmyra, sago, and other palms, are the most common trees and the most characteristic of the country. The cocoa-nut tree is applied to various purposes. The nut

CHAP. I.

which it produces is used for food, and yields an oil of superior quality; the shell of the nut is turned into cups and other culinary utensils; the fibre is converted into ropes; and the timber used for troughs and beams. Teak wood, which abounds in the forests, is useful for building ships; ebony, sandal, and blackwood are often employed in ornamental work; and spices, aromatic gums, and various medicinal plants are found in abundance.

Agricultural products.

One of the principal agricultural products of India is rice. In the greater part of the country this production forms the chief article of food of the higher classes only: the lower orders live on wheat or ragi. The use of rice is more general in some parts than in others. Of other grains, gram, maize, and millet are chiefly cultivated.

Mineral productions.

The minerals of India have been celebrated from the earliest ages, especially its iron, diamonds, and other precious stones.

The commerce of India.

The foreign commerce of India, which probably existed as early as the time of Solomon, king of Israel, consisted chiefly of spices, jewellery, and rich apparel. Indian merchandise was generally conveyed to the west by inland routes until the rise of the Arabs, who, in later times, appropriated to themselves the commerce with the East.

Early civilisation of the Hindus.

This extensive trade is an evidence of the high state of civilisation attained at an early period by the Hindus. Although we are but slightly acquainted with the ancient history of this people, we know that they once formed the most polished, civilised, and prosperous nation in Asia, with the exception of the Jews. They had attained an excellence in sculpture, architecture, and poetry, far surpassing the acquirements of those by whom they were surrounded, before the most celebrated nations of Europe had come into existence. They remained, however, as they were then. Being isolated for many ages from the rest of mankind by the physical peculiarities of their country, and by the exclusiveness of their national character, they maintained no beneficial intercourse with other races, with whom they were distantly connected by commerce alone. A stranger visiting a Hindu village in the times of old would have been struck with the same peculiarities which we notice now. Their mode of life was, in many essential points, similar to what it is at present; and wherever there has been any alteration, it has been for the worse.

Stationary character of their institutions.

We have a picture of Hindu society at an early period in the code of Menu. This collection of laws and maxims is supposed to have been compiled in the ninth century before the Christian era; and was evidently written some time after the Hindus had attained a considerable degree of civilisation.

The code of Menu. Cir. B. C. 900.

The Hindus were then divided into four castes, the Brahmins, the Kshatriyas, the Veishyas, and the Sudras. The three first were called the twice-born classes, and had particular privileges allowed them: the last appear to have been the descendants of a conquered

State of Hindu society in Menu's time.

CHAP. I.

and an enslaved people. Minute directions are given in the code concerning the mode of life and behaviour of Brahmins, and the conduct of princes and kings.

Internal administration.

The government was monarchical, and the king, assisted by a council and a Brahmin prime minister, was generally the dispenser of justice. The internal administration of affairs was conducted by officers, who varied in rank according to their authority, some ruling over a thousand villages, some over a hundred, and some over ten, and each village was under its own headman. The headman of the village was entitled to receive fees in kind from the peasants, and the other officers were compensated by grants of land.

The revenue.

Taxes were levied on agricultural produce, as at the present time, on certain trades, and on merchandise. The highest amount that could be exacted on grain was one fourth; but the rate of revenue was generally fixed between one sixth and one twelfth.

The principal changes since Menu's time.

Various changes have naturally taken place since the time of Menu; but the ascendancy of Brahminical influence and the distinctions of caste still continue in force. The second and third classes are now comparatively rare, and the Sudras are no longer regarded as utterly degraded; but innumerable subdivisions of caste and a new race of outcasts have since arisen.

The village communities.

The village communities, however, continue to this day. Modifications in the government of villages have taken place in different parts of the country: agreements regarding the revenue are in some places made with each individual, and in others with the headman; but each village constitutes a distinct community within itself. The ruling power, far beyond the observation of the simple villagers, has often been changed, but each village forms within itself a little world. The people are governed by their own officers, and care little to whom those officers are responsible.

The character of the Hindus.

The Hindus inhabit a country of great magnitude, which extends through several degrees of latitude and experiences many variations of climate; and they are divided, by geographical position, by their customs, and by language, into several distinct nations, which differ from each other as much as the English differ from the Irish and the Scotch. The character of the people is, therefore, different in different places. The Bengalee is weak and effeminate; the Rajput, brave and manly. The wily Mahratta is a perfect contrast to the Tamil inhabitant of Madras; and the ryots in the Telugu provinces are very unlike those upon the Western Coast. Our estimate of the Hindu character must, consequently, be very general.

The Hindus are polite and gentle in manner, simple in their tastes and habits, and constant in the affection which they bear to their family and friends. Their most common failings are timidity, untruthfulness, indolence, and litigiousness. They are brave when led by men whom they esteem; they are honest when entrusted with valuable property placed without suspicion in their hands; they are grateful, kind, and affectionate when kindness and affection are shewn to them. They do not, however, appear to live

CHAP. I. according to any fixed standard of goodness—to act, in a word, from principle.

The upper classes are peculiarly cleanly in their habits. Though neither energetic nor enterprising, they are most patient and persevering in all their undertakings, and their application to business is frequently astonishing. There is much in the Hindu character that an Englishman can admire, if only he honestly makes the attempt to discover the points with which he can sympathize, rather than those from which he must differ; and we sincerely trust that the bands of sympathy between the two races may daily be drawn closer.

The ancient history of India. We know very little regarding the ancient history of the people, for the accounts which we have received of the first Indian sovereigns are so mixed with Hindu fables, and so interwoven with the traditions of the Hindu religion, that it is difficult to discern between the narratives of real heroes and of imaginary deities.

The origin of the Hindus. It is the general opinion, that the Hindus are not the original inhabitants of India. They appear to have invaded the country from the north-west; to have settled at first in the extreme north of Hindostan; and afterwards to have penetrated into Southern India. The first kingdom mentioned by Hindu writers is that of Oude, where two dynasties, known as the races of the Sun and of the Moon, are supposed to have originated. The earliest person, however, who is entitled to be named in history, is Rama. He appears to have been

The kingdom of Oude.

Rama.

CHAP. I.

a prince of Oude, who invaded the Deckan, and who so highly distinguished himself by his prowess in war, that he was, according to the usual custom of ancient nations, venerated and deified by posterity.

War between the Pandus and Curus.

The next recorded event which was probably founded on fact, is the war between the Pandus and Curus, two branches of the royal family, for the throne of Hastinapura near Delhi. The Pandus were victorious; but, grieved at the loss of their friends and relatives in the war, they retired to the solitary regions of the Himalayas, where they died. Krishna, the sovereign of Guzerat, was an ally of the Pandus.

Hindu states on the Ganges. Cir. B. C. 1400.

It is supposed that this war took place in the fourteenth century before the Christian era, at which time six independent states existed in the valley of the Ganges, connected, however, with each other by alliance and commercial intercourse.

The kingdom of Magada.

One of these states was called Magada, and it appears that an unbroken line of kings reigned there from the date of the war which we have just mentioned, to the fifth century of the present era. They possessed great influence over the surrounding kingdoms, and were even allied with nations west of the Indus. The two most celebrated of these kings were Chandragupta, or, as the Greeks called him, Sandracottus, with whom a treaty of alliance was concluded by Seleucus, one of Alexander's successors; and Asoca, in whose reign the kingdom appears to have been widely extended and happily governed.

Chandragupta.

CHAP. I.

Vikramarka and king Bhoj.

No authentic information is given regarding the other kingdoms which existed in those times, until the birth of Vikramarka, who reigned at the city of Oojein, in Malwa. Several stories of the justice and the intelligence of this sovereign are related by the Hindus, with whom he is a favourite hero. The era which is named after him, and is generally used in Hindostan Proper, commences B. C. 56. King Bhoja, who flourished at the end of the eleventh century, was also a popular sovereign among the Hindus.

Ancient history of Southern India. Cir. B. C. 1000

The history of Southern India is better known than that of Hindostan. It is uncertain at what time the Hindus colonised this part of the country ; but it must have been at a comparatively early period. The existence, however, of several languages, which are, in their origin, entirely distinct from Sanscrit, the ancient language of the Hindus, and yet connected with each other, indicate the long occupation of this region by the original inhabitants.

The kingdom of Pandya. Cir. B. C. 450.

The country was divided into several states. The most remarkable of these were the kingdoms of Pandya and Chola, which flourished in the southern part of the peninsula. The capital of the Pandyan princes, who were frequently at war with the neighbouring kingdom of Chola, was Madura, and their territory comprehended the present districts of Madura and Tinnevelly.

The kingdom of Chola.

The capital of the Chola state was Conjeveram. This kingdom was, at one time, of great extent, and included the country as far north as the river Godavery.

CHAP. I.

Smaller states of Southern India.

There were smaller states between these kingdoms and the sea, in the Telugu and Canarese countries, and in the northern districts as far as the Vindhya mountains; but the accounts of them are confused and uninteresting.

Salivahana.

Salivahana, after whom the Hindu era commencing A. D. 77 is named, ruled in the Mahratta country. He appears to have been a powerful monarch, but the common narrative of his life and adventures is fabulous. He is said to have conquered Vikramarka, the celebrated king of Malwa; but this popular statement must be incorrect, because he lived many years after that prince.

We have thus endeavoured to mention all the most important events in the early times of which we have been writing, and to point out those portions of Hindu tradition that appear to have some ground in truth: but, as Mr. Elphinstone remarks, "no *date* of a public event can be fixed before the invasion of Alexander; and no *connected* relation of the national transactions can be attempted until after the Mahomedan conquest."*

* History of India. Vol. I. p. 19.

CHAPTER II.

INDIA UNDER THE EARLY MUSSULMAN DYNASTIES.

FROM B. C. 328 TO A. D. 1556.

Expedition of the Persians—of the Greeks—Seleucus—the Kingdom of Bactria—the Mahomedan invasion—Mahmud of Ghazni—his last Expedition—the Siege of Somnat—Mahomed Ghori—Kutb-ud-dien—the Slave Kings—the House of Khilji—the Toghlak dynasty—Mahomed Toghlak; his mad acts—Feroze Shah; his good reign—Tumerlane—the slaughter at Delhi—Anarchy in India—Baber—the first Battle of Paniput—Baber's character—the Rajputs—Battle of Sikri, and Baber's victory—Humayun—Shir Shah dethrones him—Shir Shah's useful reign—Humayun recovers the throne—his flight into Persia—his return, restoration, and death.

Foreign invasions of India.

THE wealth and importance of India have often attracted the attention of foreign conquerors; and the Hindus have never offered a uniformly successful resistance. Many centuries ago the Persians under Darius invaded and subdued the countries bordering on the Indus; but it does not appear that he advanced further than the Great Desert, which is described by Herodotus, the Greek historian, as the eastern boundary of the world. Tribute was demanded from the small portion of India

Expedition of the Persians

Mo.

CHAP. II.

B. C. 328.

which the Persians had overrun; but the slight dependence on that people seems to have been soon forgotten.

Expedition of the Greeks under Alexander.

Alexander the Great, claiming India as a portion of the Persian empire which he had conquered, invaded the Punjab with a large army. He overcame the Indian monarch, Porus, who offered a gallant opposition, and advanced as far as the Hyphasis, or the modern Sutlej, where his troops rebelled, and refused to follow him any further. Having left a few garrisons in the country, and having formed alliances with several of the native princes, he returned to Assyria through Scinde and Beloochistan.

Seleucus.

Seleucus, who obtained a portion of Alexander's empire after the death of the conqueror, formed with Chandragupta, or Sandracottus, king of Magada, a treaty which appears to have been favourable to the Indian prince.

The kingdom of Bactria.

The kingdom of Bactria, or the modern country of Balkh, to the north of Cabul, which was a part of the dominions of Seleucus, became, in course of time, independent, and was governed by a dynasty of vigorous and enlightened kings. Under these sovereigns the Bactrians invaded and conquered a larger portion of India than Darius or Alexander had visited; but, although their power in India lasted for more than a century, they left no permanent impression upon the inhabitants of the land.

CHAP. II.

A. D. 1001.

The Mahomedan conquerors of India,

But in later days enemies of a far different character invaded Hindostan. These were the followers of the Mahomedan religion: they thoroughly conquered the greater part of the country, and founded in it a monarchy which continued in full power for several generations.

Mahmud of Ghazni.

The first chief of that creed who invaded India, was named Mahmud. He came from Ghazni, which is situated to the north-west of India, in the mountainous country beyond the Punjab. Finding himself at peace in his native land, after a long and arduous struggle for the throne, he began to look about for further employment for his own restless spirit, and for the many warlike men by whom he was surrounded.

His expeditions into India.

India seemed to promise the best field for acquiring booty; and, therefore, inviting to his standard those who were eager for adventure and for war, he entered the country with a considerable force. He made twelve expeditions into the neighbouring districts of Hindostan, and, after each, returned to Ghazni with an enormous amount of plunder and wealth.

The siege of Somnat.

A. D. 1024.

The last expedition nearly proved fatal to him and to his army. He had advanced to Somnat, where there was a fine, rich, old temple. It was strongly fortified, and defended by a large and courageous garrison, who, for a long time, resisted the assaults of the Mussulmans. Roused by this attack upon their favourite pagoda, the neighbouring rajahs gathered round Mahmud's army,

CHAP. II.

A. D. 1024.

and he was obliged to raise the siege to meet this new foe. The battle raged long and fiercely. The excited Hindus fought nobly; and the enemy were giving way before them, when Mahmud leapt from his horse, fell upon his knees in the sight of his soldiers, prayed aloud for victory, and then, remounting his charger, led them on once more. He was successful. The Hindus fled: and the garrison of Somnat, in desperation, left their stronghold, forced a way through those who opposed them, and departed from the coast in boats. When the conqueror entered the temple, he struck the largest of the idols down with his own hands, and spoiled the pagoda of all its treasures.

Mahmud's stay in Guzerat, and return to Ghazni.

On his return to his own country, Mahmud remained some time in Guzerat, and appointed a rajah over the people of that province. Proceeding on his march, he found that the road by which he had entered India, was occupied by a large force under the Rajah of Ajmir, and he consequently resolved to turn aside, and to try a new route along the sands to the east of Scinde. The march was awful. Thousands were killed by fatigue and thirst and heat, and his army was almost entirely destroyed.

Mahomed of Ghor.
A. D. 1176.

It is unnecessary to mention Mahmud's successors, as the account of them has little connexion with the history of India. The last of the line was overthrown by Mahomed Shahab-ud-dien, or, as he is usually called, Mahomed Ghori, the most illustrious of the house of Ghor, and the

CHAP. II. A.D. 1176. founder of the Mahomedan dynasties in this land, who received his name from a district of the Hindu Koosh, near Turkestan. He extended his conquests towards Delhi and Ajmir, which were finally subdued by his general, Kutb-ud-dien.

Kutb-ud-dien. A.D. 1206. Kutb-ud-dien was originally a slave of Mahomed's, who, having no son, brought him up with the greatest care, and promoted him to the highest offices in the state. After Mahomed's death, Kutb-ud-dien and two other slaves became independent, and succeeded to power in different parts of the kingdom. The former ruled at Delhi.

The Slave-Kings; and the House of Khilji. The successors of Kutb-ud-dien are known by the name of the Slave-Kings. After them followed the house of Khilji, and during the reigns of these kings, the Mahomedans extended their conquests towards the south of India.

Mahomed Toghlak. A.D. 1325. The family of Toghlak were the next rulers of Delhi. The second sovereign of this line, named Mahomed Toghlak, was a madman. He desired to change his capital from Delhi to a city in the Deckan, and he ordered all the inhabitants of the former place to leave their abodes, and to follow him towards the south. He attempted to invade China, and sent an army of 100,000 men over the Himalaya mountains for that purpose; but they were speedily defeated, and so great were their sufferings on the homeward march, that scarcely a man returned. He actually hunted his subjects for amusement, enclosing a large circle of country with his troops,

His madness and caprice.

CHAP. II.

A. D. 1325.

and ordering every poor peasant within the space thus enclosed to be killed, because he had driven some of them into rebellion by his tyranny; and this contemptible sovereign, who could value life so low, having one day lost a tooth, buried it with royal pomp, and built over it a splendid tomb!

The good reign of Feroze Shah. A. D. 1351 to 1388.

His successor was a better man, and, perhaps, appeared still better than he was by coming after such a monster. Feroze Shah has left behind him the noblest name of all the early Mahomedan kings. He attended to the good of his people; built hospitals, and bridges, and tanks; and constructed the first canal ever known in India, which, after his reign, became useless, but has since been restored, once by Akber, and in later times by the English. He died at the age of ninety.

The nvasion of Tamerlane. A. D. 1398.

Ten years later, during the reign of one of Feroze Shah's grandsons, Tamerlane or Timur, a cruel, savage barbarian, invaded India. He found the country an easy prey. On his march to Delhi, he committed the most horrible excesses, and burning villages and smoking houses marked his road. His march being, on one occasion, impeded by the multitude of prisoners whom he had taken, it is said that he inhumanly ordered a hundred thousand of them to be murdered, sparing only those under fifteen years of age. He took possession of Delhi, which had surrendered on his promise of protection. But awful

CHAP. II.

A. D. 1398.

The sack of Delhi.

cruelties ensued. Tamerlane's followers began, according to their usual custom, to plunder, and, when the inhabitants resisted, a general massacre took place: the streets were strewed with the dead, and the city was filled with lamentation, and mourning, and woe.

State of the country after Tamerlane's departure.

After proclaiming himself Emperor of Delhi, Tamerlane returned to his own country with an enormous amount of treasure, and hundreds of men as slaves, leaving the provinces which he had overrun desolate and deserted. For many years after this invasion there was anarchy in India. The empire was thoroughly disorganised. Everywhere independent kings arose; party fought against party; and, although there was an Emperor in name, his power extended over only a very small part of the former Mahomedan dominions. It was not until Baber, the sixth in descent from Tamerlane, invaded India, as his ancestor had done, and reconquered Delhi, that peace and quietness were, in a measure, restored. This monarch was not bent like Tamerlane on plunder only; but he came to found a new kingdom in the land of the Hindu.

Invasion of Baber.

A. D. 1524.

Ibrahim Lodi was, at that time, the nominal Emperor, and in his reign several rebellions occurred, during one of which the Governor of the Punjab applied for assistance to Baber, who gladly came to his aid. After several actions in the north-west, Baber advanced towards Delhi, where Ibrahim came out to meet him with a large army.

The battle of Paniput.

April 21st 1526.

A battle was fought at Paniput. Baber's force was the smallest; but neither party seemed in-

CHAP. II.

A. D. 1526.

clined to risk an engagement, and both commanders entrenched themselves in their camps. Ibrahim first came out to the attack, he was himself slain, and his army totally defeated. By this battle the throne of Delhi passed into the possession of Tamerlane's descendants, who formed the line of kings generally known by the name of the Great Moguls.

The character of Baber.

Baber, the new conqueror, was a man of a jovial and sociable disposition. He wrote a pleasing memoir of his life, in which he affords us an open and candid estimate of his character. He does not hide his faults ; but, notwithstanding that, he reveals a love for the good, and true, and beautiful, which will endear him to the hearts of his readers in every age and land.

Baber becomes Emperor of Delhi.

Baber reigned at Delhi for five years only, during which his time was fully employed in bringing into subjection those who still resisted his authority. The Mussulman rulers were soon conquered, but the Hindus were not so easily subdued.

The Rajputs.

We have already related how Mahmud of Ghazni and other Mussulman sovereigns frequently met with stubborn resistance from the inhabitants of India : and, now that we have come to the beginning of the Mogul dynasty, it is right that we should mention those from whom that resistance was principally received. The north-western provinces of India were inhabited by the Rajputs, a warlike race who belonged to the second of the four great classes into which

CHAP. II. A. D. 1526.

the Hindus were divided. They were a brave and free people. They were never thoroughly subdued by the Mussulmans, and it was only owing to the kind treatment which they experienced from some of the Emperors of Delhi that they ever submitted to the rule of the Moguls.

Baber's war with Sanga.

Such were the men against whom Baber had now to contend. A number of Rajputs, under Sanga, Rajah of Mewar, advanced towards Agra to attack him. A desperate battle took place. Part of Baber's army was at first beaten; but the Rajputs did not take advantage of their success, and gave him time to fortify his camp, and prevent their attacking him again. His soldiers were disheartened by their first defeat, and it appeared likely that the Rajputs would gain the victory. But Baber did not despair. Collecting his principal officers around him, he prayed them not to desert his cause nor to despond, and spake to them of glory and honour; and all present swore to be true to him,—to conquer, or to die. Baber then led his army again to battle, and the revived spirit of the Mussulmans was so good that they speedily drove the enemy from the field.

Battle of Sikri. March 16th 1527.

Siege of Chanderi. Jan. 20th 1528.

During the remainder of his reign Baber had much trouble with the Rajputs. While he was one day besieging the fort of Chanderi in Malwa, a desperate scene took place. The Rajputs, having put their women and children to death, fought until every one of their number was slain.

CHAP. II.

A. D. 1528.

Death of Baber.

He also experienced opposition with his own people in Oude and Bahar: but, at the time of his death, the former Mussulman empire was almost entirely under his control. His death is thought to have been brought on by his superstitiously invoking it upon himself, to save the life of his favourite son, Humayun. It is true that he performed a ceremony for that purpose; and he most likely died from the effect which it produced upon his mind.

The accession of Humayun. A. D. 1530.

The condition of Baber's family, upon his death, was far from prosperous. His dominions were divided between his two elder sons; Camran receiving the countries of Cabul, Candahar, and a portion of the Punjab; and Humayun, the eldest, succeeding to the title of Emperor. By this arrangement the latter was prevented from obtaining men from the lands beyond the Indus to recruit his army, as his father had done.

Shir Shah dethrones Humayun. A. D. 1540.

At the beginning of Humayun's reign, many disturbances occurred, and he was unable to repress them with promptness and decision. His most formidable opponent was Shir Shah. This remarkable man was a Patan, who, having raised himself by his great bravery, and still greater skill, to a high position in Bahar, had attained such power that he was able to oppose his sovereign, and to drive him from the throne.

The useful reign of Shir Shah.

When in Humayun's place, Shir Shah exerted himself for the improvement of the country and for the good of the people: and, although

CHAP. II. A. D. 1540.

he was Emperor for only five years, he did more for both objects in that short time than any of his predecessors had done. He improved the existing system of collecting revenue; rendered the administration of justice easier and smoother than it had previously been; constructed numerous public works of great utility; and his subjects felt sincere regret when death put an end to his short but useful reign.

His death. May 22nd 1545.

He was killed during the siege of a Rajput town in 1545; and was succeeded by his eldest son; but his family governed badly, and, when Humayun afterwards made an attempt to recover the kingdom, he found so many divisions in the country, so feeble a discipline in the army, and so much corruption in the court, that he had little difficulty in accomplishing his object.

Humayun recovers the kingdom A. D. 1555.

Humayun's retreat from India.

Humayun had, in the mean time, suffered much. After his defeat by Shir Shah, he fled to Persia, and, on their way thither, he and his followers suffered severely from the fatigue and hardships of the journey. During this eventful march, when his father was a wanderer and an exile, Prince Akber, the future sovereign of India, was born.

He is assisted by the king of Persia.

When the exiled Emperor reached the court of the king of Persia, he pleased the latter so much by a change in his religious opinions, that a considerable army was placed at his disposal, with which he succeeded in driving his brother Camran out of Cabul and Candahar, and in finally recovering his former kingdom from the family of Shir Shah. He died, however, a year after his restoration, from the effects of an accidental fall, and was succeeded by his illustrious son. CHAP. II. A. D. 1555.

CHAPTER III.

THE GREAT MOGULS.

FROM A. D. 1556 TO A. D. 1744.

Akber—the prime minister, Behram—Akber's long and noble reign—his useful measures—Jehangir—Nur Jehan—Rebellions at the close of the reign—Shah Jehan—his treatment of his sons—their characters—the Emperor's illness—Struggle between his sons for power—Aurangzib and Morad fight against Dara—Dara's defeat—Aurangzib defeats Shuja—Aurangzib's triumph—Shah Jehan's death—the Mahrattas—their rise—their mode of warfare—Sevaji—an example of his treachery and cunning—Wars with the Mahrattas—the Emperor enters the Deckan—his impolitic treatment of the Rajputs—Rebellions—Aurangzib's death—Decay of the Empire—Invasion by Nadir Shah—Massacre at Delhi—Dissolution of the Empire—Rise of independent Powers—a new people come to conquer and to rule—State of India under the Mahomedans.

PRINCE Akber ascended the throne with bright prospects before him. He was very young when his father died, and the kingdom was consequently placed in charge of the chief minister, Behram, who governed it with the greatest care and ability. Under this intelligent, but arbitrary, states-

CHAP. III.

A. D. 1556.

Akber's long and noble reign.

man, the country was almost completely brought into subjection; and, when Akber himself took charge of the government, on attaining his majority, he found it in a tolerably quiet and peaceful condition. Akber's reign was a long and useful one. He was the best Mussulman king that ever ruled in India, because he was the most thoughtful of the happiness and welfare of his subjects. It can be said in his praise, that at no time, while the Mahomedans were in power, was the country so peaceful, or so well governed, and at no time were all classes so happy. One of his first objects was to bring together the different races under his command; to teach them how to work with each other; and thus to increase the strength of the kingdom without obtaining men from the neighbouring countries, from which the armies of Hindostan had been hitherto recruited. He employed the Hindus in high offices of state; he abolished several unjust taxes which had been imposed upon them; he improved Shir Shah's system of revenue; he strengthened the administration of justice; he forbad all cruel and inhuman punishments; he exerted himself to suppress the custom of suttee; in short, he did everything in his power to make his people happy and prosperous. If there is one spot in the long line of the Mahomedan rulers, on which we can look with delight, it is the reign of Akber.

His schemes of usefulness.

The accession of Jehangir. A. D. 1605.

He was succeeded by his son, Selim, who assumed the title of Jehangir, or 'The Conqueror

CHAP. III.

A. D. 1605.

of the World.' He was a slothful and careless king; but his dominions had been brought into such admirable order by his father, that he enjoyed peace and quietness during the greater part of his reign.

Marriage of the Emperor with Nur Jehan. A. D. 1611.

The most interesting event of Jehangir's reign was his love for a beautiful and accomplished lady named Nur Jehan. During his father's life-time, Prince Selim had become attached to her; but, as Akber disapproved of his marrying her, she was given to a nobleman of high rank. After he became Emperor, however, he resolved to have his own way, caused her husband to be put to death, and made her an inmate of his harem. But his love for her abated; and he suffered her to remain in retirement without showing her either kindness or attention. She succeeded, however, in regaining his affection. He afterwards married her, gave her the title of Empress, and was greatly influenced by her during the remainder of his life.

Rebellions at the close of the reign.

The last years of Jehangir were disturbed by rebellions, caused by the wildness of one of his sons, and by Nur Jehan's love of power. In one of these insurrections he was taken prisoner by a nobleman, named Mohabat Khan, who had been driven into rebellion by the Empress's ill-treatment. Jehangir died soon after his rescue, and was succeeded by Shah Jehan, the son who had rebelled against him, and whom he desired to be excluded from the throne.

The accession of Shah Jehan, Oct. 27th, 1627.

During the reign of Shah Jehan there were wars in the Deckan and Cabul; but that which distinguished it more than wars or tumults, was the manner in which he treated his sons. It had always been the custom for the Emperors of Delhi carefully to abstain from bestowing any high office in the state upon a member of the royal family. Shah Jehan was the first to alter this custom, and the innovation ultimately proved fatal to him. He treated his sons with the greatest confidence; placed them in responsible situations; and gave them the command of his armies. Their names were Dara, Shuja, Morad, and Aurangzib. They were all of very different characters. Dara was high-spirited and passionate; Shuja was sensual; Morad, the youngest, stupid and self-willed; and Aurangzib, crafty, cautious, scheming, and ambitious.

CHAP. III.

A. D. 1627.

The Emperor's treatment of his sons.

In 1657 Shah Jehan was taken alarmingly ill, and, being unable to carry on the government, he entrusted it to the charge of his eldest son, Dara. His other sons immediately commenced a contest for the crown, and declared war against their elder brother. Shuja, who was in Bengal, was the first to advance; but, during the preparation for war, Shah Jehan recovered, and Dara restored to him the supreme authority and power. Shuja, however, pretended to disbelieve the report of this change when he heard it; advanced towards Delhi with his army; and was defeated by Soliman, Dara's son.

Illness of Shah Jehan, and contention between his sons.

A. D. 1657.

In the meantime Aurangzib and Morad, the former of whom was in the Deckan, and the

Dissimulation of Aurangzib.

CHAP. III.
A. D. 1657.

latter in Guzerat, were not idle. Aurangzib pretended that he did not wish to be Emperor, that he desired to spend the remainder of his life in the services of religion, and that he would disinterestedly help Morad against his other brothers, who were, he affirmed, incapable of carrying on the government efficiently.

The defeat of Jeswunt Sing. April, 1658.

Prince Morad, believing these professions, advanced to join his army. A Rajput chief, named Jeswunt Sing, had been sent by Dara to oppose Aurangzib; but he purposely waited until Morad had arrived, so that he might triumph over both of the princes at once. He was, however, signally defeated.

Dara is defeated. June.

The two brothers then marched against Dara, who felt so certain of success that he refused to wait until his son Soliman could come to his assistance. A fierce battle took place. The princes were in the thickest of the fight; and Morad's howdah was covered with arrows and darts. An accident gave the victory to the rebel brothers. Dara, from some unknown cause, dismounted from the elephant on which he had been seated during the greater part of the engagement, and his troops, seeing the empty howdah, imagined that their leader was killed, and immediately fled in terror. While still on the field of battle, Aurangzib, covered with dust and blood, went up to Morad, and wished him joy of the victory and the throne.

On their arrival at Agra, they took their

A. D. 1658.

Aurangzib proclaims himself Emperor. August 20th.

father, Shah Jehan, prisoner. It was now time for Aurangzib to put away deceit. He therefore publicly proclaimed himself Emperor, threw his brother Morad into prison, and assumed charge of the government.

Battle between Aurangzib and Shuja. Jan. 3rd, 1659.

But he had still to contend with his other brother, Shuja, who was advancing against him with a large army. Another severe battle ensued, which he nearly lost by the perfidy of the Rajput, Jeswunt Sing, whom he had admitted into his favour, and who now treacherously attacked the rear-guard of his force. But victory was on his side. While their troops were fighting around them, Aurangzib and Shuja fought with each other on their elephants. One of Shuja's officers, rushing before his leader, made his elephant run against Aurangzib's, and brought it down upon its knees. Aurangzib was just about to descend from it, when an attendant prevented him, saying, "Stop—you descend from the throne." The Emperor remained and was saved. But what Aurangzib was withheld from doing Shuja did, and by that means lost the battle. Shuja for some time continued to give trouble to the new Emperor, but he was at length conquered and put to death by a Rajah with whom he had taken refuge. For a short time he had been assisted by Mahomed, Aurangzib's son, who had deserted his father's cause for the sake of Shuja's daughter, to whom he had become attached ; but the young prince was defeated by the Emperor, and imprisoned for life.

CHAP. III. A.D. 1659. The fate of Dara. Dara also fell into his brother's power. He tried to escape, but he was seized by a treacherous chief to whom he had twice done a kindness, and was delivered into the power of Aurangzib. He was imprisoned for a short time, and then murdered. Death of Shah Jehan. Dec. 1666. A few years afterwards, the deposed Shah Jehan died, and Aurangzib was left, with no one to oppose him, as the master of the large Empire of Delhi.

Rise of the Mahrattas. But a new nation had arisen in the Deckan. The Mahrattas, tribes of rude mountaineers, principally living in the country around Bombay, were now being united into a powerful state, by a great chief, who had lately arisen among them. Year by year they gained greater power; they kept Aurangzib in a state of constant warfare during the remainder of his reign; and, as they increased in strength, it seemed highly probable that they would rescue India from the Mahomedans, and restore the government to Hindu kings and princes.

Their method of warfare. Their mode of warfare was very different from that of the Moguls. Their armies were chiefly composed of light and active horsemen; they seldom waited to fight a battle, but rode rapidly from place to place, plundering as they went; if attacked, they would separate and flee, only to unite again, and fall upon small detached parties, and the baggage-guards of the enemy when scattered in pursuit. They were, in fact, more like several bands of robbers, united under the

CHAP. III.

A. D. 1662.

same leader and actuated by the same motive, than the army of a warlike and powerful nation.

Sevaji.

The name of the chief whom we have mentioned was Sevaji. He rose to power first by small acts of robbery, and then by greater. He gradually collected a band of hardy men around him; day by day he increased in power, and, taking, one after another, the hill forts of his native country, he at length became master of a considerable territory, and an object of danger to Aurangzib.

An example of his treachery and cunning.

The Government of the neighbouring kingdom of Bejapore attempted to subdue him, and to arrest his rising power; but he conquered the army which was sent against him in the following way. He pretended to be in a state of great alarm, and proposed a truce to its commander, requesting a private meeting, to which each party should come without arms and with only one attendant. This proposition was agreed to. The general came to the interview unarmed; but Sevaji had concealed a suit of light chain armour and helmet under his turban and long white robe, a small weapon formed like the claw of a beast being on his hand, and a dagger up his sleeve. As the Mussulman drew near, the Mahratta pretended to be frightened, and when the former advanced to embrace him, he put his armed fingers into his body, and stabbed him with his dagger. His troops then attacked the unsuspecting forces of his fallen adversary, and gained an easy victory over them.

CHAP. III.

A. D. 1665.

Rapid rise of Sevaji.

By similar treachery and cunning, Sevaji extended his power; his armies rapidly increased; and he led them throughout Southern India in search of plunder and employment. In 1665 he was crowned, with great splendour, as Rajah of the Mahrattas.

Aurangzib's wars in the Deckan.

After the death of Sevaji, the Mahratta power was supported by his son and successors; and, during the rest of his reign, Aurangzib was engaged in warfare against this new enemy. The Emperor's army was also employed against the Rajahs of Bejapore and Golconda, the latter of whom gallantly defended his capital during a siege of seven months. On the Mahrattas, however, Aurangzib could make no impression. He remained for years in the Deckan engaged in constant warfare against them, but as soon as they were beaten on one side they arose on another, and his large army could not move after them with sufficient rapidity.

His impolitic treatment of the Rajputs.

There were also troubles in other parts of the Empire. Aurangzib was a zealous Mahomedan, and was anxiously desirous of propagating the creed in which he believed; but the mode of conversion which his religion enjoins is not calculated to win the affection of others. All the Emperors of Delhi, from Akber downwards, had treated the Rajputs with kindness and consideration; but Aurangzib, in his zeal for his religion, thought fit to persecute them, to insist on their becoming Mahomedans, or to pay a tax from which Akber had wisely exempted them. The Rajputs,

CHAP. III.

A.D. 1679.

irritated by this unwise and unjust treatment, rebelled against their oppressor. They were not restored to obedience during his lifetime; and they refused to assist his successors in times of trouble and war, and thus accelerated the downfall of the Empire.

Aurangzib's death, and decline of the Empire. Feb. 21st, 1707.

In the midst of warfare and turbulence Aurangzib died. The Empire had begun to decline in his reign: but it rapidly decreased in power after his death, for his successors were feeble and unskilful monarchs, who wanted both the ability and the power to keep their large kingdom in subjection. Its destruction was quickened by an invasion of Nadir Shah, King of Persia, which, in horror and savage cruelties, greatly resembled the expedition of Tamerlane.

Invasion of Nadir Shah. Nov. 1738.

Annoyed with the Emperor for not delivering into his power some Affghans who had sought refuge near Ghazni, he invaded India, conquered the army which had been sent to oppose him, and captured the city of Delhi. For two days after he had taken possession of the town, tranquillity prevailed; but, a report being spread on the third night that Nadir Shah was dead, the inhabitants rose against the conquerors. Murder and violence ensued; and in the morning Nadir Shah was observed riding through the scene of destruction, and giving orders that the inhabitants of every street where the dead body of a Persian was found should be put to death. About thirty thousand were killed; and after this ter-

Massacre at Delhi. March, 1739.

CHAP. III. rible slaughter, the conqueror withdrew, laden with treasure and satiated with blood.

A. D. 1739.

Dissolution of the Mogul Empire.

After this invasion, the empire was completely disorganized. The Deckan was under a governor, called the Nizam, who threw off all obedience; Bengal was taken by another; Oude was seized by a third; the Sikhs, a new nation, which had arisen at the beginning of the 16th century, exercised authority in the Punjab; and the Mahrattas continued to increase in power, and though their Rajah was weak and powerless, and kept a prisoner at his Court, the principal officers of state—the Peishwa, or the prime minister, at Poona, and the Commander-in-chief, at Nagpore—kept up the strength of this warlike nation.

Rise of the English power in India.

But just at this time another power arose, which was to conquer and rule all, whether Mussulmans, Mahrattas, or Sikhs. During the 17th century, a few traders from an island in the far West, settled here and there in India. At first they attended only to the merchandise about which they had come; but they were, at length, obliged, by stern necessity, to take the sword into their hands, and gradually they acquired dominion, and province after province fell into their possession, until in the end all the land was theirs.

State of India under the Mahomedans.

We have now related the principal events of Mahomedan sovereignty in this country. To some periods we cannot look back without a shudder of horror: at other times the monarchs were wealthy, and the nation prosperous; but the people were never really cared for, except in the reigns of Feroze Shah, Akber, and Shir Shah; and during all the long years from Mahmud to Aurangzib, with only a slight gleam of light now and then, the peninsula of India was darkened by the most barbarous cruelties committed by tyrannical oppression, by continual civil wars and confusion, and by the wild excesses of arbitrary power.

CHAPTER IV.

EARLY EUROPEAN SETTLEMENTS IN INDIA.

To A. D. 1744.

Intercourse between India and Europe—the age of maritime adventure—Bartholomew Diaz rounds the Cape of Good Hope—Discovery of America—the first voyage round the Cape to India performed by Vasco de Gama—Cabral's voyage and contest with the Zamorin—Vasco de Gama second expedition—Early Portuguese settlements—Alphonso Albuquerque captures Goa and other towns—the Portuguese empire in the East—the Dutch trade with India—the English take a part in the same commerce—the East India Company—Contests between the three rival nations—the massacre of Amboyna—the second East India Company—Union of the two Companies—the settlements at Madras—Bombay—Fort St. David—and Calcutta—the French settlements in India.

Before we relate the progress of English power in the East, it will be interesting to mention the intercourse which existed, in former times, between India and Europe. This country was, as we have previously stated, early celebrated for its commerce and its wealth. We do not read, however, of any direct communication between its merchants and the merchants of Europe, where Indian manufactures were highly valued, except a few voyages undertaken by the Greeks in the first and second centuries. The commodities of India were conveyed to the shores of the Mediterranean, either by the inland trade through Central Asia, or by Arabian merchants to the Persian Gulf and the Red Sea, whence they were carried by caravans to the Egyptian and Syrian ports. They were there received by European traders, who, in the middle ages, principally belonged to the powerful republics of Genoa and Venice, which were greatly strengthened and enriched by this profitable commerce.

The age of maritime adventure.

At the end of the fifteenth century, however, an eager spirit of enterprise and adventure was awakened in Europe. The kingdoms of Portugal and Spain were among the first to profit by it, and several mariners of those countries succeeded in discovering distant regions which had never before been visited by Europeans.

Discovery of the Cape of Good Hope. A. D. 1487.

The Portuguese extended their researches along the western coast of Africa, each voyage affording them a more accurate knowledge of that extensive continent than they had previously attained. At length Bartholomew Diaz, a Portuguese captain in command of a small squadron, reached the southern extremity of the peninsula, and sailed round the celebrated promontory, which he named the Cape of Storms, on account of the tempestuous weather which he had experienced there. The

CHAP. IV. A. D. 1487. king of Portugal, however, delighted at a discovery, which afforded him the promise of a profitable communication with India, gave it a more pleasing name. He called it by its present title, the Cape of Good Hope.

No immediate results. The Portuguese did not immediately take advantage of their countryman's discovery, and ten years elapsed before an expedition was prepared in order to make the new route to India of avail.

Discovery of America. A. D. 1492. Meanwhile a far greater enterprise had been effected by their neighbours and rivals, the Spaniards, a party of whom had, under the command of Christopher Columbus, discovered the islands of the New World, which they at first believed to be a portion of India, and through which they imagined that there existed a short and speedy route to this country. This important discovery increased the desire for maritime adventure, which had, for some time past, been generally felt throughout Europe; but, while the Spaniards continued their researches in America, the Portuguese, under the direction of their sagacious king, Emanuel, made preparations for fresh discoveries towards the East.

The first voyage round the Cape to India. A. D. 1497. At the beginning of July 1497, Vasco de Gama, an experienced naval officer, sailed from Lisbon in command of three vessels, with instructions to proceed round the Cape of Good Hope to the shores of India. After a voyage of nearly eleven months, during which they visited many places in Africa, Vasco de Gama and his com-

CHAP. IV.

A. D. 1498.

panions landed at Calicut, upon the coast of Malabar. He there entered into communication with the Zamorin, as the sovereign of Malabar was styled, who, though at first inclined to favour him, was afterwards induced, by the advice of the Mussulman merchants, to shew him decided opposition. Vasco de Gama himself was imprisoned by one of the king's officers, but shortly afterwards released; when, having disposed of his cargo to the inhabitants of the place, most of whom were favourable to him, he set sail for Portugal, where he arrived after an absence of two years and two months. This important voyage was undertaken about the time when Baber, the founder of the Mogul Empire, ascended the throne in his native country, and before the Mahomedan power was extended over Southern India.

Cabral's voyage, and contest with the Zamorin.

A. D. 1500.

The king of Portugal received Vasco de Gama, upon his return to Europe, with marked honour and distinction; and, soon afterwards, prepared a more powerful expedition than the former, to continue the intercourse which had been so prosperously begun. Cabral, the commander of this fleet, being driven by a storm to the westward, discovered Brazil which proved in after times a most valuable possession to Portugal. His reception at Calicut was, in the first instance, friendly, as Vasco de Gama's had been, and he was permitted by the Zamorin to establish a factory near the town; but, owing to the misconduct of the Portuguese, as well as to the enmity of the Mahomedan traders, a severer op-

CHAP. IV.
A.D. 1500.

position than before was offered, the newly established factory was destroyed, and Cabral, after taking revenge by a partial destruction of the shipping and the town, departed for Cochin, the king of which was a discontented dependant of the Zamorin. After lading his vessels at the harbour of Cochin, Cabral returned to Portugal, and informed his sovereign of the hostility and opposition which he had encountered.

Vasco de Gama's second voyage.

Emanuel, desirous of founding an empire in the East, speedily prepared a larger and stronger armament than had yet sailed for India, and appointed the veteran mariner, Vasco de Gama, to the chief command.

Intercourse between Portugal and India.

From this time forward frequent expeditions were despatched from Portugal to India with the combined objects of commerce and of war. The ports of Cochin and Cannanore were generally selected for the former purpose: and effectual aid was afforded to the Rajah of Cochin against the Zamorin, who twice invaded his dominions, and was defeated, on the last occasion, by the courage of a small party of Portuguese soldiers.

Alphonso Albuquerque.
A. D. 1510.

In 1510, Alphonso Albuquerque who had, for some time previously, been appointed Viceroy of India, obtained the chief command in the Portuguese possessions. He was a man of eager, daring, and ambitious spirit; and he immediately proceeded to realize the schemes of conquest and dominion, to which he had for a long time past aspired. His principal object was to gain possession of a

CHAP. IV.

A. D. 1510.

secure and strongly fortified harbour, which might be converted into a central port for the Portuguese fleet, and the capital of a Portuguese empire. His first attempt was upon Calicut, from which he was repulsed with severe loss. He subsequently captured Goa, during the absence of the Rajah, who had not afforded him the slightest cause for provocation. This city, being situated in a central position on the Western Coast, was admirably adapted for his purpose: it was for many years the capital of the Portuguese dominions in the East, and it remains to this day in their possession.

The Portuguese empire.

His next conquests were Malacca, in the Malay Peninsula, and the island of Ormuz, in the Persian Gulf, both favourable positions for the purposes of commerce: and, at the time of his death in 1515, the empire of the Portuguese had attained its full extent. They possessed, indeed, only a few factories and forts on the coast of India: but their fleets commanded the Indian Ocean, and they exclusively maintained the trade with Europe.

The Dutch trade with India.

At the end of the sixteenth century, however, the Dutch began to take a part in the commerce of the Spice Islands and of India. They, in like manner, established factories in the places most desirable for trade, and they proved to be formidable rivals to the Portuguese, whose power and interest in the country gradually decreased before these and other opponents. The Dutch trade was principally with the islands of the Indian Archipelago, and the capital of their eastern possessions

CHAP. IV. A. D. 1600.

was Batavia, a town which they bnilt on the northern coast of Java: but they subsequently obtained Negapatam, Pulicat, Chinsura, and other places on the continent of India.

The English trade with India.

At the same time that the Dutch appeared as rivals to the Portuguese, the English made their first endeavours to obtain a share in the same profitable trade. They had previously attempted to open a direct route for their commerce; but they soon discovered that their only chance of success lay in adopting the same channel for it as the Dutch and Portuguese. Some merchants of London combined for this purpose in the last year of the century, and obtained a charter in A. D. 1600, as "The Governor and Company of Merchants trading to the East Indies." This was the origin of the powerful East India Company, which was established when Elizabeth was Queen of England, and Akber Emperor of Delhi.

Disgraceful rivalry between the three nations.

The English, Dutch, and Portuguese were for many years constantly at war with each other: and the Indian trade, which was ample enough to have occupied the energies of all these three nations, was conducted in a very unbecoming spirit of rivalry and hatred. Piracy was common, and cruel treatment of each other of frequent occurrence. The massacre of Amboyna was the most melancholy instance of this jealousy. The Dutch garrison murdered in cold blood the eighteen Englishmen and their dependants who were stationed on that island, notwithstanding a treaty concluded between the East India Companies of

The massacre of Amboyna. A. D. 1621.

A. D. 1621.

England and Holland, by which it had been agreed that the trade should be conducted by the merchants of both nations in a friendly and peaceable manner.

Rivalry between the English merchants.

The English East India Company had, moreover, to contend with their own countrymen, as well as with their opponents of foreign nations. Private adventurers, on whom they bestowed the contemptuous name of 'interlopers,' endeavoured to interfere with the trade: and the mismanagement that prevailed at the end of the seventeenth century, both in their Indian settlements and in England, induced certain merchants of London to establish a rival company. The directors of the two companies heartily exerted themselves to supplant each other, and to obtain from the English Government a charter, which would afford the successful party the exclusive right of trading with India. These disgraceful contests continued until the year 1708, when the contending parties, finding themselves injured mutually, made an amicable settlement with each other, and formed an association which has, from that time, been known by the name of "The United East India Company."

The United East India Company.

A. D. 1708.

The new Company consisted of a body of proprietors, who possessed shares in the money by which the undertaking was carried on, and from whom twenty-four persons were chosen to direct the affairs of the Company, and to manage all matters connected with its policy and trade. These arrangements were continued, with various modifi-

CHAP. IV. A. D. 1708. cations, until the year 1858, when the dominions of the Company were placed under the direct authority of the Crown.

Origin of Madras. A.D. 1639. The attention of the united Company was almost entirely directed to the continent of India. The trade of the English had at first been principally with the Spice Islands, where they had been brought into collision with the Dutch: but they soon abandoned the commerce of that region to their energetic rivals, and founded settlements at various places in Hindostan. They possessed, however, nothing besides the factories, or houses which they had built for commercial purposes, until the year 1639, when they were permitted by the Rajah of Chandragherry to erect a fortress at Madras. They had, some time previously, been in possession of a factory at Armogum, or rather at Dugarajapatam, about thirty miles south of Nellore: but it was not found to be an advantageous place for trade, and was consequently abandoned.

The acquisition of Bombay. A.D 1662. The island of Bombay was given by the Portuguese to Charles the Second in 1662, as part of the dowry of the Princess Catherine of Portugal, whom he married; and it was, a few years later, ceded to the Company on the condition of their paying annually a certain sum to the sovereign.

Fort St. David built. Fort St. David was built at Tegnapatam, near Cuddalore. The town had been purchased by the Company, and afterwards became the principal station on the Coromandel Coast.

CHAP. IV.

A. D. 1662.

Origin of Calcutta.

A. D. 1700.

In the year 1700, Fort William was constructed at Calcutta, where the English had purchased some land, and, soon afterwards, they were permitted, in consequence of services which Dr. Hamilton, an English physician, had rendered to the reigning Emperor, to acquire a larger amount of territory around Calcutta and Madras.

French settlements in India.

The East India Company at this time encountered other rivals, with whom they had afterwards a more arduous struggle than they had experienced with the Dutch or Portuguese. About the middle of the seventeenth century, the French, who had formed an East India Company in imitation of the English and the Dutch, attempted to found a settlement at Surat. They failed in that quarter: but they subsequently obtained possession of Pondicherry, with a considerable territory around it, where they established a settlement which prospered rapidly, and upon which the smaller stations of Mahé, on the Western Coast, and Chandernagore, near Calcutta, were dependant. The contests with this latter power ended in the final triumph of the English, and in the establishment of their extensive Empire in the East, to the history of which the following narrative is principally devoted.

CHAPTER V.

THE RISE OF ENGLISH POWER IN INDIA.

FROM A. D. 1744 TO A. D. 1753.

War between England and France—the French in India—Dupleix—the English in India—Sepoy corps—Labourdonnais takes Madras—Siege of Fort St. David—Petty war in Tanjore—Peace in Europe: but the war continued in India—State of affairs in Southern India—Nazir Jung and Mirzapha Jung—Anwar-ud-dien and Chunda Sahib—Struggle for the thrones at Hyderabad and Arcot—the French take one side and the English the other—M. Bussy—the French victorious—Salabut Jung made Nizam—Dupleix' triumph and delight—Mahomed Ali besieged at Trichinopoly—Robert Clive takes Arcot—Gallant defence of that city—Victory at Arnee—Defeat of Rajah Sahib near Madras—Lawrence relieves Trichinopoly—Surrender of the French garrison at Seringham—Chunda Sahib murdered—Lawrence defeats the French at Bahoor—Clive takes Covelong and Chingleput—returns to England.

WE have now to relate the story of British conquest and rule in India; and we know no tale more deeply interesting than the true one, which tells us how a few men, far away from the country of their birth and love, won for her

CHAP. V.

A. D. 1744.

an empire of surpassing wealth, extent, and power, and afterwards governed it with so much ability and moderation, that they added to her fame and honour, and at the same time conferred the blessings of prosperity and good government upon the Indian people.

War between England and France.

In 1744 war broke out between France and England, and soon reached India, where both of those nations had, as we have already stated, several flourishing settlements.

Monsieur. Dupleix.

The French were at that time the greatest in number. Their chief city was Pondicherry, and their governor was an intelligent and ambitious statesman, named Dupleix, who had shewn himself most skilful in the management of intrigues and treaties in native courts. He was the first to discover that the soldiers of India, if commanded by European officers, are almost equal in bravery to the troops of Europe, and to form the design of using the frequent quarrels of the Indian princes for the advantage of his country. The first desire of his heart was to conquer India; and he employed all the knowledge and power which he possessed for the accomplishment of that object.

The English in India.

The English had no such leader. They were few in number, and knew more of trade than of war. They adopted, however, the policy of Dupleix, by taking native soldiers into their service and by training them under the superintendence of English officers. The number of these troops was, at first, small: but it was increased, as the

CHAP. V.
A. D. 1746.

English power in India extended, and the sepoys, as the native soldiers are called, proved themselves, until lately, their devoted and courageous adherents.

Labourdonnais attacks Madras.

Soon after the war had begun, the French Government permitted Labourdonnais, the governor of Bourbon and the Isle of France,* to collect a fleet, and to attack Fort St. George, the chief settlement which the English then possessed in the Carnatic.

The capture of Madras. Sep. 10th.

It was not long before he appeared off that fortress. After only five days' defence the English surrendered the town and fort of Madras, which Labourdonnais promised to restore upon the payment of a moderate ransom. This promise, however, displeased Dupleix, who was very jealous of the successful commander. He sent the English to Pondicherry as prisoners, and treated them in a manner at once ungenerous to them, and disgraceful to himself.

Attacks on Fort St David. Decr. 1746, and March, 1747.

Monsieur Dupleix next attempted to take Fort St. David, the capture of which would have rendered him the sole master of the Carnatic; and he asked for help from the Nabob, whom he persuaded to join him in an alliance against the English. But a strong fleet arriving with troops from England, the siege of Fort St. David was immediately discontinued: and the French retreated to Pondicherry, where they were, in their turn, besieged.

War in Tanjore.

But the English, though now the most powerful party, were not strong enough to capture

* Now called Ré-union and Mauritius.

CHAP. V.

A. D. 1749.

that town, and they consequently abandoned their contest with the French, and took part in a petty war which had lately been commenced in the neighbouring province of Tanjore. The Rajah, who had been dethroned by his brother, entered into a bargain with them to assist him against the usurper, agreeing to give them the fort of Devicottah as the price of their aid. A small English force was sent to attack the fort. After a short time, however, peace was restored; the reigning prince surrendering Devicottah and a small portion of the adjacent country, on condition that the English would no longer help his brother, whose cause they disgracefully abandoned.

Capture and cession of Devicottah.

Meanwhile peace had been proclaimed in Europe between France and England: but the war did not cease in India. The men of these nations could not, indeed, be the chief parties in the strife; they could not attack each other's armies, nor besiege each other's towns; but they assisted certain native princes who were in open warfare, and, taking different sides in the contest, were arrayed against each other as before.

Peace in Europe, but war continued in India.

We must now describe the state of affairs in Southern India, that the events which follow may be better understood. There were, at the time of which we are writing, two large kingdoms in that part of India. The ruler of the first and largest was called the Nizam, whose Court was held at Hyderabad, and who, once in reality,

State of affairs in Southern India.

CHAP. V.

A. D. 1750.

but now in name only, governed his kingdom as the dependent of the Emperor. The sovereign of the other was the Nabob of the Carnatic. His capital was Arcot, and he ruled under the Nizam.

Contest for the thrones of Arcot and Hyderabad.

The thrones of these kingdoms were, about this time, vacated. To the former, Nazir Jung, a son of the last Nizam, succeeded: to the latter, a prince named Anwar-ud-dien. Both of them had rivals. The opponent of Nazir Jung was one of his nephews, Mirzapha Jung; and that of Anwar-ud-dien was Chunda Sahib, the son-in-law of a former ruler. The two latter joined forces, and begged an alliance with the French. This request was eagerly and joyfully granted. It was the very thing Dupleix desired. He immediately sent 400 French soldiers and 2000 sepoys to their aid. A battle was fought, and ended in favour of the usurpers. Anwar-ud-dien was killed; and his son, Mahomed Ali, fled with the remnant of his army to Trichinopoly. The French, under Bussy, the bravest and acutest leader they ever had in India, gained many victories, and seated Mirzapha Jung on the throne. The new Nizam did not, however, enjoy his triumph long. He was killed in battle, while attempting to put down a revolt, and Bussy raised Salabut Jung, Nazir Jung's younger brother, to the throne in his stead. Chunda Sahib also gained the power which he had desired.

Exultation and triumph of Dupleix.

This was the hour of Dupleix's triumph. The Nizam and the Nabob owed their authority to him; he was nominated Governor of Southern

CHAP. V.

A. D. 1750.

India; the highest dignities and honours were bestowed upon him; all his wishes seemed to be fulfilled; and, in the height of his joy, he raised a pillar near the site of his chief victory, upon which he placed inscriptions setting forth his own praises, and around which a town arose named the City of the Victory of Dupleix.

Apathy of the English.

The English favoured the other party; but while the French had done much for their allies, they had done little. They had sent a small force to help Mahomed Ali, whom they still owned as Nabob of the Carnatic, but their assistance was of little avail. He was closely besieged in Trichinopoly; and, seeing the French every where victorious, he was on the point of surrendering that city, deserting his allies, and joining their enemies, when an event took place which completely altered his views.

The meditated attack upon Arcot.

At this time a young captain in Fort St. David proposed to the English council an attack upon Arcot, the capital of the Carnatic. By this movement, he argued, Trichinopoly would be relieved, as Chunda Sahib would be sure to abandon the siege of that place, when he heard that his chief city was in danger. The members of the council approved of this plan, and the proposer himself was permitted to carry it into effect.

Robert Clive.

The young soldier's name was Clive; and it is chiefly to his great courage and thoughtful skill that the English Empire in India owes its existence. He was a man of bold and high spirit, of a

CHAP. V. A. D. 1751.

proud and fiery temper; but, at the same time, of genius, tact, and foresight. He had been at first sent out to India as a civilian; but he exchanged a service unsuited to his character for the life of a soldier, and soon shewed by his bravery and daring that the army was his proper profession.

Clive's advance upon Arcot. August 26th.

On the 26th of August, 1751, he left Madras with a small force of 200 Englishmen and 300 sepoys. He marched rapidly to Arcot. Though the weather was stormy, he still held on his way. Through lightning, rain, and thunder, he led his little band, until they reached the ancient fortress, which the enemy abandoned almost at the very moment that he marched in. Upon his arrival, he began to put the deserted citadel in order. He repaired the crumbling walls; strengthened the battlements to sustain a siege; quieted the fears of the natives who still remained within the fort; and prevented any outrage on the property which had been left there for safety. He made frequent sallies against those parties of the enemy which lingered round their former stronghold. In all of these he was successful: but, amidst all, he still urged forward the defences for the great siege which he was expecting.

Chunda Sahib despatches an army to Arcot. September 23rd.

He had not long to wait. The news of his having taken the capital was quickly carried to Chunda Sahib at Trichinopoly: and a strong force, which soon amounted to 10,000 men, 150 of whom were French, was forthwith sent from the main army to its relief, under the command of Rajah Sahib, the Nabob's son. CHAP. V. A. D. 1751.

The dauntless bearing of the little garrison.

Meanwhile the occupants of Arcot had suffered much from death. Only 120 Englishmen and 200 sepoys were left; but their hearts were strong, and, dauntless to the last, they awaited the assault. The siege lasted fifty days. The overwhelming army brought against them steadily maintained the attack; the breaches increased day by day; hunger, as well as their foes, fought against the gallant little garrison: but hunger, and danger, and death drew them nearer to each other. The sepoys were starving; but they came to their young leader, and asked leave to give all the remaining rice to their English comrades; the water in which it was boiled being enough, they said, for them.

The unselfishness of the sepoys.

The promised assistance from Morari Row.

Relief from Madras was attempted, but failed. There was, however, aid at hand. An army of Mahrattas, led by a chief named Morari Row, undecided whether to favour the French or English arms, remained inactive on the frontiers of the Carnatic, not very far from Arcot. The noble defence of that place inspirited their leader: and, when Clive asked him for help, he answered, that, as he now saw Englishmen could fight for themselves, he would willingly be upon their side.

The assault. Nov. 14th.

Rajah Sahib, hearing of this offer, felt that no time ought to be lost, and gave a last summons

CHAP. V. A. D. 1751.

for the garrison to yield. After trying all the means of insult, bribery, and threats in vain, he prepared for the final assault. He selected for it the anniversary of the Moharrum, the greatest of the Mahomedan feasts. His soldiers, maddened with bhang, and frantic with the recollection of the saddening events that festival recalls, were led on to the breaches.

The victory.

Clive was, however, prepared. The enemy was beaten back at every quarter, and retired, leaving 400 dead on the spot where they had fought. A desultory fire was kept up by the besiegers from the afternoon of the following day until midnight, when it ceased. The next morning, when the sun rose, the vast army which had been so long around Arcot was gone.

The battle of Arnee, and Clive's return.

Soon after this triumph, Clive received help from Madras, and, thus strengthened, he pursued the retreating enemy. Overtaking Rajah Sahib's army near Arnee, he gained a complete victory, the results of which were important, as 600 sepoys disciplined by the French deserted to his camp, and the enemy's treasure fell into his hands. Having captured on his way the large pagoda at Conjeveram, which had been held by a French garrison, he returned to Fort St. David. His object was gained. The siege of Trichinopoly languished, the resources of the enemy were crippled, and Mahomed Ali was generally owned as Nabob of the Carnatic.

CHAP. V.

A. D 1752.

Rajah Sahib is again defeated by Clive. February.

About three months afterwards, Rajah Sahib, with a large army, of which 400 were Frenchmen, advanced against Fort St. George. Clive, who had returned to Madras, went out to meet him; but he would not wait for a battle: he retreated without a blow, afraid, it would appear, of the very name of Clive. That officer, however, overtook the enemy's forces at Covrepauk, where he defeated them with considerable loss. After this battle, Rajah Sahib's troops disbanded, the French portion of them returning to Pondicherry. On his victorious return to Fort St. David, Clive passed the pillar and city which Dupleix had raised; when he ordered both to be utterly destroyed, wisely judging that this token of power would inspire with awe the mind of a people who are materially influenced by pomp and show.

Reinforcements sent to Trichinopoly. March 17th

The siege of Trichinopoly was still carried on: and it was, at this time, thought necessary to relieve that city more effectually than had yet been done. The Government therefore resolved to send Clive thither; but, in the mean time, his old commander, Major Lawrence, returned from England, and was, of course, appointed in Clive's stead. The latter went as second in command.

The English are joined by new allies.

Upon their arrival at Trichinopoly, the English found that Mahomed Ali had lately been reinforced by 14,000 men from Mysore, 6,000 Mahrattas, and troops from Tanjore.

Being unwilling to sustain an attack from this

CHAP. V.

A. D. 1752.

Capitulation of the French at Seringham. June 3rd.

formidable force, the French retreated to Seringham, a strongly fortified pagoda situated on an island of the same name close to Trichinopoly, where they were besieged by the English and their allies. Many attempts were made to relieve their countrymen by the French at Pondicherry; but they were all defeated by Clive's unwearying watchfulness, and, after a few weeks of bold defence, the garrison surrendered.

The murder of Chunda Sahib.

Meanwhile Chunda Sahib had been deserted by his troops; and, after the capitulation of his French allies, he gave himself up to the leader of the Tanjore forces, who had promised him protection but who deliberately broke his word, and beheaded the poor, helpless captive; and this, we grieve to say, without a word of remonstrance from the English general.

Trichinopoly in possession of the English.

Trichinopoly, which had been the scene of constant warfare for the last two years, was now in the possession of the English, who held it for their ally; and, leaving a sufficient garrison there, Major Lawrence returned to Fort St. David. Before returning, however, he attempted to take the strong fort of Gingee, in order to establish the authority of Mahomed Ali in that part of the country, but was repulsed in the attempt. Soon afterwards he met the French army in force near the village of Bahoor, between Fort St. David and Pondicherry, where he was again triumphant.

Action at Bahoor. August.

Clive had, in the meantime, been sent to

CHAP. V.

A. D. 1752.

Clive takes Covelong and Chingleput. Sept. and Oct.

reduce the forts of Covelong and Chingleput, near Madras. His party was chiefly composed of recruits who had just arrived from England; but this disadvantage gave him an opportunity of shewing how good a soldier and how skilful an officer he was; for, even with such men, he performed the duty assigned to him. Not long afterwards, he returned to his native country, for the benefit of his health, which had for some time past been failing.

He returns to England.

Situation of the English in the Carnatic.

He left the Coromandel coast in a far different state from that in which he had found it on his arrival, eight years before. The French power was then becoming greater day by day: it was now rapidly declining. The schemes of Dupleix were then steadily advancing: they were now completely crushed. The English were then occupied only with their invoices and ledgers: they were now masters of the Carnatic, showing by their courage in battle and by their firmness in times of trial, that they were worthy of the great power which they were shortly to obtain.

CHAPTER VI.

THE BLACK HOLE AND SPEEDY RETRIBUTION.

FROM A. D. 1753 TO A. D. 1757.

Continuation of the war—Truce between the French and English—Clive's return—Gheriah destroyed—Surajah Dowlah—Capture of Calcutta—the Black Hole—Approach of the avenger—Calcutta retaken—the Nabob's army beaten—Peace with the Nabob—Chandernagore taken—Inconsistent behaviour of Surajah Dowlah—Conspiracy against him—Meer Jaffier—the English engage in the plot,—which is nearly defeated by Omichund—His avarice and cunning—He is disgracefully outwitted—the English march towards Moorshedabad—the battle of Plassey—the victory—the English reach the capital—Meer Joffier is made Nabob—Disappointment and death of Omichund—Murder of Surajah Dowlah.

THE war was continued after Clive's departure, but neither the English nor the French shewed much vigour in its prosecution. Trichinopoly was in the hands of the former: but constant quarrels

CHAP. VI.
A. D. 1754.

about the possession of that city arose between them and their allies, which ended in the alliance being dissolved and many of the native princes deserting to the French.

Negotiations with the French.

But peace with France was near. The French Government did not approve of all that Dupleix had done. He was recalled from the scene of his triumphs, honours, downfall, and defeat ; and returned to his native land, where persecution and an unhonoured death awaited him. A commissioner named Monsieur Godheu was sent out to treat with the English, in whose favour the negotiations ended, as their officers, being on the spot, knew the importance of the object for which they were treating better than the French officer, who had not been in India before.

Clive returns to India. Oct. 1755.

Although there was peace between France and England both in India and in Europe, the English Government clearly foresaw that war would soon break out again. Desiring, therefore, to provide for the safety of their Indian possessions before hostilities really took place, they resolved to send out Clive once more, as the fittest man for the post of danger. They appointed him Governor of Fort St. David; and the king gave him a commission as Lieutenant Colonel in the royal service.

The destruction of Gheriah. Feb 13th, 1756.

His first exploit after his return was to destroy a horde of Mahratta pirates, who had for years infested the western seas. Their chief stronghold was a fort named Gheriah. It was

CHAP. VI. A. D. 1756.

attacked both by sea and land, and the power of the pirates was completely broken by its fall.

Saddening reports from Bengal.

But greater deeds than these were before him. Soon after his arrival at Fort St. David, news of spirit-stirring events was brought from Bengal. The Nabob of that country had taken Calcutta: the captive Englishmen had been murdered in the foulest manner: the English name had been disgraced; and the thoughts of their countrymen in the south were now turned only towards revenge.

Aliverdy Khan, Nabob of Bengal.

The provinces of Bengal, Orissa, and Bahar, in the north east of India, had been for a long time under a powerful ruler, named Aliverdy Khan, who, like most of the other Nabobs and Rajahs, had formerly governed under the Emperor of Delhi, but was now quite independent, except in name. He died in April 1756.

The character and conduct of Surajah Dowlah.

Aliverdy Khan was succeeded by his grandson, Surajah Dowlah, who was of a remarkably cruel and selfish disposition. From his youth he had entertained a bitter hatred against the English; and, soon after he ascended the throne, he shewed it openly. The English traders at Calcutta, foreseeing the threatened war with the French, had begun to place the walls of Fort William in repair. This proceeding annoyed the Nabob, and he ordered them to stop the repairs, but his order was entirely disregarded. Enraged at this insult, and at a refusal to deliver up one of his subjects who had taken refuge at Calcutta, he assembled an army, and marched against that town.

Ay.

CHAP. VI.

A. D. 1756.

The siege and capture of Calcutta.

June 18th to 20th.

Fort William was ill prepared to sustain a siege. The walls were old, the garrison small, and their weapons in bad order. Nevertheless, the fort was defended for three days: but the English found the enemy too strong for them, and, when the time for an assault drew near, their hearts failed them. The governor, the commandant, and many others ran away, and found safety on board the ships in the river. A hundred and ninety men were still left in the fort: and these chose Mr. Holwell, a civilian, for their leader. On the third day the place was taken, and quickly over-run by the savage soldiers of the Nabob, all eager for plunder. The Nabob himself was soon on the spot. He ordered the prisoners to be brought before him, and greedily inquired after the treasure which he fancied was in the place. He treated them, however, with kindness, and promised them that their lives should be spared. He then gave them over to the charge of a guard. The soldiers led them away and placed them all—they were a hundred and forty-six in number—in the common dungeon of the fort, a dark, dismal room, only twenty feet square. The unhappy men, after the promises of safety which they had heard, could scarcely believe that their jailors were in earnest. But they were soon undeceived. They were all thrust into the little room, and the door was locked upon them.

The Black Hole.

June 20th.

They were to pass the night there. Filled with desperation at the thought, they used every means to free themselves. By turns they struggled,

CHAP. VI. A.D. 1756.

implored, yelled, bribed. But their guards were deaf to their cries; and even held torches up to the barred window, so as better to see their victims, and to mock them in their agony. They begged that the Nabob might be told of their situation. The Nabob, their jailors answered, was asleep, and must not be disturbed. The heat was intense, for it was the middle of the hot weather; and their thirst became unquenchable. They begged for water, and water was brought: but they scrambled for the scanty supply, and spilt it, and the soldiers would bring no more.

Sufferings of the prisoners.

As the night wore away, their sufferings increased. Entreaties, oaths, prayers rang through the room. They trampled on each other, and fought one with another in their despair. But this gradually subsided. Heat and thirst had done their work: and, one by one, the sufferers dropped down to die in that foul dungeon. When the door was opened in the morning, only twenty-three were found alive, and they were scarcely able to move.

The Nabob returns to his capital in triumph.

The Nabob was ignorant of these horrors; but when he heard of them, he shewed no signs of anger against the murderers, nor feeling for the murdered. Soon afterwards, he returned to his capital in triumph, boasting of his grand deeds, and glorying in his splendid victory.

Approach of the avenger.

But vengeance was near. News of these sad events had been sent to Madras, where a force was immediately assembled and embarked on the

16th October, in Admiral Watson's fleet, which was lying in the roads. Clive was placed at the head of the army, which had been prepared for departure with the utmost despatch. Owing to adverse winds, however, it did not reach Bengal before December.

Re-capture of Calcutta. Jan. 2d, 1757.

But the moment he landed, Clive marched quickly forward. He took several forts as he advanced; defeated the Nabob's army; retook Calcutta; and captured the fort and town of Hooghly. Surajah Dowlah, hearing of these events, came to meet him with a larger army than the one which had just been beaten: but Clive defeated it also, and drove it back with severe loss.

Conclusion of peace. Feb. 9th.

The Nabob was thoroughly frightened by these rapid movements, and earnestly begged for peace. Clive, although exceedingly unwilling to do so, was obliged to accept this offer, because war had broken out between France and England; and, if he had been engaged in warfare with the Nabob, the French could have attacked him with greater advantage than if he were able to attend to their movements only. A treaty of peace was, therefore, entered into, by which all the possessions of the English in Bengal were restored to them, the duty on their merchandise passing through the Nabob's country was taken off, and leave to fortify Calcutta was granted.

The capture of Chandernagore. March 23rd.

Clive now turned his attention to the French, who had, as we have stated, a large settlement at Chandernagore, a little north of Calcutta. He

CHAP. VI.

A. D. 1757.

resolved to attack that place, and asked permission from the Nabob, who, after a great deal of hesitation, granted it. The fleet and army moved up the river, and, after a short but stubborn resistance, Chandernagore fell.

Irritability and inconsistency of the Nabob.

This conquest made the English more powerful than they had yet been in Bengal. The Nabob was very dissatisfied. He felt how dangerous his new allies were, and he imagined himself unsafe while they continued in the country. He was looking out for an opportunity to break the peace he had himself desired, and to get rid of the English, whom, at the same time, he most heartily feared. These feelings made his behaviour very inconsistent. One day he pretended to be very friendly to the English, and the next entreated the French commander in the Deckan to help him against them; one day he treated Clive's letters in the most contemptuous manner, and the next sent answers full of the grossest flattery; one day he abused the English resident, Mr. Watts, threatening him with the most horrible death, and the next received him at the durbar with every mark of respect, and presented him with a dress of honour. This conduct, and the constant ill-usage with which he treated his subjects, so disgusted all classes, that a conspiracy was entered into by his principal officers, to dethrone him, and to make Meer Jaffier, the Commander-in-chief of his troops, Nabob in his stead. This plot was disclosed to Clive and the members of council at Calcutta. The latter

Conspiracy against him.

The English take part in the plot.

CHAP. VI.

A. D. 1757.

wished to have nothing to do with the affair: but Clive allayed their fears, persuaded them to support Meer Jaffier, and to enter into correspondence with him.

The under-hand proceeding of Omichund.

The plot, in which the English were now engaged, proceeded favourably: but, as the time drew near for its being carried out, it was almost defeated by Omichund, a Hindu merchant of considerable influence. He had been a party to the scheme throughout, but was, at the same time, in the confidence of the Nabob. He resolved, therefore, to take advantage of his peculiar position, and, being very covetous, to add to his riches by the events then taking place. He informed Clive, therefore, that he would reveal every thing to the Nabob, unless a bond for thirty lacs of rupees were given him, as a reward for secrecy.

He is disgracefully outwitted by Clive.

The Council at Calcutta were disheartened; but Clive, using his own weapons against the artful miser, persuaded them to prepare two agreements; one, on white paper, being the real one, in which Omichund's name did not appear; the other, being a false one, on red paper, in which all that he had asked for was promised. Clive's proposal was adopted. All signed the agreements, except Admiral Watson, who refused to have any thing to do with the matter. Clive determined, however, that this should be no hindrance to the scheme; and he had the wickedness to forge the Admiral's name upon the papers, the latter of which being shown to Omichund, his greediness was satisfied and his silence secured. The real

CHAP. VI. A. D. 1757. treaty was, of course, the only one with which the conspirators were concerned.

The advance to Moorshedabad. Meanwhile, Clive wrote a friendly letter to the Nabob, to allay the suspicions he was beginning to express: but, at the same time, desired Mr. Watts to hurry forward the preparations for the revolt. Meer Jaffier, however, giving him great uneasiness by his hesitating conduct, Clive resolved to act at once, and to march forthwith for the scene of action.

Declaration of war. He wrote to Surajah Dowlah, accusing him of bad faith in seeking help from the French; and telling him that the English were on their way to his capital, where they would submit the matters under dispute to the principal men of his court. This was in reality to declare war: and the Nabob, feeling that it was so, put his army in motion, and proceeded against the advancing English.

Amount and position of the English force. Clive, in the meantime, had marched from Chandernagore with a small force, consisting of 900 Englishmen, 2100 sepoys, and eight pieces of cannon. As he drew near the enemy, he wavered. He had heard nothing lately of Meer Jaffier. His situation was dangerous. He was with a handful of troops in a hostile land, and, if he were unable to conquer his enemies, who far out-numbered them, the power of England, not only in Bengal, but throughout the whole of India, would be completely crushed. He was encamped near a river, and, if he crossed it, there could be no retreat. He consequently called a council of war, and asked the opinion of his officers, whether they should cross the stream and fight, or remain where they were.

Clive regains his self-reliance.

The greater number, and Clive among them, were against immediate action. After the council, however, he withdrew to a grove of mango trees, and there he spent an hour in quiet thought. In that hour he determined to dare all. Clive was himself again. He returned to the camp, and ordered the men to prepare for an advance upon the morrow.

The encampment at Plassey.

After a day's march, he came within sight of the enemy, who was encamped near the village of Plassey. The hostile force was very large. There could not be less than 35,000 men, 15,000 of whom were cavalry; and they had 40 pieces of cannon, under the command of a French officer. Clive's little army bivouacked in a grove of mango trees, about two miles from them; and all the following night the shrill sounds of the rude clarions and cymbals, and the distant hum of that huge host were heard in his camp.

The battle of Plassey. June 23rd.

The battle began at sunrise, with a cannonade from the Nabob's army. It did not do much damage, as the English were protected in the grove by a high bank of mud. Their few guns returned the fire, and, being well aimed, did considerable mischief. This continued until noon, when a heavy shower of rain damaged the enemy's ammunition.

The retreat.

After the rain had ceased, the cannonade was continued till two o'clock in the afternoon, when the small party of English were cheered by the

CHAP. VI. A. D. 1757.

exciting news that the enemy was retiring. One of the Nabob's chief officers had been killed by a cannon ball; and this had so thoroughly frightened him, that he yielded to the treacherous advice of his courtiers, and ordered a retreat, which, for a short time, was conducted in an orderly manner.

The victory.

But Clive, advancing from the grove, had taken a small tank which had been occupied by the French during the day, and which afforded him a commanding position for his guns. He then dashed forward, and attacked the entrenched camp to which the enemy was retiring. His success was complete. The retreat was turned into a rout: and, on every side, the Nabob's strange, barbaric host gave way and fled.

Clive's reception of Meer Jaffier.

The battle was thus won by Clive, who pursued the enemy for six miles, when he halted for the night. He was soon afterwards visited by Meer Jaffier, who came to congratulate him on the victory which he had gained. Meer Jaffier was doubtful how Clive would receive him, for he had given no assistance to his allies, except, perhaps, by his not interfering in the action, and by his aiding neither one side nor the other. Clive, however, received him in a friendly manner, treated him kindly and courteously, and saluted him as Nabob of Bahar, Orissa, and Bengal.

Installation of the new sovereign. June 29th.

They advanced together to Moorshedabad, the capital, to seize the treasury of the late Nabob, and to secure the allegiance of the people; and the new sovereign was proclaimed with great pomp in that city, the brave Englishman handing him to the throne in the midst of the thousands who had assembled to witness the ceremony.

Reading the treaty.

The principal men engaged in the revolution retired soon afterwards to the house of a wealthy and influential Hindu, where the treaty was read, and the subject of reward to the English discussed.

Final arrangements.

The treasure found in Surajah Dowlah's palace was less than had been expected. Meer Jaffier promised, therefore, to pay at once half of the sum which he had agreed to give, and the rest within the next three years: liberal presents were given to the English officers: and it was agreed that the English should enjoy all their former privileges; that they should possess the Zemindary of the country south of Calcutta, as far as Calpee; and that their goods, when passing through the Nabob's territory, should be almost entirely free from taxation.

The fate of Omichund.

When the parties retired, as we have stated, Omichund accompanied them, fully expecting to receive the large sum which had been promised to him. He was very much astonished, however, to hear a treaty that was very different from the one of which he had a copy. When the reader ceased, he was told that the red treaty was a sham, and that he was to receive nothing. He immediately fainted; and, on his recovery, it was found that his mind had been affected by the shock. He was an idiot for the remainder of his days, and not long afterwards died unhonoured and unwept.

CHAP. VI.

A. D. 1757.

The flight, arrest, and murder of Surajah Dowlah

We have also to relate the death of another actor in these events. Surajah Dowlah, as soon as he had ordered the retreat at Plassey, fled from the field of battle. He hastened to his palace at Moorshedabad; but, when he heard that Meer Jaffier and Clive had entered the city, he left it in disguise, and, with only two attendants, took his way by night from that which once had been his own. In his flight, however, he was recognised by a man, who had in the previous year been cruelly mutilated by his orders. He was arrested, and brought, as a prisoner, into the presence of his successful rival. Meer Jaffier wished to spare his life: but Meeran, the heir apparent, who was as cruel as his victim had been, persuaded his father to give over the poor, fallen sovereign to his care. This request was granted: and in the dead of night the unhappy man was inhumanly murdered in a distant corner of the palace.

Triumphal return of the English to Calcutta.

After every thing had been settled between Meer Jaffier and Clive, the latter returned to Calcutta with his little army. A hundred vessels, containing treasure, floated down the river to Fort William, accompanied by the boats of the fleet with their colours flying and their bands playing—a striking contrast to the scene on the same river, when the late Nabob had gone upwards in triumphal show, but one short year before.

CHAPTER VII.

CONQUEST OF THE CARNATIC, AND THE TREACHERY OF MEER JAFFIER IN BENGAL.

FROM A. D. 1756 TO A. D. 1760.

Temporary quiet in the Carnatic—Renewal of hostilities—Troops sent to Tinnevelly and Nellore—the French attack Trichinopoly,—which is relieved by Captain Calliaud—Arrival of a French army—Count de Lally—his character—Capture of Fort St. David—Recall of Bussy—Lally invades Tanjore—Siege of Fort St. George—Colonel Coote arrives from England—Captures Wandewash and Corangoly—the battle of Wandewash—the French defeated they are besieged in Pondicherry—Colonel Forde defeats them in the Northern Circars—Pondicherry taken—Fate of Lally—Shah Alum invades Bahar—flees before Clive—Meer Jaffier's ingratitude—the Dutch help him—Defeat of the Dutch expedition—Clive leaves Bengal.

WHILE Clive and his soldiers were fighting in Bengal, their brethren in arms on the Coromandel coast were not inactive. For some time after the treaty which we have already mentioned, there was peace and quiet; but the storm of

CHAP. VII.

A.D. 1757.

war broke out with renewed fury, when hostilities were again declared between France and England.

Troops sent to assist Mahomed Ali in Tinnevelly and Nellore.

Mahomed Ali was left in undisturbed possession of the throne in the Carnatic, but he found it neither an easy nor a quiet seat. Rebellions arose, which he was unable to subdue, and even his own brother set his authority at defiance. The English, being his allies, felt themselves bound, as they had made him Nabob, to assist him against all his enemies. The Rajah of Mysore had claimed Trichinopoly, as the price of the aid which he had afforded, when it was relieved from the attacks of the French. This town was therefore defended by the English from all unlawful claimants; and, at the same time, English troops were sent to enforce the Nabob's authority in Madura and Tinnevelly, where they were stubbornly opposed by the Poligars, and the half savage tribes which inhabited those provinces. For the same reason, a force was also ordered to Nellore, where an assault made by the English was repulsed.

Trichinopoly relieved by Capt. Calliaud. May 26th.

Observing that the English were thus fully employed, and that their forces were at places so far distant from each other, the French took advantage of the opportunity thus afforded them to attack Trichinopoly. Captain Calliaud, who commanded the detachment in Madura, as soon as he heard of the movements of the French, marched rapidly across the country; entered the city unobserved by the besiegers; defeated all their designs by his activity and vigour; and forced them to retreat to Pondicherry.

CHAP. VII.

A. D. 1758.

Troops arrive from France. April 28th.

For some time after this unsuccessful attack on Trichinopoly, little was effected by either party, until a fleet appeared off Pondicherry, with a well-appointed armament from France. This force was commanded by Count de Lally, an officer, who, although an Irishman by birth, had taken service under the French sovereign. He was a passionate and ill-tempered man, very jealous of his officers, quite ignorant of the character of the natives, and unable to treat properly, either the zeal of the one or the peculiarities of the other.

The capture of Fort St. David. June 1st.

The way in which he commenced the campaign seemed to promise him success. The very evening he landed, he proceeded to attack Fort St. David. The fort was badly defended; and, after a short resistance, fell into his hands.* Delighted with this triumph, he returned to Pondicherry, fully resolved to give himself no rest, until he had driven the English out of India.

Lally's unwise proceedings.

His great eagerness, however, made him act unwisely. He recalled M. Bussy, who had been very successful in the Nizam's country, and made an enemy of that officer by treating him with unmerited disrespect. All his other measures likewise rendered him unpopular among those who served under him.

* This is the last we hear of Fort St. David, which had once been a place of great importance. The French destroyed it; and it was never rebuilt.

CHAP. VII.

A. D. 1758.

French expedition to Tanjore. June 18th to August 18th.

He was in great want of money to carry on the war, and, in consequence, invaded the territories of the Rajah of Tanjore, from whom he expected to obtain supplies. But the expedition failed. The peasants, whom he allowed his soldiers to ill-treat, rose against him; and he was obliged to return in confusion, without the treasure which he so much required.

Siege of Fort St. George. Dec. 12th, 1758, to Feb. 17th, 1759.

Having succeeded in obtaining a little money from private individuals at Pondicherry, he laid siege to Madras, which he reached on the 12th of December, with a force of 2700 French and 4000 sepoys, whom he quartered in Black Town. The siege of Fort St. George lasted two months, during which period the place was gallantly defended by Major Lawrence and Mr. Pigot, the Governor. On the 14th of December, the garrison made a furious sally upon the French in Black Town, but they were unable to take the enemy by surprise, and it was only through the indifference of Bussy that their small party was enabled to return in safety to Fort St. George. But the siege was badly conducted, owing to mutiny and disunion in the French camp; and the besiegers retreated to Pondicherry, upon the arrival of an English fleet, which, towards the close of the second month of the siege, appeared off the town.

Occurrences after the siege.

Major Lawrence took the field as soon as the siege was raised. Several trivial engagements took place; many forts exchanged masters; but nothing worthy of especial mention occurred.

Arrival of Colonel Coote. Oct. 27th.

In the following October, Colonel Coote arrived with considerable reinforcements from England; and, instead of proceeding to Calcutta as he had originally intended, remained at Madras and assumed the command of the army. One of his first exploits was to take the important fort of Wandewash, which surrendered to him after a short defence; and, leaving a small garrison there, he proceeded to another fort, not very far distant, named Carangoly. While the English commander was thus employed, Lally captured Conjeveram, and, advancing quickly to Wandewash, he attempted to recover it from its present possessors. He did not, however, attack the fort immediately; and, while he was preparing for the siege, the English army returned to relieve the place.

The battle of Wandewash. Jan. 22nd, 1760.

A severe battle ensued, in which the French were thoroughly defeated. At the beginning of the action, Lally imagined that a portion of the English infantry wavered under the fire of his artillery. Eager to take advantage of the confusion which he expected to find in the English ranks, he placed himself at the head of his cavalry, and ordered them to charge. They refused. He suspended officer after officer on the spot, and implored the men themselves to obey him, even though their officers would not. They answered his appeal; but they had not advanced far, when a slight fire from the English threw them into disorder, and they precipitately retired, leaving their general to fight, if he pleased, alone.

CHAP. VII.

A. D. 1760.

Finding himself thus deserted, Lally joined the French infantry, which, under his leading, advanced in a firm and orderly manner. Strong in numbers, they bore down the part of the English line which was opposed to them; but, the flanks of the English army closing in around them, a deadly conflict ensued. The soldiers fought hand to hand; bayonets were crossed; and, the sepoys standing aloof, this fierce struggle was carried on by the Europeans alone; but, after a time, the French retreated in confusion. Exhortations, threats, example, were all unable to stop the fugitives. Bussy threw himself from his horse, and, fighting hard himself, tried to turn them back. All was in vain: Bussy was taken prisoner; and the English were left masters of the field.

The siege and capture of Pondicherry. Jan. 16th, 1761.

After the battle of Wandewash, the English triumphed slowly, but surely, on every side. One by one, the enemy's forts fell into their power; until, in the month of May following, the French were compelled to retreat to the fort of Pondicherry, to which the English army laid siege. Lally made a last desperate struggle to free himself, but he was again defeated; and a rigid blockade was kept up until January, when the English took the place, the fortifications of which they entirely destroyed.

Colonel Forde's successes in the Northern Circars. From October 20th, 1758, to May 12th, 1759.

In the meantime Clive had sent Colonel Forde to the Northern Circars, a large tract of country on the sea coast, extending from Ganjam to Guntoor, which the French had received from Salabut Jung, for their services in placing him upon the

CHAP. VII.

A. D. 1758.

throne. After Bussy had left them, they were commanded by an officer named Conflans; but he was by no means equal to their former leader. He was totally defeated at the village of Condore near Pittapore in the district of Rajahmundry; the French garrison at Masulipatam surrendered on the 6th of April, after a siege which had lasted for exactly a month; the French influence at the court of the Nizam was destroyed; and a large tract of country round Masulipatam was ceded to the English.

The battle of Condore. Dec. 9th.

The two hill-forts of Thiagur and Gingee were now all that belonged to the French in India: but these places did not long remain in their possession. By April, 1761, not one military post in the country was left in the power of the French.

The final triumph over the French. April 5th, 1761.

Soon after the fall of Pondicherry, Lally returned to Europe. He was there put on his trial by the French Government in consequence of his failures in India; was convicted of treason and extortion; and ended his days ignominiously on the public scaffold.

The death of Lally. May 6th, 1766.

We must now return to Bengal. Meer Jaffier had not been long upon the throne, when it appeared quite evident that he could remain on it only by the help of those who had placed him there. His country was in danger on every side. The eldest son of the Emperor of Delhi assembled an army to attack him, and was aided by many of the neighbouring Nabobs, the strongest of whom was Suja Dowlah, the governor of Oude. Meer Jaffier

Meer Jaffier's insecurity.

The Shahzada invades Bahar.

CHAP. VII.

A. D. 1758.

was very much frightened by these preparations, and immediately applied to the English for help. Clive readily undertook the defence of the man whom he had himself made Nabob: and, although the small army which he commanded had been weakened by sending Colonel Forde to the Northern Circars, he ordered it forthwith to join the Nabob's forces.

Lays siege to Patna.

The Emperor's son, Shah Alum, had laid siege to Patna: but Clive wrote to Ramnarrain, a brave Hindu soldier, who commanded the fort, to defend that post to the last, for he was coming to the rescue with men who never turned their backs.

Retreats before Clive.

But there was little need of courageous resistance. The very fact that Clive was coming struck such terror into the heart of the enemy, that in a short time the whole of the large army which had caused so much anxiety to Meer Jaffier, dispersed, to assemble again no more. The Nabob, in the fulness of his gratitude, bestowed upon Clive, as a personal estate, the whole of the rents paid by the Company for the lands to the south of Calcutta.

Treachery of the Nabob.

His gratitude, however, did not last long. He imagined that he was not safe upon the throne, so long as those who had made him Nabob remained in the country. He looked about, therefore, for aid from some foreign power by whose assistance he might be enabled to expel the English from Bengal.

Meer Jaffier secretly applies to the Dutch for assistance.

He knew that no native prince could hope to oppose them with success, and that the French possessed, at this time, no power in the north, and were too weak to send help from the

CHAP. VII. A.D. 1759.

south. In this dilemma he applied to the Dutch, who had, as we have already stated, a small settlement at Chinsura, two miles above Chandernagore and twenty beyond Calcutta. Although their nation was not at war with England, the Dutch authorities at Chinsura agreed to assist him; and wrote for reinforcements from Batavia, the capital of the Dutch possessions in Java, whence seven ships of war arrived in the Hooghly soon afterwards, and on board of them was an army of 1500 men.

Defeat of the Dutch fleet. Nov. 24th.

Meer Jaffier pretended to be very much alarmed, when he heard of their arrival; but he was unable to conceal the real state of affairs from Clive, who immediately resolved that the Dutch ships should not be allowed to proceed up the river. He strengthened the fort at Tanna, which commanded the approaches to Calcutta, and made vigorous preparations for defence; but the commodore of the English fleet engaged the Dutch with spirit and success, and effectually prevented their proceeding to Chinsura.

Their land forces opposed by Col. Forde.

The Dutch troops had previously been disembarked, in order that they might march thither by land; and Colonel Forde, who had a short time before given up his independent command in the Northern Circars, was sent, with a small force, to oppose them. On their way, they encamped one evening in a position where the English commander thought that he could advantageously attack them: but, as he knew that the two na-

CHAP. VII. A. D. 1759. tions were at peace, he wrote to Clive for instructions how he was to act. Clive was amusing himself with a game at cards, when Col. Forde's hastily written note was brought to him. He did not move from the table, nor interrupt the game he was playing, but scribbled on the back of the letter a few words in reply. "Dear Forde," he wrote, "fight them immediately: I will send you the order of Council to-morrow."

Battle near Chinsura. Nov. 25th. Colonel Forde's action was as quick as his leader's decision. He engaged the enemy as soon as he received this permission, and routed them with so severe a slaughter that few of their number reached Chinsura to tell the tale. Immediately after the action he marched straight to that fort; but the garrison, disheartened at the defeat which their countrymen had reported, and fearing the powerful and energetic enemies whom they had made, acknowledged that they had been in the wrong, agreed to pay the costs of the short-lived war, and asked for peace and forgiveness. Their submission was accepted, and thus the expedition from which Meer Jaffier had expected so much was brought to an end in failure and disgrace. The ingratitude and treachery of the Nabob was overlooked.

Clive's second return to England. Feb. 1760. Three months after these events, Clive, who had in so decided a manner upheld the interests of his country in Bengal, returned to his native land, where he was received with marked distinction, and was rewarded with honours and with fame.

CHAPTER VIII.

CHANGES, WARS, AND TROUBLES IN BENGAL.

FROM A. D. 1760 TO A. D. 1767.

Shah Alum invades Bahar again—Ramnarrain is defeated—Siege of Patna—Battle near Patna—Pursuit of the enemy—Death of Meeran—Return of the troops—Deposition of Meer Jaffier—Meer Cossim—the Emperor defeated—Meer Cossim's character—Condition of Bengal—Marder of Ramnarrain—Disputes with the Nabob—the English take Patna—It is retaken by Meer Cossim—Meer Jaffier restored—Battle of Geriah—Monghir captured—Meer Cossim's rage—the English advance—the massacre at Patna—the Nabob flees to Oude—the Emperor, Suja Dowlah, and Meer Cossim against the English—they are defeated—Mutiny among the sepoys—Battle of Buxar—Clive's return—the English receive the sovereignty of Bengal—Reformations in the civil service and the army—Clive suppresses a formidable mutiny—Leaves India for the last time—His character.

As soon as Clive had left Bengal, troubles arose on every side. Shah Alum, who had lately become the Emperor of Delhi, invaded the country again; and he was assisted by Suja Dowlah, the powerful ruler of Oude, whom he had re-

CHAP. VIII.
A. D. 1760.

cently appointed grand Vizier of the Empire. A large army was assembled under these two princes and advanced to Patna, which was still commanded by the brave Hindu, Ramnarrain, whom Clive had held in high esteem.

Ramnarrain is defeated.

Ramnarrain applied to the English for assistance: but, before he had time to receive reinforcements, he engaged the Emperor's army, and was defeated.

Col. Calliaud defeats the Emperor and his allies.
Feb. 22nd.

Immediately on hearing of these events, Colonel Calliaud, who had lately come from the Carnatic to assume command of the army in Bengal, marched rapidly forwards; effected a junction with the army of Meer Jaffier, which had been placed under the orders of prince Meeran; and compelled the enemy to retire from Patna. The Emperor attempted a forced march to Moorshedabad; but Colonel Calliaud quickly pursued him, prevented him from laying siege to the capital, and tried to bring him to another battle. Anxious, however, to avoid an engagement, he returned and again besieged Patna, which, in the hurry of pursuit, had been left by Colonel Calliaud with a small and feeble garrison.

Gallant defence of Patna.

The fortress was gallantly defended by a surgeon named Fullerton, who repulsed two assaults, and kept the besiegers at bay, until the place was relieved by Captain Knox, who had marched from Moorshedabad to Patna, under the scorching sun of India, in thirteen days, himself marching on foot to encourage his men.

CHAP. VIII.

A. D. 1760.

Battle under the walls of Patna.

Meanwhile the Deputy Governor of a neighbouring town, named Poornia, had assembled an army, and was advancing with 12,000 men, to the assistance of the Emperor. Captain Knox resolved to prevent the junction of the two armies; and, consequently, when these forces drew near Patna, he crossed the Ganges, and, with only 200 Englishmen and a few sepoys, totally defeated them in sight of the walls of the town, where the garrison were anxiously watching the well-contested strife.

The death of Meeran. July 2nd.

Colonel Calliaud arrived soon after this action and joined in the pursuit of the defeated army; but on the march his troops were obliged to halt during a severe thunder storm, in which prince Meeran was killed by a flash of lightning, as he was listening to a story-teller in the retirement of his tent.

Mutiny of the Nabob's troops.

Without their leader the Nabob's soldiers were unmanageable, and Colonel Calliaud was compelled to return. He remained at Patna, while Meeran's troops proceeded to Moorshedabad, to demand the arrears of pay which had for a long time past been due to them. Meeran had been, for the last year or two, the real ruler of the country: and, after his death, Meer Jaffier, who had fallen into his dotage, was unable to satisfy the demands either of his army or of his English allies.

Interposition of Meer Cossim.

The former were in a state of mutiny: they stormed the palace; and they would have murdered their sovereign, if Meer Cossim, his son-in-

CHAP. VIII. A.D. 1760.

law, had not discharged a part of their arrears from his own private resources. The latter also were in urgent need of funds.

Arrival of a new Governor. July.

It was evident that this state of affairs could not last long. A new Governor had arrived at Calcutta, and he found that the Nabob had not paid the whole of the allowances due to his army, nor of the sum which he had agreed to give the English for placing him on the throne. This gentleman, whose name was Vansittart, resolved, therefore, with the consent of the Council, to deprive Meer Jaffier of all real authority by placing the administration of affairs in the hands of Meer Cossim.

Deposition of Meer Jaffier. Oct. 16th.

Early in October, 1760, Mr. Vansittart proceeded to Moorshedabad for this purpose: but Meer Jaffier would not accede to the proposal, and preferred to resign his position as Nabob. The English Governor accepted his resignation, and Meer Cossim succeeded to the throne, agreeing, in return for the services of the English, to bestow upon them the revenues of Burdwan, Chittagong, and Midnapore.

Defeat of the Emperor. Jan. 15th, 1761.

Soon after this change, Major Carnac, who had succeeded Colonel Calliaud in command of the army, advanced against Shah Alum. Only one battle took place, which ended in the defeat of the Emperor, who was compelled to agree to the terms of his conquerors, and to acknowledge Meer Cossim as the ruler of Bengal.

CHAP. VIII.

A. D. 1761.

Meer Cossim, the new Nabob.

But the warfare in that province had not yet ceased. Meer Cossim, the new Nabob, was not the puppet sovereign, that the English expected him to be. He was, on the contrary, a man of great ability and of remarkable energy. He fully comprehended the peculiar position in which he was placed, and felt that, while the English remained in the country, he would be a ruler in name only. While, therefore, he set heartily to work to bring his dominions into order, and to fill his empty treasury, he was secretly preparing to resist the demands of his powerful allies. He had under him an Armenian general of great ability, who was endeavouring to bring his army into a fit state for effective service: and he left Moorshedabad to reside at Monghir, a strong town which was situated a little higher up the river.

The state of Bengal.

Troubles were gathering around the English, which were brought on by their own mismanagement and misrule. The state of Bengal was very sad. The English were covetous and tyrannical: and their evil example was followed by their native servants and by others who fraudulently assumed their name and power. The tone of English society in India has happily changed since that time: and the majority of those in authority, while they remember with affection the land from which they are separated, sincerely desire to promote the welfare of the people by whom they are surrounded.

8

CHAP. VIII.

A. D. 1761.

Meer Cossim's treatment of Ramnarrain.

The first measure, which was the forerunner of trouble, was as unwise, as it was unprincipled. Meer Cossim was in great need of treasure, and what he required, he asked permission of the English to extort from Ramnarrain, the faithful commandant of Patna, who was supposed to be wealthy, but who had hitherto refused to submit the accounts of his government to the Nabob. Mr. Vansittart, contrary to the advice of Colonel Calliaud and Major Carnac, who were both recalled from Patna, ordered the troops to withdraw from that city, leaving Ramnarrain in the power of the tyrant, who first plundered and oppressed, and subsequently murdered him.

Discontent against the English.

The conduct of the Governor in this affair disgusted all the native noblemen, and, for a time, destroyed their confidence in the honour of Englishmen. Many joined the Nabob, when he openly waged war; and the knowledge of this feeling of discontent made him declare his intentions sooner than he would otherwise have done.

Disputes with the Nabob.

An occasion of quarrel soon arose. Disputes occurred about the custom-house duties in Bengal. The Company's officers had lately engaged in the inland traffic, and had insisted on their goods passing through the country free from taxation: but the Nabob very naturally desired that both the native and the English merchants should in future, be taxed alike, and, upon the latter refusing to pay a small duty of nine per cent, he abolished the custom-house duties altogether. This

CHAP. VIII.

A. D. 1763.

measure greatly annoyed the Council at Calcutta: and, being eager to act on the offensive first, they sent instructions to Mr. Ellis, their principal agent at Patna, to seize the citadel at that place. He promptly obeyed; and Patna was taken. Meer Cossim's rage, when he heard of this event, was furious, and it was not appeased by the tidings that Patna had been recaptured on the following day. In revenge, he murdered a civilian named Amyatt, who was returning to Calcutta after having accompanied an embassy to his court.

Capture and recapture of Patna. June 24th and 25th.

An English force was immediately sent to oppose him: and the Council, imagining that it was the wisest measure to adopt, set up Meer Jaffier, as ruler once more. The poor old man, now more than seventy, bent with age, weak with disease, and perfectly imbecile, again accepted the empty title of Nabob.

Restoration of Meer Jaffier. July 7th.

After two or three slight engagements, a pitched battle was fought at Geriah. The day was in favour of the English: but it was after a severer action than had hitherto been fought in India. A detachment of sepoys, dressed and disciplined in the English manner, was commanded by a European adventurer named Sumroo, who showed great courage in the engagement, and led his forces forward in such a dashing manner, that, at one time, the English line was broken, and two of their cannon taken. They were attacked both in the front and in the rear: but their

The battle of Geriah. August 2d.

CHAP. VIII. A. D. 1763.

unyielding courage triumphed. The enemy's endeavours were all in vain, and he was forced to retreat to his entrenchments near Monghir. These fortifications were soon afterwards stormed and carried gallantly, and Meer Cossim fled to Patna.

Capture of Monghir. October 1st.

Soon afterwards Monghir was taken. When Meer Cossim heard that his favourite city had fallen, he was beside himself with fury; and intimated to the commanding officer that, if any further advance was attempted, all the English prisoners in Patna, where he was then staying, should be put to the sword. Mr. Ellis and Mr. Hay, the senior civilians there, begged the same officer to march instantly, come what would, without regarding them. The English advanced; and Meer Cossim faithfully kept his word. He ordered every prisoner in the place to be murdered. He could find, however, no one but the renegade Sumroo, and a few sepoys, to perform his will.

The massacre at Patna. October 3rd.

Mr. Ellis and his companions were invited to a supper, and, immediately on entering the room where it was laid out, they were assaulted. Mr. Ellis was killed on the spot. The others defended themselves desperately with plates and bottles which they had seized from the table: but Sumroo's sepoys fired upon them from the roof, and, one by one, they fell. All, but one, were massacred. Even a little helpless child was murdered by the ruffians.

CHAP. VIII.

A. D. 1763.

Soon after this bloody deed, Patna was again taken by the English, and Meer Cossim fled to Oude, where he was received by Suja Dowlah, with whom the Emperor of Delhi had also taken refuge.

Reconquest of Patna. November 6th.

In the following year, the armies of these three sovereigns advanced against the English, and a battle was fought under the walls of Patna, near which the English forces under Major Carnac were awaiting their arrival. The confederate princes were completely routed, and again retreated into Oude.

Defeat of the confederates. May 13th, 1764.

Soon after this engagement, the English army was in imminent danger. An alarming mutiny broke out among the sepoys, who demanded higher pay than they had hitherto received: and it was not suppressed without very severe measures being taken by Major Hector Munro, who had relieved Major Carnac in the command. Twenty-four of the ring-leaders were blown from the cannon's mouth: and obedience was immediately enforced.

Alarming mutiny among the sepoys.

Discipline having been restored in this prompt and energetic manner, Major Munro followed the enemy, whom he engaged at Buxar. After a contest of three hours, the army of the Emperor, Suja Dowlah, and Meer Cossim was defeated; and the Emperor, perceiving that the cause which he had upheld was irretrievably lost, surrendered to the English commander.

The battle of Buxar, and surrender of the Emperor. October 23rd.

Suja Dowlah, however, was still, at the head

CHAP. VIII. A. D. 1765. Defeat of Suja Dowlah. May 3rd.

of an army, and had entered into an alliance with a neighbouring Mahratta chief. The English now acted on the offensive; invaded the territory of Oude; captured the towns of Allahabad and Lucknow; and finally gained a decided victory over the enemy at Corah. Soon after this battle, Suja Dowlah surrendered to General Carnac, who was again in command of the English troops: and thus the two greatest enemies, whom the English had yet encountered in the north of India, were, at the same time, prisoners in their camp.

Return of Clive. May 3rd.

Meanwhile Clive, who had arrived from England on the day this victory was won, was upon his way to the English camp. Disheartening accounts of the state of Bengal had reached England. Frequent tidings were received of the bad conduct of the English there, which was ruining the newly-won country within, and of the dangers which threatened it from without. The Court of Directors and the English Government clearly perceived that something ought speedily to be done to counteract the evil consequences of this state of affairs. They dreaded lest they should lose the authority and power which had been so recently gained; and they felt persuaded that Clive, who had been made a peer for his former services, was the only person capable of saving their new possessions. They had, therefore, bestowed upon him the chief power in Bengal; and requested him to return thither, with the avowed object of restoring that province to peace and order.

CHAP. VIII.

A. D. 1765.

Lord Clive's decision.

Lord Clive, when he reached Madras on his outward voyage, learnt that the enemy had been defeated, that the Emperor had surrendered, and that the English sepoys had returned to their obedience. He heard also that Meer Jaffier was dead. These tidings convinced him that the time which he had long foreseen had arrived,—that the English must take the chief power into their own hands.

The English receive the sovereignty of Bengal. August 12th.

Soon after his arrival at Calcutta, therefore, he proceeded to Allahabad, where, on the 12th August 1765, the emperor gave him a grant, by which the East India Company received the right to the revenues of Bengal, Orissa, and Bahar; and by which all the territory they had gained in other parts of India was confirmed to them. There was still to be a Nabob in name: but the real sovereignty was, for the future, to belong to the English.

Reformation in the Civil Service.

When he had thus placed the government upon a new footing, Clive undertook the difficult task of reformation among his own people. The pay of the Civilians, which had hitherto been very small, was raised, so as to remove all inducements to take presents from the natives. They were not permitted to carry on private trade, for that had hitherto made them think more of their own gain and good, than of the Company's. They were for the future to aim at higher and nobler objects: they were to be henceforward not merchants, but

CHAP. VIII.
A. D. 1766.

rulers of provinces; not petty traders, but governors of kingdoms.

Mutiny among the officers.

Having effected a reformation in the Civil Service, he turned his attention to the affairs of the army. The officers were, in future, to receive double batta, only when they were on service in the field, and not at all times and in all places. This innovation caused a mutiny. Two hundred officers resigned at once: but Clive was not to be moved; he sent to Madras for others to replace them, and, in the end, by his indomitable firmness and courage, suppressed a rebellion which, to a man of less ability and resolution, would, most probably, have proved insurmountable.

Clive's final return to England. January, 1767.

He had done the work which he had come out to do: and, directly afterwards, returned to England, where he was persecuted to the death by the people for whom he had won India.

The character and achievements of Clive.

This is the last time that we shall mention Robert Clive. He was a great, though not a good, man; and he had done great deeds. He obtained for England one of the choicest portions of her Empire. He accomplished what Dupleix had only dreamed of doing. Emperor, kings, princes bowed to the might of a small island in the far West, and held their dominions at her pleasure. Fair and fertile provinces owned her sway, to be increased, ere long, by yet richer and nobler possessions.

CHAPTER IX.

THE FIRST WAR WITH HYDER ALI.

FROM A. D. 1767 TO A. D. 1769.

Rise of a new enemy in Southern India—the kingdom of Mysore—the adventures and progress of Hyder Ali—Hyder Ali usurps the throne of Mysore—Extension of his dominions—Alliance against Hyder with the Mahrattas and the Nizam—Treachery of the Mahrattas—Advance to Mysore—Defection of the Nizam—Colonel Smith's retreat—the battle of Changumma—the battle of Trinomalee—Defeat and repentance of the Nizam—Tippoo's foray at Madras—Gallant defence of Amboor—Captain Calvert's spirited message—Defeat of Hyder near Amboor—Hyder retires to the Western Coast—Invasion of Mysore—Capture of forts below the ghauts—Supersession of Colonel Smith—Hyder's return and partial success—Reappointment of Colonel Smith—Peace concluded with Hyder.

PEACE in the south of India did not last long. The French had been conquered : but a new enemy

CHAP. IX.

A. D. 1767.

had arisen. In the centre of Southern India there is a large and wealthy country called Mysore. It had been governed for several generations by Hindu Rajahs: but, during the occurrences which we have been relating, a change had taken place in the government of the Mysore territories.

The adventures of Hyder Ali.

In the year 1767, it was under the rule of a Mahomedan named Hyder Ali, who subsequently proved one of the bravest and most skilful foes that the English ever encountered in India. In early life he had been an adventurer and a robber: but he had risen, by dashing bravery and wholesale cheating, to so great a height of power, that he had gathered around him a large band of devoted followers; had rebelled successfully against his master, the Rajah; and had made himself sovereign in that master's place. After he had succeeded in gaining the object of his ambition in Mysore, he had invaded the neighbouring countries; and had extended his conquests upon every side: province after province had fallen into his power, and had been formed by him into a strong Mussulman kingdom.

Alliance with the Nizam and the Mahrattas, against Hyder.

At this time the English entered into alliance with the Nizam and the Mahrattas to check his progress. The ruler at Hyderabad was Nizam Ali. He had dethroned his brother, Salabat Jung, whom Bussy had raised to power; and he was now supported by the English, to whom he had given the Northern Circars, with the exception of Guntoor, in return for military help which

CHAP. IX.

A. D. 1767.

they promised to afford him, whenever he required it.

State of the Carnatic.

Mahomed Ali was still the Nabob of the Carnatic, and, although kept upon his throne by the power of the English, he governed the country himself, except a small portion of territory around Madras, which he had placed in their possession.

Treachery of the Mahrattas.

These sovereigns, with the Mahrattas, were the allies of the English. The Mahrattas began the war. They invaded Hyder's country: but he bribed them to leave it, and without hesitation they deserted the alliance; plunder, or gain of any kind, being all that they desired.

Treachery of the Nizam.

Meanwhile, the English and the Nizam's armies had advanced into the heart of Mysore, where Nizam Ali also received money from Hyder, and, with consummate treachery, went over to his side.

Col. Smith's retreat.

Colonel Smith, who commanded the English, was, in consequence of this desertion, obliged to retreat. He returned towards Madras: but day after day he was annoyed by the numerous cavalry of the enemy, which completely surrounded him, cutting off his baggage and supplies of food, and taking prisoner every straggler from the ranks. Amidst all, however, with difficulty, danger, and death on every side, he retired in an orderly, soldier-like manner, through a country of which he knew scarcely anything.

The battle of Changumma. September 3rd.

At Changumma, the enemy attacked him, and received a defeat. Continuing his retreat after this engagement, he arrived at Trinomalee, where he was

CHAP. IX. A. D. 1767.

very much disappointed at not finding those supplies of which he stood in absolute need. Hyder, aware of this circumstance, again drew near to battle, expecting to find the English army weak and dispirited from want of food. But a hidden store of rice had been found by accident, and they were better prepared to fight than they had been for many weeks before.

The battle of Trinomalee. September 26.

The two armies were drawn up in battle order on the plain before Trinomalee. On the English right there was an extensive swamp, over which Hyder expected that they would pass, and hoped, while they were making the attempt, to throw them into confusion. Colonel Smith, however, observing a small hill on one side of the swamp, ordered his troops to march round it, and to fall without warning upon the flank of the enemy. Hyder imagined from this movement that they were retreating, and advanced towards the same hill, in the opposite direction, to cut them off. The two armies met unexpectedly. Hyder's artillery was not up; but the English had theirs, and used it well. Their rapid firing threw into confusion the enemy's cavalry, which formed the vanguard, and which had completely covered the advance of the infantry and artillery. They fled on all sides; and the victory was decided by the English infantry, who speedily put the unsupported infantry of the enemy to flight. Hyder's troops could not withstand the impetuous charge: and the rout, in every quarter, was complete.

CHAP. IX.

A. D. 1767.

Defeat and repentance of the Nizam.

Ladies also were in the battle. The Nizam's women, mounted upon elephants, had been placed in the rear to witness his anticipated triumph. When the retreat began, orders were sent for the elephants to be driven from the field: but a voice from one of the howdahs was heard to say, that her elephant at least should remain, for it was not accustomed to precede its master's standard. They remained, therefore, until the flag had passed, and the English shot and shell were falling thick and fast around. This successful battle induced the Nizam to ask leave to join the English again, and his request was, after some time, granted.

Tippoo's foray at Madras.

Meanwhile Tippoo, Hyder Ali's favourite son, had been sent, with the cavalry, to invade the country round Madras. He did his work thoroughly, riding about from house to house, burning, plundering, and destroying everything upon which he could lay his hands, up to the very gates of Fort St. George: but, when he heard that his father had been defeated, he returned to join the main army.

The gallant defence of Amboor. From Nov. 10th to Dec. 7th.

Colonel Smith, owing to the small number of his troops, and to the deficiencies in his commissariat department, was unable to take immediate advantage of the victory at Trinomalee; and Hyder, after capturing a few weak forts which had been held by the English, laid siege to Amboor, a very strong rock-fortress, at no great distance from Vellore. It was defended by an Eng-

CHAP. IX.

A. D. 1767.

lish officer named Calvert, a few Europeans, and 500 sepoys of the 10th Madras Native Infantry.

Captain Calvert's spirited behaviour.

Hyder tried every possible means to take the place. Unable, however, to effect his object by surprise or by assault, he attempted to persuade Captain Calvert to surrender, affirming that he had done all that a brave man could do. "Hyder," answered the English officer, "has not yet given me an opportunity of shewing my valour." Hyder Ali next attempted bribery, and offered the highest favour that he could bestow, ample riches and the command of half his army, as the price of surrender. "Your master," was the spirited reply to the messenger, "had better regard the lives of his men in future; for, as sure as I am alive, I will hang the next who brings such a message." Twenty-six days did this brave man hold out; and, when Colonel Smith came up, he had the pleasure to see the flag of England still flying at Amboor. For their behaviour in this affair, the 10th Madras Native Infantry still have the word "Amboor" upon their colours.

Hyder retires to the Western Coast.

Soon after this ineffectual siege, Colonel Smith defeated Hyder in the field, near Amboor; upon which the latter withdrew towards the Western Coast, leaving his opponents in full possession of the Carnatic.

Invasion of Hyder's territories.

Upon the departure of Hyder, the Government of Madras resolved to carry the war into the enemy's own territories. There were two ways of effecting their object. One was to invade the

CHAP. IX.

A. D. 1768.

country below the highlands of Mysore, which forms a triangle between Vaniambady, Dindigul, and Palghaut: the other was to ascend into Mysore Proper, and to besiege Bangalore, the second city of the kingdom. One or the other of these schemes ought to have been adopted: but it was unwisely resolved to attempt both of them at once. Colonel Wood was sent to execute the former measure, and soon made himself master of the country which we have mentioned. He took the forts scattered over it; but left them defended by insufficient garrisons. He was afterwards sent to supersede Colonel Smith, who had conducted an army into the country of Mysore, and who, having excited the displeasure of the council at Madras, had been recently recalled.

Hyder's return and partial success.

Meanwhile Hyder had repelled a party of English from Bombay, who had landed on the Western Coast, and had fled from him in a manner disgraceful to their name. He then returned to face his foes in the east, and he was, for a short time, successful against them in both the quarters which they had attacked. He gained some advantages in the country of Mysore, principally against the troops of Mahomed Ali; and, descending from the table-land into the low country about Coimbatore, by passes unknown to the English, he retook the ill-garrisoned fortresses in that province.

Peace concluded with Hyder. April 4th, 1769.

In consequence of these events, the Madras Government was anxious to conclude a peace;

CHAP. IX.
A. D. 1769.

but some disagreement occurred regarding the conditions, as they would not accept the very reasonable and moderate terms which Hyder offered: and Colonel Smith, once more in command of the English troops, prepared to attacked him again. But Hyder, frankly acknowledging that he was unwilling to meet Colonel Smith in the field, avoided the English army, marched rapidly to Madras, and, appearing before Fort St. George, informed the Government that he had come to solicit peace. His own terms were now accepted; and a treaty was drawn up, in which each party agreed to restore the places they had taken during hostilities, and to assist the other in all defensive wars. When the conditions of peace were definitely arranged, Hyder returned to defend his own country, which was in danger from the Mahrattas.

CHAPTER X.

CHANGES IN THE GOVERNMENT OF INDIA, AND WAR WITH THE MAHRATTAS.

FROM A. D. 1767 TO A. D. 1780.

State of Bengal—Discontent in England—Changes effected by Warren Hastings—the Company stand forth as dewan—Tranquillity and good government in Bengal—the Regulating Act—Feuds in the Council Chamber—Treaty with Suja Dowlah—Expulsion of the Rohillas—Arrangements regarding Corah and Allahabad—Death of Suja Dowlah, and treaty with his successor—Intrigues of Nuncomar—his trial and execution—Mr. Hastings gains a majority in the Council—State of affairs at Bombay—Dissensions among the Mahrattas—Capture of Tanna—Alliance with Ragoba—Interference of the Government of Bengal—Treaty of Poorundher—Mahrattas prepare for war—Operations against the Mahrattas—the march from Bombay—the retreat—Halt of the Bengal corps—Col. Goddard's march to Surat—his successes—Capt. Popham takes Lahar—the capture of Gwalior—Peace concluded with the Mahrattas.

WE now return to the affairs of Bengal, which after Clive's departure, had again fallen into dis-

CHAP. X.
A. D. 1767.

order. The reforms which he had made were not properly carried out. Private trade was still permitted; the collection of money was entirely entrusted to the agency of native officials; and the revenue, in consequence, was far less than it ought to have been.

Discontent in England.

The effects of these errors were felt in England. The proprietors of East India stock did not receive the profits they had expected: and their discontent became at last so great, that the English Parliament was obliged to take notice of a country and a government which had hitherto been left almost entirely to themselves.

Change effected by Warren Hastings.
May 11th, 1772.

Meanwhile Mr. Warren Hastings, the Governor of Bengal, had resolved, with the consent of the Court of Directors, to effect a thorough change in the administration. The collection of revenue was placed under the control of English gentlemen; and thus, after seven years during which the country had been their own, the English became, in deed as well as in name, the sole rulers of Bengal.

Tranquillity and good government in Bengal.

Under Warren Hastings' government at this period, the people enjoyed a season of quiet to which they had long been strangers; and many persons from other places came to settle in the territories of the Company, where peace and plenty prevailed.

The Regulating Act.
July 1st, 1773.

The English Parliament about this time passed a bill, by which it was decreed that the affairs of all

CHAP. X.

A. D. 1773.

India should be directed by the Governor of Bengal, who was henceforward to be called the Governor General, and who was to be assisted by four members of Council. A new Court of Justice was to be established at Calcutta; and no one was allowed to take presents of any kind from a native of the country. This was called the Regulating Act. The first Governor General under it was Warren Hastings; and the first councillors were Mr. Barwell, Mr. Francis, General Clavering, and Colonel Monson. Mr. Barwell was then in India; but the three latter had not been in the country before.

The new Supreme Council. Oct. 21st, 1774.

As soon as the Council had taken its seat, quarrels arose upon every question which was brought before it. The three councillors from England soon began to entertain a thorough hatred towards the Governor General, and opposed him upon every occasion. Mr. Barwell, however, always voted upon his side. There were thus two parties in the Council Chamber at Calcutta: and, as the one against the Governor General was at first the most numerous, he possessed, for a considerable time, but little authority or power.

Expulsion of the Rohillas. April 23rd.

The first cause of dispute was Hastings' conduct towards Suja Dowlah, the Nabob of Oude, to whom he had rendered assistance in expelling from Rohilcund certain troublesome Affghan chiefs who had conquered that country. Hastings had, unjustly we think, consented to aid the Nabob in this project. He had sent a

CHAP. X. A. D. 1774.

small force into Rohilcund under Colonel Champion, who speedily subdued the Rohillas; and he had given their country to Suja Dowlah, who had treated them with the greatest cruelty.

Arrangements regarding Corah and Allahabad.

He had received money for this proceeding on behalf of the Company; and he had also ceded to Suja Dowlah the provinces of Corah and Allahabad, which had formerly been given to the Emperor of Delhi who was unable to protect them from the incursions of the Mahrattas, on the condition of his paying fifty lacs of rupees more, and protecting his weak neighbour, Cheyte Sing, the Rajah of Benares. But this arrangement was annulled by the majority in the Council. Suja Dowlah died in February 1775, and a new treaty was made with his son and successor, who agreed to resign all his claims to the territory of Benares, in exchange for the provinces of Corah and Allahabad.

Intrigues of Nuncomar.

But the chief event of this time was the fate of Rajah Nuncomar, a wealthy but vicious brahmin of Calcutta. When Nuncomar observed that the majority in the Council desired, in every way, to annoy the Governor General, whom he also hated, he accused Mr. Hastings of having taken bribes, especially from a wife of the late Meer Jaffier, a lady who had been appointed guardian to the infant Nabob. Mr. Francis and his party were delighted when they heard of this accusation. They espoused Nuncomar's cause, treated him with every token of respect, and commenced an illegal trial of their superior.

CHAP. X.

A. D. 1775.

His trial and execution. Aug. 5th.

While, however, these transactions were taking place, Nuncomar was unexpectedly brought before the new Court of Justice on a charge of forgery, an offence which he had committed many years before. He was tried, found guilty, and hanged. The sensation among the Hindus was great. Nuncomar was a brahmin, and of noble birth; and for both these reasons they looked up to him. Thousands crowded to see the execution: but, though there was great excitement, no attempt was made to rescue him. His death put an end, of course, to the unfair trial of the Governor General.

Mr. Hastings gains a majority in the Council.

The quarrel was still continued: but Warren Hastings gradually gained more power than he had at first possessed; for General Clavering and Colonel Monson both died, and by their deaths he obtained a majority in the Council.

State of affairs at Bombay.

Meanwhile important events had taken place in a part of India, which we have scarcely noticed. While the other presidencies had been disturbed by wars and tumults, the Government of Bombay had enjoyed a season of quiet. They were now to have their share of warfare. They had, for some time past, been very covetous of several places near Bombay, which would be of use to them for trading, and in particular of the island of Salsette which the Mahrattas had a few years previously taken from the Portuguese.

Dissensions among the Mahrattas.

There had for sometime been dissensions among the Mahratta chieftains for the position of Peishwa,

CHAP. X. A.D. 1774.

or prime minister, who possessed the chief power in the administration of the Mahratta territories; and the Government of Bombay attempted to avail themselves of these disputes to gain what they had so long desired. While the Mahrattas were thus occupied with their own affairs, the Government of Bombay sent a small force to take possession of Salsette, in order to prevent it from falling into the hands of the Portuguese who were preparing to recapture it; and soon afterwards they entered into an agreement with Ragonath Row, or Ragoba, one of the chiefs who claimed the office of Peishwa, to help him against his rivals, if he would cede to them that island, and other places around Bombay, in return for their assistance.

Interference of the Government of Bengal.

Upon Ragoba's consenting to this arrangement, a force was sent to aid him, but the Government of Bengal, which now possessed supreme authority over the other governments peremptorily interfered. They ordered the recall of the troops, which had already been despatched to the scene of action; and desired Colonel Upton, an officer whom they had sent from Bengal, to negotiate with Ragoba's opponents, who, on their parts, agreed to give up Salsette and the adjacent islands, if the English would cease to uphold the cause of Ragoba.

Treaty of Poorundher. June 3rd, 1776.

The Mahrattas prepare for hostilities.

For some time the Mahrattas were quiet: but it was soon discovered that they were engaged in plot against the English. There was a prospect of

CHAP. X.

A. D. 1778.

further war between France and England: and news reached Calcutta that a French officer was at Poona, the capital of the Mahratta country, and was instructing the Mahratta army in the art of war.

Operations against the Mahrattas

Mr. Hastings immediately ordered a small detachment to march across from Bengal to Bombay; and desired the Government of the latter place to despatch a second force from Bombay to co-operate with it. This order was immediately obeyed. Four thousand men were sent under Colonel Egerton, who was soon compelled by illness to relinquish his command, and was suceeded by Colonel Cockburn; and two civilians accompanied the detachment to negotiate with the enemy. Divided authority of this nature was decidedly bad.

The march from Bombay.

The Bombay forces marched towards Poona. Ragoba was with them, having been taken into alliance again; but he had not brought a Mahratta force, as he had promised. It would join, he said, as soon as the English had gained some decisive advantage. This answer did not produce the effect which he intended. The commanders grew afraid. The enemy was in sight; but their hearts failed them, and they actually turned their backs without trying their opponents' strength.

The retreat. Jan. 11th, 1779.

The Mahrattas were strong in cavalry, and their horsemen galloped round and round the retiring party, keeping off all supplies of food, and cutting off all who might be compelled

CHAP. X.

A. D. 1779.

to fall out of the ranks by illness or fatigue. If they apprehended an attack, they immediately drew off to a little distance, but held themselves in readiness to return directly the march was resumed.

Failure of the expedition.

Back marched the detachment in disorder and disgrace. But in two days they halted; and a treaty was entered into with the enemy, who permitted them to return unmolested to Bombay, in exchange for their giving up every thing that they had desired to obtain. Two gentlemen were sent, as hostages, to the Mahratta camp; and Ragoba, making the best terms that he could for himself, surrendered to one of his rivals.

Halt of the Bengal corps.

Meanwhile the detachment from Bengal had done nothing. Colonel Leslie, its commander, had lingered on the road, and had meddled in the quarrels of certain petty princes, with which he ought not to have interfered.

Col. Goddard appointed to the command. Dec. 3rd, 1778

Mr. Hastings, disapproving of this delay, decided on recalling him, and appointed in his stead a brave and energetic officer named Goddard. Immediately on receiving the news of his appointment, the new commander marched forward rapidly. Messages reached him from the Bombay corps; he received contradictory orders from the civilians who accompanied it; but he continued his march to Surat, without regarding the messages or the advice of others. The Mahratta cavalry frequently menaced him; but they did

Reaches Surat. Jan. 30th, 1779.

CHAP. X.

A. D. 1780.

not dare to attempt an attack on his well disciplined little army.

His subsequent successes.

Colonel Goddard undertook no offensive operations against the enemy for a year after his arrival at Surat. That period was spent in attempts at negotiation: but in January 1780, he took the field again; captured Ahmedabad on the 15th of February; and in the following April defeated the Mahratta army.

Appointment of Capt. Popham.

While Colonel Goddard was conducting the campaign in the west, Warren Hastings had sent a small force under Captain Popham, to assist a new ally—the Rana of Gohud, a district in the province of Agra—against the common enemy.

Capture of Lahar. April 21st.

He could not have sent a better or a braver officer. Captain Popham's first exploit was the capture of Lahar. The place was defended desperately, and the assault was badly contested. A hundred and twenty-five of the assailants were slain: but their unflinching courage prevailed, and the fortress was taken.

Storming of Gwalior. August 3rd.

Captain Popham next attacked Gwalior, a place which was generally considered too strong to be captured even by the English. It was built on a very high rock, and was defended by a numerous and determined garrison. Early in the morning of the 3rd of August, 1780, the English soldiers surrounded it; by the help of their scaling ladders, they clambered up the steep rock; took the enemy by surprise; and, with very little loss of life, became masters of that renowned stronghold.

CHAP. X.

A. D. 1780.

Termination of the campaign.

The campaign lasted only a short time longer. Warren Hastings was engaged in a far more important war, to which he was obliged to give all his time and attention, and for which he required all the treasure at his command.

The treaty of Salbye. May 17th, 1782.

After some negotiation peace was made with the Mahrattas: and most of the conquests were restored to them, that had been achieved since the treaty of Poorundher, the name of the agreement which had previously been concluded with Colonel Upton.

CHAPTER XI.

INVASION OF THE CARNATIC BY HYDER ALI.

FROM A. D. 1780 TO A. D. 1784.

Hyder's invasion—Carelessness at Madras—Col. Baillie's defeat—Sir Hector Munro retreats—Panic at Madras—Hastings sends reinforcements—Sir Eyre Coote's arrival from Calcutta—Wandewash relieved—Repulse at Chillambrum—Battle of Porto Novo—Hyder defeated—Capt. Pearse's march from Bengal—Second battle—the victory of Sholingur—Vellore relieved—War with the Dutch,—whose settlements are taken—Hyder approaches Madras again—Sir E. Coote resigns his command—Col. Brathwaite's defeat—Mysoreans repulsed at Tellicherry—Tippoo sent to the Western Coast—is defeated at Paniani—Hyder's death—Tippoo's return—Genl. Mathews invades Mysore—takes Bednore—his foolish security—Tippoo re-appears—retakes Bednore—his faithlessness—Siege of Mangalore—Col. Fullarton's march—Peace with Tippoo Sultan.

MADRAS was now in very great danger. Hyder Ali was coming down with his tens of thousands upon the plains of the Carnatic. It was a fact well known throughout India that he had, for a long time past, been assembling a large army

CHAP. XI. A.D. 1780.

for that purpose; that he had invited the Nizam and other Mussulman sovereigns to assist him; and that he had been joined by adventurers from every part of the land. But the Governor and Government of Madras were unaware of these preparations. No well-trained army was ready to oppose the foe: no stores were prepared for the troops: and, worse than all, the members of Government were divided by disgraceful quarrels, similar to those which had lately prevailed in Bengal.

Hyder invades the Carnatic. July.

They were not fully awakened to the truth of the case, until the smoke from villages which Hyder had fired in a semicircle round Madras, was seen from St. Thomas's Mount; until he had plundered Porto Novo; and news arrived that Conjeveram had fallen into his hands.

Frantic efforts of the Government.

Then the Government awoke. They wrote to Bengal for treasure. They sent a force to Conjeveram, which had been deserted by the enemy, and gave the command of it to Sir Hector Munro. They recalled Col. Baillie, who had been sent with a detachment to Guntoor, about which there had been serious disputes with Nizam Ali.

Return of Col. Baillie's detachment.

That officer immediately returned with the intention of joining Sir Hector Munro at Conjeveram. Hyder resolved to prevent this movement; and prepared to attack him before he could effect the junction. Sir Hector Munro sent a thousand men, under Colonel Fletcher, to reinforce Colonel Baillie; and, although the spies, who were in Hyder's pay, attempted to mislead the party, Colonel Fletcher successfully performed the object which he had in view.

Col. Baillie's defeat. September 10th.

Colonel Baillie was within nine miles of Sir Hector Munro's encampment, when, early in the morning, soon after he had begun his last march, he found himself surrounded by Tippoo's army, which had, for several days before, annoyed him. A few of the enemy's cannon opened fire upon the little band. Men were ordered forward to capture these guns. They obeyed. The guns were taken in a gallant manner, but numberless horsemen gathered round the little party and obliged it to retreat to the main body. These horsemen formed the advanced-guard of Hyder's army, and had been sent forward to cover his artillery and infantry. Upon approaching the English they drew off; and Colonel Baillie found himself under the fire of fifty field pieces. The English returned it; but they had very few guns, and their powder and shot were soon exhausted. Two cases of gunpowder blew up: and the sepoys, who had hitherto fought steadily and bravely, were thrown into confusion. The English soldiers were eager to dash forward. 'Lead us on, lead us on,' was their cry: but Colonel Baillie would not. He was bewildered by his situation, and wearied with his exertions. He stepped out before his men with a flag of truce, and ordered them to surrender. Excited by this triumph, Hyder Ali and his troops disgraced themselves by the most savage cruelty, sparing but few of their fallen enemies.

CHAP. XI.
A. D. 1780.

Sir H. Munro's retreat.

When Sir Hector Munro heard of this event, he retreated towards Madras, throwing his guns away that he might march the quicker, and left the field open to Hyder, who subsequently took Arcot and several other forts, and laid siege to Vellore.

Energetic proceedings of Warren Hastings.

The news caused a painful sensation at Madras. But Warren Hastings, when he heard it, acted quickly and well. Within fifty-two days, he sent reinforcements to Madras, under Sir Eyre Coote, the Commander-in-chief in Bengal; ordered a detachment to march thither from Bengal by land; collected treasure from every place, where he could obtain it; dismissed the dull-headed Governor; entered into negotiations with the Mahrattas; in short, did everything that lay in his power to meet the danger boldly.

Sir E. Coote's arrival. November 5th.

Sir Eyre Coote did not take the field immediately after his arrival. He found the army badly equipped and inadequately provided for, and he was obliged to occupy himself, at first, in preparing it for active service. On the 17th of January in the following year, he began to act against the enemy, his first object being to relieve those forts which still held out against Hyder. Chingleput and Wandewash, the scene of one of his early victories, were succoured. The latter town had been bravely defended by Lieutenant Flint, who had been sent there, when it was found that the commandant under Mahomed Ali was not to be trusted. Sir Eyre next proceeded to Pondicherry, which the French had attempted to retake; and then

CHAP. XI.

A. D. 1781.

advanced to Cuddalore, where he remained for some time without undertaking any farther offensive movement. In June, he attempted to capture Chillambrum, a fortified pagoda thirty miles from Cuddalore; but the party which was sent upon the expedition was repulsed with considerable loss.

Failure at Chillambrum. June 18th.

Hyder Ali's movements.

Hyder Ali had not been near the English army for a long time: but he had been fully employed in other places. He had taken Amboor, Thiagur, and other forts, and had over-run the whole of Tanjore but the capital. The news of the failure at Chillambrum induced him to draw near the position of the English, and he marched rapidly to Cuddalore, near which town he prepared a strongly fortified encampment. Sir Eyre Coote had long wished to bring him to battle: and a favourable opportunity was now offered for it. Hyder also seemed to desire an engagement, although he had, up to this time, shunned meeting the English army in the field.

Sir E. Coote's preparations.

But Sir Eyre Coote though confident of victory, calmly prepared for defeat. The English fleet remained, at his request, close in shore, so as to afford him the means of leaving the coast in case of a reverse.

The battle of Porto Novo. July 1st.

At seven in the morning of the 1st July, 1781, the English marched out of their camp in battle order. They continued to advance, until they came in sight of Hyder's army, which was drawn up across the road to Cuddalore, with its left on a range of sandbanks that ran parallel to the sea, at the distance

CHAP. XI. A.D. 1781. of a few hundred yards. Its right was upon some hills a little way inland; and, along the line, several powerful batteries were placed so as to fire from different directions across the plain, where Hyder expected that the English would make their attack.

The reconnoisance. The English General spent about an hour in making himself fully acquainted with the position of the enemy, his men remaining during that time under a slight fire, to which they were ordered not to return a single shot. His plans were at last made. He perceived that the enemy wished him to advance straight across the plain, where he would be exposed to the fire of all the hostile guns, and where Hyder's cavalry could charge with advantage, if his troops were thrown into confusion. Dividing his army, therefore, into two columns, he turned to his right, and advanced along the space between the sand-banks and the sea.

The attack. Hyder also rapidly changed his position. The first column of the English army met the enemy at an opening in the sand-banks. They formed in the plain beyond, under a severe cannonade; and waited, with passive courage, until the second column had taken possession of the sand-banks which they had already passed. The General, riding along the ranks, exhorted his men to be patient, and to reserve their cartridges 'for a time.' At length an aid-de-camp galloped up to inform him that the sand-banks had been carried. Immediately he received this information, he ordered the artillery to open fire: and the order was obeyed so effectually, that the enemy in that quarter was speedily put to flight. CHAP. XI. A.D. 1781.

The victory.

Meanwhile the second column had been engaged in a severe struggle on the sand-banks: but they had repulsed the enemy triumphantly; had taken the position which they desired; and, in a short time, the whole of Hyder's army was in full retreat.

Hyder's dismay.

During the action, Hyder had been seated on a neighbouring hill, surveying the scene below. When he was told that a retreat had been commenced, he would not believe the report, and grossly abused the men who brought it. Nothing could induce him to move, until a favourite servant seized his feet, thrust on his slippers, and made him mount a horse, upon which he fled rapidly from the field.

Results of the victory.

This victory was very important. It restored the terror of the English name; effaced the unfavourable effects of Colonel Baillie's defeat; and put an end to the hopes of final conquest, which Hyder had begun to entertain.

Junction with the Bengal detachment. August.

Tippoo was attempting to retake Wandewash, when the news reached him, and he immediately effected a junction with his father, who had retired to Arcot, intending to prevent Sir Eyre Coote from meeting the detachment, which was expected from Bengal. But Sir Eyre marched along the road to the east of the Pulicat lake, a route which had never been used by an army

CHAP. XI.
A. D. 1781.

before, and effected his object, without approaching Hyder's position.

Col. Pearse's march from Bengal.

Colonel Pearse, the commander of this detachment, had marched from Calcutta through countries of which very little was at that time known; and had shewn much tact and skill in his negotiations with a people half inclined to be unfriendly.

A second action at Pollilore. August 27th.

After receiving this reinforcement, Sir Eyre returned towards Arcot and Vellore. Hyder's army again drew near to intercept him: and another battle was fought on the very spot, where Colonel Baillie's soldiers had been so cruelly massacred the year before. The bones of many of them still lay upon the ground, and their countrymen passed over these sad memorials, as the army advanced to fight the authors of that unmanly and useless outrage. The action was an indecisive one. Hyder claimed it as a drawn battle; but the English, although they did not gain a complete victory, caused the enemy to retreat, and encamped upon the field.

Battle of Sholingur. September 27th.

On the 27th of September, however, another battle was fought near the hill of Sholingur, at no great distance from Vellore. Hyder was taken by surprise. He maintained his ground for some time: but finding himself worsted, he ordered a retreat; and, while that movement was being effected, he gave directions for his cavalry to charge over and over again, although they were repulsed in each encounter, in order that his ary might be enabled to retire in safety. The ıy's loss was about 5000 while that of the ish was only a hundred.

CHAP. XI.

A.D. 1781.

ıe 20th Madras Native Infantry highly dis- ıished themselves in this action; and, in me- ' of the good service which they performed he occasion, they still bear the name of "Sho- ır" upon their colours.

The 20th Madras Native Infantry.

r Eyre Coote was enabled by this battle to ve Vellore, which had been blockaded by the ıy, and had been considerably reduced by famine. ı after, he retired to Madras, in the neigh- hood of which he quartered his troops dur- the monsoon.

The relief of Vellore.

uring this campaign, war broke out with the :h. Their possessions in India were taken by English. Sadras and Pulicat soon fell: and ıpatam yielded after a short attack from the and from a small land force under Sir Hector ro.

War with the Dutch.

ıe principal event of the next campaign which nenced in the following January, was the ıre of Cuddalore by Hyder. He subsequently opted the siege of Wandewash, which Sir ;, for the fourth time in his career, relieved. long afterwards, Sir Eyre Coote marched to Madras. His army was thinned by sick- : he was himself very ill; and, on arriving ;, he left his beloved troops to join them again nore.

Renewal of the campaign. Jan. 1782.

CHAP. XI.

A.D. 1782.

The best praise that can be given to Sir Eyre Coote is to mention the extreme love and veneration with which the sepoys for years after regarded his memory and name.

Col. Brathwaite's expedition and defeat. Feb. 16th to 18th.

After Negapatam had been taken from the Dutch, some of the troops who had been engaged in its capture were sent, under Colonel Brathwaite, into the kingdom of Tanjore, where for some time they did good service against the enemy. The expedition, however, ended sadly. Colonel Brathwaite was one day encamped, with only two thousand men, on a plain, where his guides assured him that he was at some distance from the enemy, a large number of whom had lately assembled in the neighbourhood. The spies were, as usual, in Tippoo's pay. Though warned, Colonel Brathwaite would not move from the ground which he had chosen, and remained in fancied security, until he found himself surrounded by overwhelming numbers of the Mysoreans. The little band defended themselves bravely for two days. They formed into a square, and resisted every effort which was made during that time to break it. But numbers at last prevailed. An impetuous charge in which the French distinguished themselves, was successful.

Cruelty of Tippoo's troops.

The same scene of indiscriminate slaughter ensued, as at Perambaukum, where Colonel Baillie's force was in a similar position: but the carnage was stayed by the exertions of the French officers, who formed a brilliant contrast to the savages with whom they served.

CHAP. XI.

A. D. 1782.

Proceedings on the Western Coast.

About the time that this event took place, the enemy received a severe repulse on the Western Coast by Major Abington, who had been sent to reinforce the Nairs and the English at Tellicherry, who had for two years defended themselves in a noble manner against all the attacks of Hyder's forces.

Engagement at Paniani. November 29th.

Hyder, upon hearing of the repulse sustained by his troops, immediately sent his son to their assistance. When Tippoo reached the Western Coast, Colonel Humberstone, who had joined Major Abington with reinforcements, and had taken command of the little army, was advancing to besiege Palghaut. Upon his approach, the English troops retreated to Paniani, where he attacked them, and was defeated with considerable loss.

Death of Hyder Ali. December 7th.

During Tippoo's absence, Hyder Ali died at Chittore: and the principal officers of the army determined, if possible, to keep his death a profound secret, until the return of Tippoo, to whom they sent the news of that event. Everything went on as usual. Hyder's body was embalmed; and, in every march, it was carried before the army in a closed palanquin, as if the person inside were still alive, but very ill. One effort at rebellion was made, for the secret could not be kept; but a stop was put to it at once.

Inaction of General Stuart.

The death of Hyder became, by some means, known to the English Government, who urged General Stuart, the commander of their forces to take immediate advantage of it. But he would

CHAP. XI. — A. D. 1783.

not, and idled away his time until the favourable opportunity for action had passed.

Siege of Cuddalore. June 7th to 25th.

Throughout the present war Hyder had been assisted by French troops. They were now commanded by Monsieur Bussy, who had, however, lost that distinguished energy and decision which had enabled him to perform such brilliant exploits thirty years before. General Stuart at this time laid siege to Cuddalore, which the French then held, and he was carrying it on with success, when news arrived of peace between England and France, which put an end to the ill-timed siege.

Accession of Tippoo to his father's throne.

In the meantime, Tippoo, as soon as he had heard of Hyder's death, had left the Western Coast, and hastened to the camp in the Carnatic, where he was acknowledged as the sovereign of Mysore, and the leader of his father's army.

Renewal of action on the Western Coast.

His departure was the signal for the renewal of action in Malabar. The English troops were removed from Paniani to Merjee near Honore; they were reinforced by several regiments from Bombay; and this augmented force was placed under General Mathews, with orders to press forward at once.

Invasion of Mysore from the west. January.

There are two ways by which the kingdom of Mysore can be attacked from the west. One, through a gap formed by the hills about Palghaut, leading into Coimbatore, which then formed part of Tippoo's dominions: the other, by one of the passes in the mountains which separate Mysore from the sea. The latter method was adopted, the fort of Honore was taken; and the army advanced to the Hussaingherry Pass: the difficulties of the ghaut

CHAP. XI.

A. D. 1783.

were overcome by the courage of the troops, although they met with fierce resistance; and, finally, Bednore, the capital of that part of Mysore, fell into their hands.

General Mathews's inaction at Bednore.

But General Mathews remained inactive there. He seemed to forget that there was still an enemy in the field; he sent away many of his best regiments to the coast again; and was culpably ignorant of Tippoo's movements. Time passed away. He was still at his ease, still doing nothing, when he was surprised to find himself one morning surrounded by Tippoo's army. The new sovereign had rapidly marched across to the place, where there was the greatest danger. He invested Bednore; cut off the means of retreat to the coast; and, in a short time, forced the garrison to surrender. The terms which he offered were favourable; but he did not keep to them: and all the prisoners captured there were sent into a long, dark, dreary captivity, which in most cases ended in death by poison or the sword.

Capitulation of Bednore. April 30th.

Gallant defence of Mangalore. From May 23rd 1783 to January 23rd 1784.

Directly after the capture of Bednore, Tippoo proceeded to Mangalore, where the remainder of General Mathews's army was stationed. The fort was almost in ruins, but it was gloriously defended by a small garrison under Colonel Campbell, and every effort of Tippoo's to take it was in vain.

A short truce.

He here heard of the peace which had been concluded between England and France. This event deprived him of the help of his French allies; and he was obliged to agree to a short truce, in the terms of which he promised to supply the

CHAP. XI.

A.D. 1783.

garrison of the besieged fort at Mangalore with as much food as they should require: but he kept the letter of the agreement, and not the spirit. The food with which he supplied them was bad and unwholesome, and he continued the works for the siege. The heroic defenders of Mangalore were at length forced by the horrors of famine to surrender their well-defended fortress, where for eight months they had bidden defiance to the flower of the Sultan's troops.

Col. Fullarton's march.

There was now much talk of peace: but Tippoo's tone was high and proud, and no terms could be agreed upon. But there was still an army in the field to oppose him. Colonel Fullarton who commanded it, had been at first perplexed by various contradictory orders from Madras: but he was at last free to advance in whatever direction he pleased. He marched boldly and rapidly across the peninsula from Tanjore and Trichinopoly to the Western Coast, proposing to join General Macleod, who commanded a force which was at no great distance from Mangalore. On his way, however, he heard of the truce. This checked, but did not stop, his advance. He altered his plans; returned towards Palghaut and Coimbatore; took both those towns; and was preparing to march upon Seringapatam, there to avenge Tippoo's broken faith with regard to Mangalore, when he received orders to suspend hostilities on account of the negotiations which were then taking place.

CHAP. XI.

A. D. 1784.

The treaty of Mangalore. March 11th.

After many evasions and delays, a treaty was concluded, by which it was agreed, among other things, that each party should restore what had been gained during the time of warfare, and that the allies of each should enjoy all the advantages of the peace.

CHAPTER XII.

THE LAST DAYS OF HASTINGS IN BENGAL, AND WAR WITH TIPPOO SULTAN.

From A. D. 1781 to A. D. 1792.

Gaining supplies for the war—Cheyte Sing—Hastings goes to Benares—the Rajah taken prisoner—Hastings in danger—Cheyte Sing defeated—Hastings at Chunar—leaves India—Various opinions regarding his character—Changes in the government of India—Mr. Fox's Bill—Mr. Pitt's Bill—Lord Cornwallis—Rumours of war—Tippoo's cruelty towards the Nairs—his war against Travancore—is repulsed—Invasion of Travancore—War with the English—Marching and counter-marching—Lord Cornwallis arrives at Madras—Bangalore taken—Advance on Seringapatam—Retreat—Operations on the Western Coast—Lord Cornwallis at Bangalore—Nundidroog taken—Second advance on the capital—the Siege of Seringapatam—Conclusion of peace—Tippoo's sons surrendered as hostages.

The expenses of the war which we have just related, were very great. It was, therefore, one of the first objects of the Governor General to obtain the means wherewith to carry it on in an

CHAP. XII.

A.D. 1781.

Supplies demanded from Cheyte Sing.

effectual and creditable manner. He applied for the necessary supplies of treasure to all the native rulers over whom he had control: and, among others, to Rajah Cheyte Sing, the zemindar of Benares. The whole of that district had been ceded to the Company by Azoph-ud-dowlah, the Nabob of Oude, in 1775: and a new grant for the zemindary had then been given to Cheyte Sing, who from that time held it under the English Government, instead of under the Nabob of Oude. When war was declared against France in 1778, a contribution was demanded from the Rajah for the defences of the State, and the demand had since been renewed each year. But Warren Hastings was not satisfied. Supplies were urgently needed, and the Rajah was supposed to be very wealthy. He had, in former times, offended the Governor General by taking part, in a measure, with the Council, and Warren Hastings was not sorry to have an opportunity of bringing him into disgrace. He was required to furnish a small force of cavalry, which he agreed to do after many delays; more treasure was demanded; and, upon his refusing to pay it, a large sum of money was imposed upon him as a fine, which he strove to the utmost of his power to evade.

Warren Hastings proceeds to Benares. August 14th.

But Warren Hastings was determined to obtain his object, and proceeded to Benares to have a personal interview with the Rajah, and to enforce obedience. He believed that the Rajah was able, but unwilling, to assist him, and was thoroughly disaffected towards the State. Cheyte Sing

CHAP. XII.
A. D. 1782.

went out a long distance to meet him; and, in the most abject manner, asked for reconciliation and forbearance; but the day after their arrival at Benares the Rajah's tone gave the Governor General so much displeasure, that, on the following morning, orders were issued for his arrest.

Arrest of Cheyte Sing. August 16th.

These orders were obeyed in a quiet and peaceable manner; and Cheyte Sing was placed in confinement. The sepoys who had accompanied the Governor General were, however, few in number. Two companies only were sent to arrest the Rajah; and they, by some unaccountable oversight, took with them no ammunition.

Insurrection at Benares.

The news immediately spread through the city, which was crowded with pilgrims, sanyasis, and brahmins from all parts of India. The people, furious at the indignities offered to their prince, rose in rebellion. They entered the palace where the Rajah was detained; slew all the sepoys; overpowered the English officers, who fought as long as they could use a sword; and released Cheyte Sing from confinement. He escaped in the midst of the tumult, and fled from Benares across the river Ganges, down the steep banks of which he lowered himself by a string hastily made of the turbans of his followers, who pressed after him to see him safely out of the city.

Extreme danger of Warren Hastings.

The situation of Warren Hastings was now very dangerous. He was left with only a few Englishmen, and a small guard, in the heart of a turbulent crowd: and all chance of life seemed to have deserted him. Calmly and quietly, how-

CHAP. XII.

A.D. 1781.

ever, he sent messenger after messenger for aid, who, with letters written on slips of paper rolled up in quills, and placed in their ears instead of earrings, passed safely through the dense, dark mass of people. But even during that time of danger, his self-possession was so great that he was able to prepare a despatch regarding the treaty with the Mahrattas, which he sent in the same manner as the other letters. In a short time, a few sepoys arrived: but he did not think it prudent to remain longer where he was, and he fled by night to Chunar, a stong fortress near Benares.

Cheyte Sing's revolt and defeat.

Cheyte Sing was up in arms, and with an undisciplined mob prepared to resist the authority of the Governor General. But faithful sepoys, under their English officers, were coming from every side. His adherents were dispersed; and he retired to the fort of Bidjeeghur, fifty miles from Benares. A force was sent against that place, upon which he fled to Bundelcund, in an exile that ended only with his life.

A new Zemindar at Benares.

His nephew was placed in possession of his estate: the annual tribute from Benares was considerably increased; and the management of the district was confided to the charge of the new Zemindar's father.

Fresh treaty with the Nabob of Oude. September 19th.

Meanwhile Warren Hastings, while at Chunar, had employed himself in settling matters of importance with the Nabob of Oude, who had failed to pay his stipulated tribute. Money was demanded from him also: but he affirmed that he

CHAP. XII. A. D. 1782. Affair of the Begums. had none to give. A new treaty was, therefore, entered into, by which he was allowed to obtain the required treasure from his mother and grand-mother, who were strongly suspected of having attempted to excite an insurrection in his dominions. It was taken by force; and one of the chief charges against Warren Hastings, when, after his retirement, he was put upon his trial in England, was founded on the permission that he had given to the improper means, by which the treasure was procured from these two princesses.

End of Hastings' administration. Feb. 8th, 1785. Warren Hastings did not stop in India very long after these events. During the remainder of his stay, he exerted himself in the management of the large country which was under his control; in making and strengthening alliances with the native states; and in promoting, in every way, the good of the people committed to his charge. He stayed long enough to see peace restored to the Carnatic, and the English name covered with new honour and renown: and he left the country sincerely regretted by the people for whom he had cared.

Trial of Warren Hastings. After his return to England, he was brought to trial upon many charges of mis-government, and unfairness in his treatment of the native princes. The trial lasted for many years, and at length ended in his acquittal.

His character. There are various opinions about Warren Hastings. Some altogether praise, and others altogether condemn, him. A middle course would be nearer the truth. We cannot think well of all that he did: but we dare not fully condemn one, who did for India great and glorious service; whom the voice of his country has pronounced not 'guilty'; and to whose memory the inhabitants of Bengal for years after looked back with mingled feelings of reverence and love. CHAP. XII. A. D. 1785.

Before he left India, important changes had been made in the government of this country. Indian affairs had been frequently discussed in the houses of Parliament, and endeavours had been made to frame bills with reference to the extending Empire of Great Britain in the East. Changes in the government of India.

In 1783, Mr. Fox, one of his Majesty's Principal Secretaries of State, attempted to bring in a bill which, if it had passed, would have taken the Government of India from the East India Company: but the scheme failed, and Mr. Fox and the ministry of which he was a conspicuous member, soon afterwards resigned. Mr. Fox's Bill. A. D. 1783.

Mr. Fox's youthful successor, Mr. Pitt, turned his attention to the same subject; and, in 1784, brought in a bill by which the authority of the Company was confirmed; but a new body called the Board of Control was instituted for the management of Indian affairs. The members of this new board were to be appointed by the Crown, and were to exercise a measure of serveillance over the Court of Directors. By this arrangement the government of India was brought under the authority both of the Company and the Crown. Mr. Pitt's Bill. Aug. 13th, 1784.

CHAP. XII.

A.D. 1786.

Lord Cornwallis appointed Governor General.

In 1786, Lord Cornwallis was appointed Governor General. He left England with strict injunctions to preserve peace in India, if he possibly could; and he assumed charge of the government, with an anxious desire to fulfil these instructions. But he found it impossible to do so. He had not been very long in India, before the great enemy of the English at Mysore obliged him to declare war.

Tippoo's preparations for war.

Since the peace of 1784, Tippoo Sultan had been secretly preparing for a renewal of strife. He had been adding to his army, improving his soldiers, and using all his influence to induce the Nizam to join him in alliance against the English. During that period he had not been entirely at peace. He had made war against the people on the Malabar Coast, and had conducted it in the most barbarous and savage manner. He had fought not only against the inhabitants, but against their religion: and his cruelty to the Nairs, a class of high-born Hindus who inhabit that coast, had inspired them with a burning desire for revenge. Many of them had fled into the country of the Rajah of Travancore, which Tippoo resolved, at this time, to invade. The shelter which the Rajah had afforded to some of the exiled Nairs was the principal cause of quarrel: but there were also disputes about two forts on the frontiers of Travancore, which the Rajah had lately purchased from the Dutch, and about a wall which he had built along the boundary between his kingdom and Mysore, and which extended for about thirty miles from the Anamullay mountains to the sea.

His savage warfare in Malabar.

Quarrels with the Rajah of Travancore.

CHAP. XII.

A.D. 1789.

Attack on the Travancore Lines. December 29th.

At the end of 1789, Tippoo appeared before this fortified wall with a large force. He made an ineffectual attempt to carry it by assault. He then attempted to enter the Rajah's territories by a mountain path, which had been discovered at a little distance from the place where he was encamped. The slight resistance offered in the first instance was overcome; and, after ordering part of the wall to be thrown down so as to afford an easier entrance to his troops, he advanced along the summit towards the quarter where the main portion of his army lay. He was soon stopped. A few Hindus, in a small tower, repulsed the numbers who were advancing with him, by a few rounds of grape shot. A panic seized the Mussulmans. They turned and fled in confusion, bearing the Sultan and his train along with them in their flight. According to his orders, the wall had, in one place, been broken down and a gap made. Into this the frightened fugitives fell by hundreds, the front ranks being unable to stop on account of those who, ignorant of the awful pit-fall, urged them on from the rear.

His narrow escape.

The Sultan himself had a narrow escape. The gap had been partly filled by the still living bodies of his soldiers; and a few attendants carried him over the writhing road. Very angry at this repulse, he determined to remain before the wall, until he could receive from Seringapatam a number of guns sufficient to ensure success.

CHAP. XII.

A.D. 1790.

Alliance with the Mahrattas and Nizam.

This unprovoked attack on the country of one of their allies, was the cause of war with the English. An English army was equipped for the field, and placed under the command of General Medows, the Governor of Madras, and close alliances were formed with the Peishwa and the Nizam. To the last Lord Cornwallis tried to preserve peace: but Tippoo treated his endeavours as signs of fear, and he was obliged, though against his will, to enter into war.

Invasion of Travancore. May 7th.

Meanwhile Tippoo had destroyed the Travancore wall, had entered the Rajah's dominions, and carried into them all the horrors that the most savage mind could imagine: but, when he heard of the English preparations for war, he returned to Seringapatam, to prepare for a severer contest and a stronger foe.

Commencement of the war.

The war began by the capture of the enemy's fortresses in the low country surrounding Coimbatore. Early in September Tippoo quitted Seringapatam, and, advancing against the English by the Guzalhutty Pass, on the 13th attacked a detachment which had been stationed at the foot of the ghaut, and by which he was repulsed with considerable loss. The English General was very desirous to bring him to a battle; but he would not allow himself to be drawn into one: and the rest of the campaign was passed in continual marching and counter-marching in pursuit.

CHAP. XII.

A. D. 1790.

Lord Cornwallis's arrival at Madras. December 12th.

But the war was to be carried on in a different manner. Lord Cornwallis came from Calcutta to command the army in person; and arranged another method of attack. His first object was to take Bangalore, the second city in Mysore. Both the pettah and the fort were gallantly carried by storm.

Advance on Seringapatam. A. D. 1791.

From Bangalore he advanced straight to Seringapatam. Tippoo was filled with fear. He fully expected that his favourite city would be taken, and he effaced every evidence which it contained of his bitter hatred to the English. Insulting pictures, of which there were many in the town, were obliterated; foul words were wiped from the walls; and the prisoners were cruelly murdered, lest reports of his barbarities should reach an English ear.

The English army falls back. May 26th.

The march to Seringapatam was very slow, chiefly owing to the paucity and feebleness of the bullocks which were employed to drag the guns. At length the army arrived within sight of the city, and Tippoo's troops, which had been drawn up before it, were thoroughly defeated. But just as victory was in his grasp, Lord Cornwallis was compelled to retreat: sickness and famine were in his camp, and he was, consequently, obliged to turn his back upon the fortress which he had marked for his own.

Occurrences on the Western Coast.

There had also been military operations in another quarter. Colonel Hartley, and, after him, General Abercromby, had been fighting on the Western Coast: and they were joined by the

CHAP. XII. A. D. 1791.

brave Rajah of Coorg, who had assembled many of his subjects who had been hitherto compelled to hide themselves on account of Tippoo's cruelties, and were now eager for revenge.

Capture of Nundidroog. Oct. 20th.

After the retreat from Seringapatam, Lord Cornwallis returned to Bangalore, where he remained to prepare for a second attack on the capital. During this season of comparative inaction, he occupied the army in taking many of the surrounding hill-forts, which the inhabitants of Mysore imagined to be impregnable. The most formidable was Nundidroog, which was built on the summit of a steep granite rock. For three weeks a cannonade was kept up, until two practicable breaches were made; and through these breaches the English soldiers climbed. Rocks were rolled down upon them. Every means of resistance was used. But all danger and difficulty were set at nought: and the hearts of the English were cheered by seeing their flag float upon the walls, from which many of their captive countrymen had been thrown by the orders of the monster who sat upon the throne of Mysore.

Second advance to Seringapatam. Jan. 1792.

Fresh men and supplies arrived; and Lord Cornwallis once more moved towards the capital. He was now joined by the Nizam's troops; and General Abercromby was to advance from the Western Coast to meet him.

The siege. From 18th to 24th Feb.

On the 5th of February 1792, he appeared again before Seringapatam. Some hard fighting took

CHAP. XII.

A. D. 1792.

place: but the English were successful, and Tippoo was obliged to cross the Cauvery, and to retire into the town, which is situated on a small island formed by two branches of that river. He made one or two desperate efforts to free himself; but they were all in vain.

Cessation of the siege. Feb. 24th.

The preparations for the cannonade were nearly completed; the trenches were dug; the guns laid; and the soldiers were longing for the assault; when orders were given that the siege should be discontinued. Tippoo, thoroughly frightened, had asked for peace.

Conclusion of peace. March 19th.

Lord Cornwallis informed him of the terms on which it could be obtained: half his kingdom was to be given up to the allies; a large sum of money was to be paid for the expenses of the war; all the prisoners were to be restored; and two of his sons surrendered as hostages, until the conditions of the treaty should be fulfilled. When Tippoo received the letter containing these terms, he assembled his chief officers in the great mosque of the town, told them what he had read, and asked them whether their voices were raised for peace or war. Devoted as they were to their Sultan, they were obliged to say, though with tears in their eyes, that peace was best. Then Tippoo yielded. His sons were sent to the English camp; the terms of the English commander were accepted; and a treaty of peace was finally concluded on the 19th of March.

CHAP. XII.

A. D. 1792.

After everything had been settled, the conquering army returned to Madras; and, for a time, the tyrant of Mysore was tamed.

CHAPTER XIII.

THE FALL OF SERINGAPATAM.

From A. D. 1792 to A. D. 1799.

The English assume temporary charge of the Carnatic—Capture of the French settlements—French intrigues—French officers take service in native states—Revenue systems—Sir John Shore—his peace policy—the Mahrattas attack the Nizam—the English keep aloof—Temporary withdrawal of the Nizam's subsidiary force—Death of Mahomed Ali—Disputed succession in Oude—Lord Mornington's arrival in India—Change of policy—Negotiations with the Nizam—Tippoo prepares for war—Lord Mornington proceeds to Madras—Assembling of the English forces—the Nizam's troops join the army—a short campaign—Advance of the English—Tippoo is beaten at Seedasoor and Malvelly—the siege of Seringapatam—the assault—the triumph—the death of Tippoo—Partition of the conquered country—Restoration of the Rajah—Colonel Wellesley's government of Mysore—Present aspect of Seringapatam.

Lord Cornwallis did not remain in India very long after the successful termination of the war

CHAP. XIII. A. D. 1792.

against Tippoo. During the war, he had thought it advisable to take charge of the country of Mahomed Ali, the Nabob of the Carnatic, whose conduct, always uncertain and suspicious, had lately been very unsatisfactory. The possession of the Carnatic was, however, kept for a short time only; and, at the end of the campaign, it was restored to the aged Nabob, under a treaty which, in some respects, differed from the one entered into with him before.

Capture of the French settlements. Aug. 1793.

The French possessions in India were taken without any resistance being offered, upon the declaration of war with that nation. They had been restored at the conclusion of the last war: but the power of the French in India had been effectually crushed, and no attempt at recapture was made, as they had, at that time, employment enough for their arms in Europe. French officers were, however, in the service of native princes, whose armies they disciplined and drilled; they still entertained the idea of reviving their country's influence; and, by their intrigues and military knowledge, occasioned great embarassment to the English cause.

Revenue systems.

Lord Cornwallis will be chiefly remembered for his administration in Bengal. He was the principal promoter of that mode of receiving the land revenue, which is known by the name of the Zemindary system. There are three methods of collecting this tax. One is the Zemindary system, by which large landholders are made individually responsible for the revenue of certain tracts of country; another is the village system, by which the inhabitants of each separate village are answerable for the rent of the land within their boundaries; and the third is the Ryotwary system, under which the settlement is made with each individual cultivator. These are the three modes of collecting revenue in India at the present time. Lord Cornwallis adopted the first for Bengal, and likewise reformed the administration of justice, and the principal regulations for the revenue and judicial departments in that Presidency were passed in his days.

Ryotwary system.

The Ryotwary system was adopted at Madras. It was begun under Colonel Read, who had charge of part of the territory taken from Tippoo Sultan in the war which has just been related; it was upheld by Colonel Munro, who shewed by his example, how beneficial it could be made to the people; and it is, at the present time, the principal system of revenue in Southern India.

Sir John Shore becomes Governor General. Aug. 1793.

Lord Cornwallis was succeeded by Sir John Shore, a distinguished civilian, who afterwards became Lord Teignmouth. Sir John Shore was eminently a peace governor; but the measures which he took to preserve the English dominions from war, were neither for the welfare of India, nor for the honour of the English name.

CHAP. XIII.

A. D. 1795.

The Mahrattas attack the Nizam.
March.

The Mahrattas were preparing to invade the country of the Nizam: but the Governor-General refrained from affording assistance to the latter, although he was in alliance with the English, and the native princes, who had admired the manner in which the English had upheld the cause of the Rajah of Travancore, because he was an ally, were disappointed at finding that they could not always depend upon the English alliance. The Mahrattas invaded the Nizam's country, as they had threatened; triumphed over his army; and forced him to conclude an ignominious peace. He was obliged to cede a large portion of his dominions; to pay a considerable amount of treasure; and to surrender his prime minister, as a hostage for the faithful performance of these conditions.

Temporary withdrawal of the subsidiary force.

The Nizam, irritated at the Governor General's refusal to afford him aid, requested that the English force which was stationed at Secunderabad might be withdrawn, and shewed every encouragement and favour to the French officers who were at his Court.

Death of Mahomed Ali.
Oct. 13th.

At the same time changes took place in the Carnatic. Mahomed Ali, the old ally of the English, died in October 1795, at the advanced age of seventy-eight, and was succeeded by his eldest son, Omdut-ul-Omrah. Lord Hobart, the Governor of Madras, was desirous of receiving from the new sovereign the cession of a portion of his dominions which had, for several years, been impoverished and misgoverned on account of the debts and mismanagement of the late Nabob, who had been constantly surrounded by usurers and unworthy counsellors, both native and European. This subject was the cause of disputes between the government of Madras and Bengal, and consequently no change was, at this time, effected in the management of the Carnatic. CHAP. XIII. A. D. 1795.

There were also disputes in the north. Asoph-ud-Dowlah, the Nabob of Oude, died in 1797, and was succeeded by his reputed son, Mirza Ali. For a time the Governor General acknowledged Mirza Ali as Nabob: but there were so many complaints of his unpopularity, and so many representations against his claims to the throne, that Sir John Shore himself visited Oude to settle the matter. Mirza, or, as he was generally called, Vizier, Ali, was eventually deposed, and Saadut Ali, a brother of the late Nabob, was placed upon the throne. The dethroned Nabob resided, after these events, at Benares. Disputed succession in Oude. A D. 1797. Vizier Ali dethroned. Jan. 21st, 1798.

But a Governor General of a very different character was on his way from England. In 1798 Lord Mornington, who afterwards became Marquis Wellesley, arrived in India. He at once saw that the peace, which then prevailed, was hollow and unsatisfactory, and that the influence of the English at the native courts was rapidly declining. Arrival of Lord Mornington. May 17th.

Lord Mornington immediately applied himself to remedy these evils. The principal power with New treaty with the Nizam, Sep. 1st.

CHAP. XIII. A. D. 1798. whom he entered into negotiation was the Nizam. He persuaded that prince to dismiss his French officers, to look up to the English alone, and to join heartily in alliance with them. The English subsidiary force returned to Secunderabad according to the provisions of a new treaty entered into with the Nizam; the brigade which had been raised and commanded by the French was surrounded and disarmed; and the French officers were conveyed to Calcutta, as prisoners of war.

Tippoo Sultan prepares for war. But a harder task than negotiation remained to be performed. The Tiger of Mysore, still unhumbled, insolent, and mad, was crouching for his last fatal bound. Tippoo Sultan was preparing for war. He was surrounded by Frenchmen, who gave him the assistance of their military knowledge; he was in correspondence with their great leader, Napoleon; he was improving his army; he was increasing the strength of Seringapatam; and he was striving in every way to gain the means wherewith to struggle successfully against his still hated enemies.

Assembling of the English forces. Feb. 1799. Fully aware of these proceedings, Lord Mornington also prepared for war, went to Madras to superintend the arrangements for the campaign, and exerted himself heartily in equipping the fine army which was assembling for the invasion of Mysore. More than 20,000 men were at Vellore, and they were joined on the march by 16,000 more from the territories of the Nizam. The latter were under the command of Colonel Arthur Wel-

CHAP. XIII.

A. D. 1799.

lesley, afterwards the Duke of Wellington, who commanded the English army in Portugal and Spain, and subsequently became England's most illustrious general. A small army was also sent from Bombay to the Western Coast: and the entire force was placed under the command of General Harris.

Tippoo is twice defeated. March 6th and 27th.

The campaign was short. Slowly, but surely, the two forces marched towards Seringapatam. Tippoo first turned towards the west. At a place, called Seedasere, his army was beaten by General Stuart who commanded the army from Bombay. Repulsed in that quarter, he proceeded to face his foes in the east. He attempted to stop General Harris's advance; but was thoroughly defeated on a battle-field of his own choosing, at Malvelly.

The English advance to the capital.

Tippoo, though defeated in both these engagements, still endeavoured to stay the march of the English, and would willingly have fought another battle: but, while he was watching for them along the route which Lord Cornwallis had adopted, he heard that they had crossed the Cauvery at a ford some distance down the river, and were in full advance for Seringapatam by another road. Back he immediately turned to guard his favourite fortress; and, after some hard fighting, during which an English detachment was one evening driven back, he was compelled to retreat into the fort.

CHAP. XIII.

A. D. 1799.

The siege of Seringapatam. From April 5th to May 4th.

In a short time the town was regularly invested; General Stuart's force joined the main army; and nothing was heard but the roar of the cannon which was directed against the devoted city, and the shrill whistle of the shot. The siege continued for a month. At length a practicable breach was made, and orders were given for the assault. The soldiers were told to lie down in the trenches, until the signal was given. Many a heart beat high: but not with fear. They were exulting in the thought that the man who had treated their captive countrymen with every kind of insult, was now within their reach, and that their hands were raised to strike him down.

The assault, May 4th.

It was noon. All was silent in the town: there was no stir of life within; and, in fancied safety, Tippoo lay in his royal palace, pretending to think that Englishmen dared not enter, and took no heed of his most favoured officers when they told him of the approaching danger. The blinding sun shone down with its fiercest heat; most of the garrison were deep in their midday slumber; the green flag flapped lazily from the battlements: when General Baird, who was to lead the British soldiers through the breach, stept out from the entrenchments, and, waving his sword, gave the signal to advance. "Follow me, lads!" he said, "and prove yourselves worthy of the name of British soldiers!" The men pressed towards the town. The alarmed garrison hastened to defend the walls, a cry spread through the city,

CHAP. XIII.

A. D. 1799.

and even the Sultan rushed to the defence. A cross-fire was immediately opened upon the English: but in seven minutes they had passed the sandy bed of the river, and, desperately fighting their way upward, had placed the red flag of England on the ramparts.

The triumph.

The first wall was thus cleared: and, as it had been arranged before the assault, the soldiers divided, half of them going to the right hand, and half to the left, to meet again on the eastern side. Those on the right, or southern, side were easily victorious: but sterner work was before the others. When they had advanced about half way, they met with a desperate resistance. The Sultan was there; and his followers fought with the madness of wounded tigers. They grappled hand to hand with the English; but were driven back with clubbed muskets or bayonet thrusts.

The death of Tippoo.

When the Sultan saw that all was lost, he attempted to return to his palace, and, on his way to it, he passed through a low, dark gateway, where the men of each side were fighting hard. He was wounded, and faint with loss of blood. His attendants begged him to proclaim his rank, that his life might be spared: but he either feared or disdained to do so, and was still struggling on, when an English soldier gave him a mortal wound, and he sank down to die amidst the foul mass of the dead, and dying, and mutilated, in that horrible gateway.

CHAP. XIII.

A. D. 1799.

Restoration of order.

The whole town was now in the possession of the English, and order was soon restored by the admirable arrangements of Colonel Wellesley, who relieved General Baird after the assault. Search was made for Tippoo, and, after a long time, his body was found in the place where he had died, but so changed that it was scarcely known. It was buried by the conquerors in the tomb which he had raised to his father.

Partition of the conquered country.

The leader having fallen, there was no farther resistance. The war was at an end. Seringapatam was kept by the conquerors: and the remainder of Tippoo's dominions was divided between the English, the Nizam, and the present Rajah, to whom the kingdom of Mysore was given. The last was a child of tender age: but he was of the ancient dynasty of Mysore kings, and was, in consequence, raised to the throne which his ancestors had held.

Colonel Wellesley's government of Mysore.

Colonel Wellesley was appointed to bring the restored realm into order, and well and nobly did he perform his task. The people were happy; roads, tanks, and bridges were constructed; and many from other parts of India came to live in Mysore, affording the best testimony to its good government and prosperity.

The present aspect of Seringapatam.

The traveller may to this day see a memorial of that time in a bridge at Seringapatam, which still bears the name of Wellesley. Not far from it are relics of the reign of tyranny which had

CHAP. XIII. A. D. 1799.

just passed away. There is Tippoo's tomb with its delicate tracery and graceful columns; his palace, now a mart for sandal-wood; and his garden house, fast falling to decay. The broken cannon lie uselessly about the town; and the cannon balls are stored in heaps, round which the tendrils of a creeper twine, the vivid green of its leaves contrasting beautifully with the rusty red of the shot,—a happy emblem of the time, when the sound of warfare shall be heard again no more.

CHAPTER XIV.

WAR WITH THE MAHRATTAS.

FROM A. D. 1799 TO A. D. 1803.

Arrangements with the Nizam—the English take possession of the Carnatic—Threatened invasion of Zemaun Shah—Vizier Ali—Insurrection at Benares—Murder of Mr. Cherry—Mr. Davis's gallantry—Arrangements with regard to Oude—Disputes among the Mahrattas—Scindia and Holkar—Treaty of Bassein—War against Scindia and the Rajah of Berar—General Wellesley advances on Poona—Marches after the enemy—Description of the Mahratta encampment—the battle of Assaye—General Lake—Capture of Alighur—the battle of Delhi—Surrender of the French officers—Release of Shah Alum, the Emperor—the battle of Laswaree—Suspicious behaviour of Scindia—the battle of Argaum—Capture of Gawilghur—Conclusion of peace.

AFTER the conquest of Mysore fresh territories were added to the English possessions. A subsidiary force had, for many years, been stationed at Secunderabad for the support of the Nizam, who had agreed to pay a sum of money for its maintenance: but the payment had, of

CHAP. XIV.

A. D. 1801.

Fresh treaty with the Nizam. October 12th.

late, been very irregular; and the Governor General now entered into a treaty with that prince, the object of which was to obtain a tract of land, in exchange for this allowance, in order that the compensation might be rendered permanent and secure. The Nizam assented to this arrangement; and gave up, for the required purpose, the districts which he had received after the fall of Seringapatam, and which are still known by the name of the Ceded Districts.

The English take possession of the Carnatic.

The dominions of the Nabob of the Carnatic were also surrendered to the English. The reigning Nabob was Omdut-ul-Omrah, the eldest son of Mahomed Ali, who owed his throne entirely to their exertions. It was discovered that he had entered into a treasonous correspondence with Tippoo, during the last Mysore war; and his country was terribly misgoverned. The Court of Directors and the Home Government, therefore, concurred with the Governor General and the Governor of Madras, as to the propriety of taking from him the territories which he managed so ill. But before the arrangements for this proceeding were concluded, the Nabob was on his death-bed, and it was thought proper not to inform him of them. After his death, however, the throne was offered to his reputed son upon the condition that the government of the country should be placed in the hands of the English. But that prince would not accept the proffered terms, and Azeem-ul-Dowla, another grandson of old Mahomed Ali,

CHAP. XIV. A.D. 1801.

was made Nabob; a liberal allowance was bestowed upon him; and all the country, from Ongole to Cape Comorin, came under the rule of the East India Company.

Threatened invasion of Zemaun Shah.

We must now turn our attention to the north of India, where more serious affairs had taken place. For some time past, Zemaun Shah, king of Affghanistan, had been preparing for an invasion of India. He had been deterred, for a season, by troubles in his own country: but his intentions now appeared so evident, that the Governor General determined to cross them altogether by persuading the king of Persia to attack Affghanistan. The Shah of Persia agreed to Lord Mornington's proposal: and the Affghan invasion was entirely frustrated.

Insurrection at Benares. Jan. 14th, 1799.

These occurrences, however, occasioned a disturbance nearer home. In the last chapter we mentioned Sir John Shore's arrangements with regard to Oude. Vizier-Ali, who had succeeded to the throne, and had, after a short reign, been deposed, hailed the idea of the Affghan invasion with delight; encouraged, as far as lay in his power, those who favoured it; and made preparations for assisting Zemaun Shah. When this conduct was made known to the Governor General, he thought it advisable that Vizier Ali should be removed to a residence near Calcutta: but the idea of this change enraged the dethroned sovereign to such an extent that he deliberately murdered in cold blood Mr. Cherry, the Resident, and two other Englishmen. It is probable that all the English at Benares would have fallen victims to this unexpected treachery, if his infuriated followers had not first gone to the house of Mr. Davis, the Judge, who, seeing the excited mob approach, retired to the roof with his wife and children, and defended himself at the head of a narrow staircase, with only a small hunting spear in his hand, until soldiers from the English camp came to the rescue. After a slight resistance, Vizier Ali fled; but he was, soon afterwards, taken prisoner, and kept in confinement during the remainder of his life.

CHAP. XIV.
A.D. 1799.

Mr. Davis's gallantry.

The reigning Nabob of Oude, who had lately expressed a desire to abdicate his throne, was induced to cede part of his territory to the English, by which arrangement his kingdom was rendered secure, as several of the ceded districts were situated in the west of Oude, and thus formed a barrier between it and foreign states; and an alliance was concluded between him and the English, the latter binding themselves to defend him from all foreign and domestic enemies, and the Nabob agreeing to establish such a system of administration in his dominions, as should be conducive to the welfare of his subjects.

Arrangements with regard to Oude.
Nov. 10th, 1801.

Peace now prevailed throughout India: but it was not of long duration. The foes against whom the English were next to turn their arms, were the Mahrattas. Two powerful Mahratta chiefs had lately risen, who had taken all authority away

Battle between Scindia and Holkar.
Oct. 25th, 1802.

CHAP. XIV. A. D. 1802.

from the Peishwa, in the same manner as the Peishwa had, in former years, taken all authority from the Rajah. Their names were Scindia and Holkar. There was at this time war between them. Holkar was in arms against Scindia and the Peishwa. He was victorious, and the poor, feeble Peishwa was obliged to flee from Poona, his capital, and to take refuge with the English, with whom he entered into an agreement, promising to maintain a subsidiary force in his country, to dismiss all European adventurers from his Court, and to yield his claims to Surat and other places near Bombay which then were in their possession. On the 31st of December 1802, a treaty was signed at Bassein, and the offered alliance accepted.

The treaty of Bassein. Dec. 31st.

Restoration of the Peishwa. May 13th, 1803.

This treaty led to a war with Scindia, whose army was partially commanded by Frenchmen, and had been brought into a better state of discipline than any native force had yet attained. English troops were approaching the Mahratta country for the purpose of restoring the Peishwa to his capital: an army under General Lake which was stationed in the provinces lately acquired from Oude, was ready to attack it on the north; and another, commanded by General Wellesley, was advancing from Mysore and Hyderabad. Holkar, not feeling himself strong enough to oppose them, had fled. General Wellesley marched rapidly to Poona to save it from the destruction which Holkar's adherents had threatened; and the Peishwa was replaced upon the throne in his former capital.

CHAP. XIV.

A. D. 1803.

War against Scindia and the Rajah of Berar.

Scindia was now invited to join the English alliance. But he still kept aloof. His army was near the frontiers of the Nizam's country, and it appeared that he was desirous to join the Rajah of Berar, another powerful Mahratta chief, who had also felt himself aggrieved by the treaty of Bassein, and who was the first to declare war against the English. Scindia attempted to gain farther time for preparation by sending evasive answers, but he was at last obliged to say that he did not approve of the treaty of Bassein, and that he would not accept the proposed alliance. The armies of the confederate princes were then marching towards Hyderabad, the capital of the Nizam: and General Wellesley, who had left Poona, and taken Ahmednuggur, one of Scindia's forts, quickly followed them, placed himself between their army and that city, and forced them to return.

General Wellesley's arrangements for an attack.

In the middle of September the two armies arrived within a short distance of each other, and the English General made arrangements for attacking the enemy, with Colonel Stevenson, who commanded the Nizam's force. It was agreed that the latter should march round some hills to the west of their position, and that the General himself should proceed towards the east, both joining three days after and giving battle to the enemy. But while thus separated from Colonel Stevenson, General Wellesley heard that Scindia's infantry was encamped quite close to him, on the banks of the Kaitna, a small river

CHAP. XIV. A.D. 1803.

which flowed near. He resolved to attack them forthwith. He sent a messenger to Colonel Stevenson, ordering him to return as rapidly as possible; and then rode on with the cavalry to reconnoitre.

Encampment of the Mahratta army.

After a short ride, he reached some high ground, from which he saw the enemy in full force, cavalry and artillery as well as infantry, encamped on the opposite bank of the Kaitna. In their rear ran another small stream, named the Juah, which joined the Kaitna a little below the village of Assaye, and formed with it an acute angle. The whole Mahratta host was spread out below him. Eighty cannon guarded the narrow stream; 50,000 trained warriors were behind them; and the tents of the camp were seen covering the plain for miles. The sounds of life came upward from that huge host, in which every manner of workman had his store, and every trade was carried on as regularly as in one of their own towns.

The battle of Assaye. September 23rd.

The English infantry had now come up. The General had made his arrangements. Numerous as the Mahrattas were, they must be engaged, and the English were led forward as if to attack the enemy's front. They had not gone far, however, when they were ordered to march to their right, and to cross the river at a ford near its junction with the Juah. Under a tremendous fire they dashed through the water, ascended the rocky banks, and formed on the plain beyond, with their infantry in advance and their cavalry in the rear. Rapidly as these movements had been made, they had been followed by the enemy, who as quickly changed his front. His left was now on Assaye and his right on the Kaitna; and his cannon swept the triangular space on which the small brave English army had deployed. No time was to be lost. The enemy's artillery were as ten to one. The infantry were, therefore, ordered forward to capture the hostile guns. Part of the line was broken by the deadly fire, and the Mahratta horse attempted to charge through it, but they were driven back by the English cavalry. There was a fearful struggle also at the village of Assaye, which had been attacked owing to the misapprehension of an order. But the village was carried: the enemy's line gave way, and the cavalry charged again. Down fell horse and rider. Resistance was in vain. The wild, irregular Mahrattas were no match for the firm front of the English dragoons and their sepoy comrades. Once only they rallied: and some, who had been past as dead, rose up and fought again. But one more charge of those terrible horses drove them back. The retreat was quickened: the whole Mahratta army fled: and England had gained one of her most brilliant victories in the East. CHAP. XIV. A.D. 1803.

Meanwhile General Lake had advanced to Delhi. On his way he had taken the strong fort of Alighur, the result of which success was, that M. Perron, the most eminent Frenchman in Scindia's service, deserted the cause that he had so long upheld. The capture of Alighur. September 4th.

CHAP. XIV.

A. D. 1803.

The battle of Delhi, September 11th.

The Mahrattas were encamped in a strong position near Delhi: a swamp was on each side of them, and the high ground on which they were located, was defended by nearly a hundred pieces of cannon. The English came within sight of this formidable array, after a march of eighteen miles: but their General resolved to attack it at once. By a pretended flight, he drew the enemy from their strong position into the open country. When the Mahrattas saw the English cavalry, which was in advance, retreating, they rushed eagerly and wildly forward, fancying that they were to obtain an easy victory. As soon, however, as the horsemen reached the infantry, they moved off to the right and to the left; and the latter, passing on, drove the enemy back, charged up to the muzzles of the guns, and, then, leaving room for the cavalry to gallop through their ranks, left them to follow the beaten foe.

Surrender of the French, and rescue of Shah Alum.

Several Frenchmen surrendered after this battle, and no French officer of note remained in the enemy's camp—the Mahrattas were left to fight their battles alone. The city of Delhi was taken out of their power, and Shah Alum, the poor old Emperor who had years ago caused so much alarm in Bengal, was released from a cruel bondage, during which he had been illtreated by several captors in succession, had been half-starved, and eventually deprived of sight.

The battle of Laswaree. November 1st.

General Lake then proceeded to Agra, which he captured; but another large army, called the "Invincibles of the Deckan," was advancing towards

CHAP. XIV.

A. D. 1803.

the city of Delhi, and he immediately retraced his steps to encounter it. As he drew near, he felt so impatient to come within sight of the enemy, that he left the infantry with orders to follow, and rode on rapidly with his cavalry alone. He came up with the Mahrattas at a village called Laswaree, where a brilliant cavalry action took place. The enemy appeared to be in retreat, as the English approached, and General Lake, therefore, ordered the few men who were with him to charge. Though it appeared like riding to certain death, there was no hesitation. At the sound of the bugle, and at the call of duty, those brave men rode on, as others have done since; dashed through the awful fire; and fought gloriously among the thick masses of their foes. But it was all in vain. They were obliged to retire for a time.

The victory.

The remainder of the army having arrived, the Mahrattas proposed to surrender their guns, and to leave the battle-field. The English leader, anxious to save life, and to give his tired soldiers rest, agreed to their proposal, and gave them an hour to consider. The hour passed away, and there was no message, no sign of retreat. And now the real battle began. A column of English infantry led the way, and were soon in the midst of the fire. Part of the line held back, and the King's 76th, some of the 12th and the 16th B. N. I., were left alone, to march on bravely through the shot and shell, and to repel a charge from the Mahratta horse. This

CHAP. XIV. A.D. 1803.

band of heroes, as General Lake called them, fought nobly; but they were cut off from the others, and it was necessary to help them. The dragoons were ordered to the front. As they rode by, they were received with cheers from the 76th, and, echoing back their comrades' hurrahs, they galloped through the Mahratta forces and beat them off. Then came the advance of the whole English line. The General put himself at their head. His horse was shot under him, and, as he was mounting another, his son was struck down by his side. But he could not stay to grieve or to assist, for the long line of English soldiers were pressing forward with the bayonet. Foot to foot, and hand to hand, the Mahrattas fought desperately: but they were driven back, although they did not cease the struggle, until every one of their guns had been taken. After this battle, Scindia's army in the north existed only in name.

Scindia's suspicious behaviour.

In the south, General Wellesley had followed up the victory of Assaye by sharp and rapid movements. Scindia pretended to desire peace, and a truce was made with him: but the Rajah of Berar was still in the field, and Scindia was, in reality, making as much delay as possible to enable reinforcements to come up to him. Advancing rapidly, General Wellesley met the Rajah's forces, with which a number of Scindia's were also found, at Argaum in the province of Berar. There was hardly half an hour of day-light left: but there was time enough to beat the enemy. The battle was a straightforward one. The steady

The battle of Argaum. November 27th.

advance of English infantry carried all before them. A few of the sepoys, who had fought courageously at Assaye, wavered under the enemy's fire; but they soon rallied, and, throughout the remainder of the day, fought as heartily as the rest. The moon arose that evening on the Mahratta forces in full retreat, and enabled the English cavalry to pursue them for several miles.

Capture of Gawilghur. Dec. 15th.

But the enemy still held out. The battle of Argaum was succeeded by the capture of a strong fort, named Gawilghur, after a severe march over steep mountains and through almost impracticable ravines. The Rajput commandant fought bravely, but the garrison did not follow his example, and the fort was taken with less trouble than the strength of its position warranted.

Peace with the Rajah of Berar. Dec. 17th.

After the fall of this stronghold, the Rajah of Berar asked for peace, which was granted to him upon his promising to cede the province of Cuttack and to dismiss all European adventurers from his service. A large portion of territory was also ceded to the Nizam, who had been a faithful ally of the English throughout the war.

Peace with Scindia. Dec. 30th.

Scindia also yielded. He ceded the tract of country situated between the rivers Jumna and Ganges, which had lately been held by French officers; renounced all claims upon the English Government and their allies, the Nizam, the Guicowar, and the Peishwa; and to submit any dispute which he might have with the Peishwa to the decision of the English Government. The Mahratta war was

CHAP. XIV. A. D. 1803.

thus brought to a close. It had lasted only five months: but in that short time many a hard-fought battle had taken place, and many a victory had been added to the battle-roll of England.

CHAPTER XV.

ANOTHER WAR WITH THE MAHRATTAS.

FROM A. D. 1804 TO A. D. 1806.

Holkar's suspicious conduct during the war—his insolent message to General Lake—General Lake's army set in motion—Pursuit after Holkar—Return of the English army—Col. Monson's disastrous retreat—Defence of Delhi—the English army, in two divisions, pursues Holkar—the cavalry defeat him near Furruckabad—the infantry at Deeg—Favourable operations in the west—Capture of Deeg—Siege of Bhurtpore—every assault repulsed—Ameer Khan—Rajah of Bhurtpore yields—Alliance between Holkar and Scindia—Marquis Cornwallis returns to India—his death—Sir George Barlow becomes Governor General—Fresh treaty with Scindia—Holkar flees to the Punjab—Pursuit after him—a treaty of peace concluded—the English abandon their allies.

DANGER was still to be expected from the Mahrattas. During the war which had just been concluded, the conduct of Holkar had been very suspicious. He seemed at first inclined to assist Scindia and the Rajah of Berar, but he refrained from doing so. The rapid victories of

CHAP. XV. A.D. 1804.

the English appear to have filled him with dismay, and he remained inactive until those chieftains had been defeated. Then, however, he began to shew what his intentions really were. He wrote to several native princes to rouse them against the English: and he plundered the territories of several English allies.

Holkar's insolent behaviour.

As these proceedings could not be permitted without remonstrance, General Lake wrote to inform him that such acts could not be tolerated, and required him to withdraw his thieving army from the frontier of the British territory. Holkar's answer was full of insolence. He professed to desire peace, but required the English to give him several rich provinces; to permit his demanding chout, or a tax from the native rulers that their countries might not be plundered; and to make a treaty with him, similar to the one which had lately been concluded with Scindia.

Pursuit after Holkar.

This was as much as asking for war. General Lake's army was immediately set in motion; and Colonel Murray was ordered to march from Guzerat towards Oogein. Holkar was, at that time, employed in plundering the territory of the Rajah of Jypoor, an ally of the English; but General Lake sent forward a detachment under Colonel Monson for the protection of that prince, and—Holkar retired towards the south. The English, after capturing the fortress of Tonk Rampura, continued the pursuit. Holkar, however, retreated so rapidly that they could not overtake him; and the troops suffered severely from the

CHAP. XV.

A.D. 1804.

heat, the fatigue of the march, and want of provisions. Thinking, therefore, that the detachment under Colonel Monson was strong enough to keep Holkar in check, and desirous of sparing his men, General Lake returned with his force towards Cawnpore. But whatever were the trials of the soldiers before, they were now increased a thousand-fold. The march back was most disastrous. Hundreds dropped down on the wayside to die, overcome by the hot winds which raged all day, by thirst, and by fatigue.

Slight successes.

Meanwhile some irregular cavalry had attacked a party of the enemy with success, and afterwards joined Colonel Monson's troops: and Ameer Khan, a chieftain in the service of Holkar, had treacherously fallen upon some sepoys and artillery, who had concluded a truce with the commander of a fort which they were besieging, on the promise of its surrender; but he was afterwards beaten by a small party of British sepoys.

Col. Monson's advance.

While General Lake was retiring, Colonel Monson continued his southward march, with the intention of joining Colonel Murray, who was advancing from the opposite direction. But as he proceeded, he found more and more difficulty in procuring supplies for his men; he heard that Colonel Murray had fallen back; and he imagined that Holkar was too weak or too dispirited, to attempt any offensive movement. He resolved, therefore, to retreat: and, leaving the irregular cavalry under Lieutenant Lucan at the place of his encampment, with orders to follow in half

CHAP. XV. A.D. 1804.

an hour, and to inform him of the enemy's movements, he turned his back on Holkar. It was an error in judgment only, for Colonel Monson himself was a brave man and a devoted soldier.

His disastrous retreat. July 8th

We have already remarked how disastrous a retreat before the Mahrattas always proves. Directly the enemy heard that Colonel Monson had commenced his march, they hastened after him, attacked and overwhelmed the small party of cavalry which had been left behind, and pursued the remainder of the detachment which had reached the Mokundra Pass, a steep and difficult defile between Kota and Neemuch. Here they attacked the retreating troops on almost every side: but the small party of English stood their ground firmly, and beat them off. Colonel Monson had at first intended only to retreat as far as the Mokundra Pass. Fearing, however, that the enemy might intercept him, he retired to Kota, the capital of a professedly friendly rajah, who nevertheless refused to admit him within the walls of the town. Backward marched the detachment in the greatest distress: the streams were overflowing their banks; the troops were in want of food; the guns had to be spiked and left behind; and the enemy's cavalry made frequent attacks. Yet no impression could be effected on it: whenever there was any fighting, success was always on the side of the English. But treachery was at work. Some of the native officers entered into correspondence with the enemy, and two companies of sepoys and some irregular cavalry went over to Holkar.

As Colonel Monson drew near a position of safety, one more desperate attempt was made to overcome him, but it was repulsed. After that action, however, all order was lost, the firm front shewn against danger was no more seen, and every one escaped, as best he could, to Agra, where the last straggler arrived on the 31st of August, about two months after the first backward step had been taken.

Reassembling of the English army.

But the year was not to close without retrieving this disaster, which was calculated to cause a feeling of disaffection against the English throughout all India. General Lake's army was speedily reassembled, and by the 22nd of September it was at Agra, ready to take the field. Holkar had advanced to Muttra, a little higher up the Jumna, and leaving his cavalry behind, sent forward his infantry and guns to capture Delhi. But he was completely baffled. The Resident, Colonel Ochterlony, and Colonel Burns placed the city in the best state of defence that they could adopt, and, with only a few native troops, defended it for eight days against Holkar's numerous army. Part of the garrison mutinied, but the remainder fought gloriously; and the courage shewn at Delhi is deserving of greater praise than any other incident in the war.

Spirited defence of Delhi. From Oct. 8th to 15th.

Division of the English army into two portions.

Defeated at Delhi, Holkar proceeded to ravage the surrounding country. General Lake, therefore, dividing his army into two portions, gave the command of the infantry and foot artillery to

CHAP. XV. A.D. 1804.

General Frazer, with orders to bring Holkar's infantry to action; and, taking with him the greater part of the cavalry and the horse artillery, started in pursuit of Holkar, who, with his cavalry, was busily engaged in plunder and excess. The chase was a long one. Holkar kept in continual motion: but the English cavalry closely followed him at every turn.

Defeat of Holkar's cavalry at Furruckabad. November 17th.

At length, one evening, General Lake heard that the enemy was encamped near the city of Furruckabad, which was only thirty-six miles in advance. Although his men had just finished a long march, he ordered them to mount again. All night they rode on rapidly. The moon was shining; they were in high spirits at the thought of meeting their chief foe; they had just heard of a victory gained by their comrades; and the cool, crisp air kept off fatigue. In the grey of the morning, they came in sight of Holkar's camp, in which the horses were still standing at their pickets, and most of the men lay sleeping by their side. A round of grape shot told them that the English were coming; and, a few moments after, the English cavalry were riding through and through the startled camp. A few of the Mahrattas had found time to mount their horses, and to flee as quickly as possible; and among these was Holkar himself, who ran away among the first.

The battle of Deeg. November 13th.

In the meantime, while General Lake was chasing Holkar's cavalry, General Frazer had destroyed his infantry. The English army came in sight of the Mahrattas on the 12th of November, and found them encamped in a very strong position in the neighbourhood of Deeg. Their right was near a village built on rising ground; their left was close to the town; a large lake was in their rear; and a long swamp lay spread before their camp. Very early on the following morning, the troops were led out to the attack. They were obliged to march some distance to the left to avoid the swamp. The king's 76th regiment, which had highly distinguished itself before, was in advance. The fortified village was quickly carried; and the soldiers ran down from it to the first range of guns, and captured them. Other regiments hastened after the gallant 76th, and supported it. During the struggle at the second battery, General Frazer was mortally wounded, and Colonel Monson assumed the command. Part of the army staid behind to keep the enemy near the swamp in check: but the rest hastened forward; battery after battery, which appeared one after another for the space of two miles, had to be taken at the point of the bayonet. At length the last was stormed and carried, and the conquering soldiers found themselves close to Deeg, the guns of which were fired at them, and compelled them to retire. Meanwhile the enemy had regained the first range of cannon, and turned them against the English, but they were gallantly retaken by Captain Norford of the 76th at the head of only twenty-eight men. The troops who had taken the batteries, had now returned to drive off the enemy's forces near the swamp, which had hitherto been kept in check by the party left be-

CHAP. XV. A.D. 1804.

hind for that purpose: but as soon as they appeared, the Mahrattas fled, and many, in their headlong flight, were drowned in the morass. The victory was complete; and the remnant of Holkar's infantry, beaten and subdued, sought refuge behind the walls of Deeg.

Reunion of the English cavalry and infantry.

After this engagement, Colonel Monson withdrew to Muttra, a little to the east of Deeg, where he rejoined the cavalry under Lord Lake. Both divisions of the reunited army had done the work set before them, having beaten the enemy at different points, and completely dispersed Holkar's forces.

Operations in the Deckan and Malwa.

In the south, Colonel Wallace had taken Chandore and Jaulnah, and subdued all Holkar's possessions in the Deckan: and Colonel Murray, who had fallen back for a time, and had thus partly caused Colonel Monson's retreat, had taken Oogein, Indore, and the whole of the province of Malwa.

The siege of Deeg. Dec. 16th to 23d.

General Lake's army proceeded, in the next place, to the town and fort of Deeg, whither many of Holkar's troops had fled for refuge after the battle. Deeg belonged to the Rajah of Bhurtpore, who had been one of the first to seek an alliance with the English at the commencement of the war, and to whom very favourable terms had been granted. He had, however, assisted Holkar in many ways; it was ascertained that he had entered into correspondence with that chief; and, at the battle of Deeg, his men had fought against the English, his guns had fired on them, and his fortress had been a refuge to their foes. It was, therefore, necessary to punish his treachery. In the middle of December, the army appeared before the town. The enemy was posted within and around it, and had, on either side, erected several formidable batteries. In a few days a practicable breach was made: and three parties were formed to carry the place, one on the right to take the batteries on the one side, another on the left to attack the fortifications on the other, and the third was the storming party. All were successful. The town was taken, and the fort was surrendered on the following day

The siege of Bhurtpore. From Jan. 2nd to Feb. 22nd 1805.

The Rajah's capital still remained to be captured, and preparations were made for the siege. Bhurtpore was a very strong place, eight miles in extent, enclosed by a high mud wall, and a broad, deep moat, and defended by a numerous and determined garrison. Many attempts were made to take it by assault: but all failed. The enemy fought desperately; they rolled down on the advancing columns large stones, jars of boiling oil, logs of wood, and every missile upon which they could lay their hands: the English soldiers fought as fiercely; they fixed their bayonets in the wall, and climbed up the dangerous stair, one here and there reaching the top, and placing the English flag on the ramparts, only to be cut down on the spot. On each occasion, however, they were obliged to retire. Some of the men who had fought bravely at Laswaree and Deeg, refused one day to advance, but, the next, retrieved their character by the most desperate valour. But all was in vain: no impression could be made on the thick mud walls of Bhurtpore.

CHAP. XV.

A.D. 1805.

Ameer Khan's marauding foray.

During the siege, Holkar, who was now too weak to do much damage himself, despatched Ameer Khan, one of his most savage retainers, to inflict as much mischief as possible on the neighbouring territories of the English, and thus to create a diversion in favour of the besieged. Gathering around him his wild horsemen, Ameer Khan invaded the Company's newly acquired possessions, leaving burning villages and trampled fields in his track. This incursion, however, did not affect the siege of Bhurtpore. The cavalry were sent after him; and, chasing him hither and thither, over mountains and through valleys, across rivers and through dark forests, they came up with him, almost destroyed his marauding band, and returned in triumph to the English army, which was still encamped before the unconquered fort.

The siege turned into a blockade.

General Lake, finding that the place could not be taken by assault, resolved to turn the siege into a blockade. But the Rajah of Bhurtpore was weary of the war. He had undertaken it to help Holkar, and, now that Holkar was powerless, he desired to desert his cause. New guns were daily received in the English camp to replace those which had become useless during the siege; fresh supplies were coming in; and there was no sign that General Lake would leave the place, until he had accomplished his object, although he had, for a time, abandoned his old quarters before the town.

Peace with the Rajah of Bhurtpore. April 17th.

The Rajah, therefore, asked for peace, which was granted to him on better terms than he could have reasonably expected. He agreed to pay

CHAP. XV.

A. D. 1805.

twenty lacs of rupees for the expenses of the war; to restore some territory which the English had formerly given him; and to leave the fortress of Deeg in their possession, until his fidelity should be fully proved.

Lord Lake's advance against Holkar and Scindia. April 21st.

Meanwhile Holkar had joined Scindia, who was again prepared for war. There had been disputes between Scindia and the English, since the conclusion of the treaty which we have already mentioned, but his conduct had grown more and more suspicious since the failure at Bhurtpore. Released from the siege of that place, General Lake, who had recently been made a peer for his former services, was free to follow Holkar and his new ally, and, at the approach of the English, they both retreated.

Return of Lord Cornwallis. July 30th.

At this time, the Marquis Cornwallis arrived from England as Governor General, with the full determination of following a different course of policy from that which had been pursued by the Marquis Wellesley. He had been instructed to make peace with Holkar, if he possibly could: but, as he was on his way to join Lord Lake he was taken ill, and died at Ghazipore near Benares. Sir George Barlow, the senior member of Council, succeeding to the post of Governor General, proceeded to carry out the views of his predecessor, and entered into negotiations with Scindia and Holkar.

His death. Oct. 5th.

Peace with Scindia. Nov. 23rd.

Scindia immediately agreed to peace. Very favourable terms were granted to him; the treaty before made with him by General Wellesley was

CHAP. XV. A.D. 1805.

confirmed; the Fort of Gwalior was surrendered to him, with part of the territories of the Rana of Gohud, one of the ancient allies of the English; a pension was given him; and estates in the English possessions were bestowed upon his wife and daughter.

Holkar flees to the Punjab.

But Holkar was still up in arms, and had fled to the Punjab, in full expectation that the Sikhs and Affghans would afford him help. Forces were sent to cut off his retreat; but he managed to out manœuvre them, and to reach the country of the Sikhs. Lord Lake's army was quickly in pursuit. It had reached the banks of the river Beah, the Sikhs had refused to aid Holkar, and that treacherous and dangerous enemy was in the power of the English; when Lord Lake was ordered to enter into treaty with him. The brave English conqueror had spoken firmly and decidedly against the new arrangements: but his voice was unheeded. That part of Holkar's territories which the English had subdued, was restored to him; he was allowed to return to them by an appointed route; and possessions to the north of the river Chumbal, which the English had at first reserved for themselves, were given up: thus honouring and enriching him, who had ever shewn himself a most unrelenting, murderous, bitter foe to England.

Peace with Holkar. Dec. 24th.

Sir G. Barlow's peace policy.

The unreasonable desire for peace which then prevailed, induced Sir George Barlow to act unwisely and unfairly. He fixed upon the river Jumna as the boundary line of the English territories on the north; broke the alliance with most of the native states upon the other side of it; refused help to the Rajahs of Jypoor and Boondee, both of whom had shewn themselves true and faithful to the English cause, and had done every thing to uphold it during the war; left them to the revenge of Scindia and Holkar, although they had stronger claims to the support of the English Government, than any other of the native princes in the north; and was only prevented from following the same selfish policy with regard to the Rajahs of Bhurtpore and Machery, by the stern remonstrance of Lord Lake, although the former had shewn in his conduct through the time of warfare a striking contrast to the loyal Rajah of Jypoor. With one voice the best writers on Indian History, and foremost among them the officer by whom the treaties with Scindia and Holkar were concluded,* condemn the unstatesmanlike, narrow, foolish policy which was then adopted. Peace was gained: but at a price far greater than that of the most protracted war; for Englishmen ought always to count Honour dearer than their lives.

* Sir John Malcolm.

CHAPTER XVI.

THE ADMINISTRATIONS OF SIR GEORGE BARLOW AND LORD MINTO.

FROM A. D. 1806 TO A. D. 1813.

Profound peace throughout British India—Mutiny at Vellore—Massacre of the European soldiers who were stationed there—the cavalry come from Arcot—Suppression of the mutiny—Causes of the disturbance—Treatment of the mutineers—Suppression of the mutiny in other places—Lord Minto becomes Governor General—Sir George Barlow is appointed Governor of Madras—Departure from the peace policy—Occurrences at Poona and Hyderabad—Embassies to Persia and Cabul—Unpopularity of Sir George Barlow—the Tent Contract—Disgraceful mutiny at Madras—Affair at Seringapatam—Return to duty—Restoration of peace and quiet. Expeditions against Java, Bourbon, and the Isle of France—Signs of approaching warfare—Disputes with the Goorkhas—Quarrel with the Burmese—Departure of Lord Minto.

THERE was now profound peace throughout the English possessions in India. Beyond them, however, there were continual wars and tumults: but Sir George Barlow still adhered to the views which he had adopted, and which were urged upon him from England; he would not interfere with disputes between the native states; and he would not use the enormous power gained by the English for those high purposes for which it had been given. Rather he rejoiced at the thought, that the quarrels of the Mahratta chieftains would keep them from warfare with the English, and turn to the profit of the English Government. But although we must condemn Sir George Barlow's policy in this respect, we must praise the manner in which he used peace for the good of those directly under him in the province of Bengal.

The mutiny of Vellore. July 10th.

In the midst, however, of the quiet that prevailed, the dwellers in British India were startled by the news of an alarming outbreak near Madras. Very early in the morning of the 10th of July, 1806, while it was still dark, the sepoys stationed at Vellore, a town which is situated eighty-four miles to the west of Fort St. George, arose and murdered the greater part of the European officers and soldiers who were residing in that place. Silently and secretly they assembled on the parade ground; marched to the barracks of the European soldiers; and, surrounding them, placed before the door a field piece, with which they frequently fired upon the unarmed men within. The English soldiers could not return the fire, for they had no ammunition, and they were unable

CHAP. XVI.
A. D. 1806.

to charge out against their numerous foes. Some of the rebels had, in the meantime, gone to watch the houses of the officers, and to murder every one who quitted them, and by these Colonel Fancourt, who commanded, was mortally wounded: others had proceeded to secure the powder magazine: and a third party had entered the houses of the English residents and slain all whom they had encountered. Soon after it was light, a few officers, who had bravely defended themselves in one of the houses, contrived to enter the barracks; led the men who still remained unwounded, to the door, where they captured the gun, and, fighting their way out, reached the top of one of the gateways where they kept their adversaries at bay. The officers were killed in the struggle; and a serjeant, named Brodie, assumed command of the survivors.

Assistance received from Arcot.

But news of these events had been carried to Arcot, which was only nine miles off; and, while brave serjeant Brodie and his comrades were fighting desperately, there was seen in the distance a cloud of dust, which told them that help was near. It was a regiment of dragoons and the 7th native cavalry galloping to the rescue. Before them, rode furiously a single horseman—the commander of the dragoons. He reached the gateway. A rope made of the soldiers' belts was let down to him. By help of this he clambered up the ramparts, where he put himself at the head of the soldiers; and led them on to one more charge against the murderers of their countrymen. Presently the dragoons came up with the galloper guns; battered in the gate of the fort; charged through and through the rebels; and did not put up their swords, until the blood of hundreds had flowed for the blood of those so foully slain.

CHAP. XVI.
A.D. 1806.

Causes of the mutiny.

Various causes contributed to this fearful mutiny. Orders had been given that the sepoys were to appear upon parade without any of the marks which Hindus wear upon their foreheads to indicate their caste; that they were to cut their beards and mustaches after one uniform fashion; and that they were to wear a turban which, they imagined, was like an English hat. Many supposed that these changes were ordered, because the Government wished to force them all to become Christians. This feeling was increased by the speeches and counsel of rebellious men, who were willing to rouse them, by any means, against the English rule. But there was something further and deeper concealed under these things. The sons of Tippoo Sultan were in confinement at Vellore. They were treated kindly, and allowed to hold intercourse with many of the inhabitants of the town. Vellore was full of those who looked back with regret to the days of Mahomedan greatness in Mysore; of men who had been secretly preparing to raise the sons of Tippoo to their father's power; and of numerous beggars, dervishes, and fakeers, who had proceeded from man to man with false stories of English oppression and with pretended promises of assist-

CHAP. XVI. A. D. 1806.

ance from Mahomedan states. The regiments at Vellore were principally composed of Mahomedans and of persons from Mysore, who eagerly listened to these idle tales. The green flag of Tippoo had been hoisted during the disturbance: and it seems certain that, even if the princes themselves did not incite the sepoys to rise in their behalf, the rebels entertained thoughts of raising again the Mahomedan dynasty, and, at the same time believed the absurd stories of the Government interfering with their religion.

Treatment of the mutineers.

The sons of Tippoo were removed to Calcutta, where they were kept under a mild restraint. The ringleaders in the rebellion were brought to trial: a few were executed; others were dismissed the service; and quiet again prevailed, although the feeling of confidence between the Madras sepoys and their officers, which existed before the outbreak, was not restored for several months. The regulations about the sepoys' dress were altered.

Suppression of the mutiny in other places.

Vellore, however, was not the only place where a mutinous spirit was shewn. At Secunderabad, Wallajabad, Nundidroog and other places, there were signs of rebellion: but it was averted by the firmness of some commanding officers, and by the good sense of others in not insisting upon the use of the turban which the sepoys disliked.

Arrival of Lord Minto.

While the trials of the men that had been engaged in this outbreak were taking place, Lord Minto, who had a short time before been appointed Governor General, landed at Madras, remained there a short time, and then proceeded to Calcutta. The Governor of Madras had returned to England, and Sir George Barlow succeeded him.

CHAP. XVI.

A. D. 1807.

Departure from the peace policy.

Lord Minto came to India firmly resolved to follow his predecessor's views with regard to the non-interference with native states, and to spend his time in the internal administration of the country: but, strong as his own wishes and the directions from England on the subject were, he was obliged to depart from the course which had been lately followed. He found that not only the interests, but the safety, of the English possessions in India were in danger by refusing to give help where it was really needed. Ameer Khan, the robber chieftain whom we have already mentioned, relying upon the English withholding assistance, invaded the territories of the Rajah of Berar; but the Governor General ordered an English force to oppose him, and he rapidly retreated to plunder in districts farther off.

Transactions at Poona and Hyderabad.

Assistance was given to the Peishwa in bringing some of his unruly people into subjection: and the Governor General also interfered with the internal affairs of another ally, and, contrary to the wishes of the Nizam, appointed, as minister at the Court of Hyderabad, a person whom he desired to see holding that station.

English embassies to foreign courts.

At this time fears were entertained by the English in India about the danger of French and Russian invasion through the mountainous countries to the North. Even now such fears have not

CHAP. XVI. A. D. 1809.

altogether died away: but at the time of which we are writing they were very strong. A splendid embassy was, therefore, sent to the king of Cabul: but no satisfactory treaty could be concluded with him on account of the domestic tumults and troubles in that land. Another embassy which had been sent to the Shah of Persia was more successful. Both these expeditions were useful in correcting the imperfect knowledge of those countries which Englishmen had previously possessed.

Unpopularity of Sir G. Barlow at Madras

Sir George Barlow, now Governor of Madras, was very unpopular at his new station. He had brought with him from Calcutta the principles of economy, which the Court of Directors had urged upon him, when Governor General: but, although he was desirous of reducing the expenses of Government, even by unpopular measures, the principal act which brought upon him the dislike of the officers in the Madras army was effected under instructions from the Bengal Government. The commandants of regiments had been hitherto accustomed to receive an allowance for providing tents for their men. This was called the Tent Contract. It was now abolished: and this proceeding irritated the Madras officers. Another source of quarrel was, that their Commander-in-chief was not allowed a seat in Council.

The Tent Contract.

Mutiny at Madras.

The discontent among the officers increased day by day. They brought serious charges against Colonel J. Munro, who had written the report about the Tent Contract, accusing him of false insinuations against the army: and, a short time afterwards, General Macdowall, the Commander-in-chief, annoyed at being excluded from a seat in Council, put Colonel Munro under arrest. There were thus two parties at Madras. The Governor was at the head of the one in favour of Colonel Munro: and General Macdowall was the leader of the other. The Governor ordered the prisoner's release; and, on the Commander-in-chief's refusing to accede to his request, released him himself. Irritated at this additional slight, General Macdowall resigned his appointment, and returned to England. After his departure, the Adjutant General and the Deputy Adjutant General were suspended, because they had published a General Order against Government, which the Commander-in-chief had written previous to his embarkation: and several commanding officers were also suspended, or removed from their commands, because they had signed memorials against the proceedings of Government. These proceedings increased the spirit of disaffection. It spread from the officers to the men. At Masulipatam there was open mutiny. At Seringapatam, the officers, annoyed by an appeal circulated by Government among the native officers and sepoys, openly encouraged their men in rebellion, and an engagement took place between a mutinous regiment, which was marching from Chittledroog to Seringapatam, and a body of faithful sepoys and European troops.

CHAP. XVI.

A. D. 1809.

CHAP. XVI.

A.D. 1809.

Return of the officers to their duty.

At Secunderabad also there was mutiny. But the officers at that station were happily soon recalled to a sense of duty. Colonel Close, the Resident at Poona, was sent to Secunderabad; and, though his counsel was at first disregarded, he succeeded afterwards in bringing matters to an amicable conclusion. The mutineers at Seringapatam and other places followed the example of their brethren at Secunderabad; and an address recording their feelings of penitence was sent to Lord Minto, who, at this time, visited Madras, where his presence seemed needful. A few officers were dismissed; others were pardoned; and quiet again prevailed.

Conquest of Java, Bourbon, and the Isle of France.

Although there was no warfare in India during Lord Minto's administration, the armies of India were employed in war and triumphing abroad. The rich and fertile island of Java was conquered; Bourbon and the Isle of France were taken; and the sepoys shewed themselves as brave and loyal while fighting in a foreign land, as they had been in their own.

Signs of approaching warfare.

But although there was peace in India at the time of Lord Minto's departure, there was occasion to believe that it would not be of long duration. Soon after his arrival, disputes regarding boundaries arose between the English and the Nepaulese, who inhabit a wild and mountainous country to the north of Bengal. The Rajah of Nepaul had, at a later period, seized some land belonging to a subject of the Company: and the

Goorkhas, a bold, fierce tribe, who were then engaged in warfare in Nepaul, had occupied a small portion of the Company's territories, and built a fort there. A detachment had been sent against them, and they had been driven back: but their conduct was so arrogant, that it was evident a war with them was near. There were disputes also with the Burmese on the frontiers of Chittagong: and, in the centre of India, there had arisen a new enemy whom we shall in a short time be obliged prominently to notice. Lord Minto thus left to his successor a heritage of war.

CHAPTER XVII.

WAR WITH NEPAUL.

FROM A. D. 1813 TO A. D. 1817.

Arrival of the Earl of Moira—the Goorkhas—they attack a small party of English on the frontier—Commencement of the Goorkha war—Arrangements for an invasion of Nepaul—Description of the country—Operations of the second division—Siege of Kalunga—Advance on Jytak—Failure of the third and fourth divisions—Success of the first division—Nalagerh abandoned—Temporary cessation of hostilities—Ramgerh abandoned—Attack on the heights of Maloun—Capture of Almora—the Nepaulese ask for peace—the terms of peace—Renewal of war—Sir D. Ochterlony turns the Chiriaghati Pass—Battle of Mukwanpore—Capture of Hariarpore—Conclusion of peace—Intrigues among the Mahrattas—the Pindarees—Description of their warfare—Foray into the Company's territories—Defeat of a Pindaree expedition—Preparations for extensive warfare.

THE next Governor General was the Earl of Moira, who afterwards became the Marquis of Hastings. He landed at Calcutta on the 4th of October, 1813. Immediately after his arrival, he was obliged to prepare for war. There was now no question about interfering with the internal affairs of neighbouring states or not. A bold and encroaching enemy was committing ravages upon the northern frontier of the English territories; one who would not listen to negotiations, treaties, or reason.

Incursion of the Goorkhas.

We have stated how the Goorkhas were bent upon extending into their neighbours' country the conquests which they had acquired in their own. In May 1814, while negotiations were under discussion between their government and the English, a party of Goorkhas attacked and destroyed a small force which had been stationed on the frontiers of Bhotwal. This was an insult which could not be overlooked. Preparations for assembling an army were speedily made: but the war was not begun immediately on account of the season which was unfavourable for military operations. The Governor General himself, who held also the appointment of Commander-in-chief, visited the upper provinces to hurry forward the preparations; and to guard the south-west of Bengal, and the north of the Deckan, from the incursions of the Pindarees, the new enemy to whom we have already alluded.

Plan of invasion.

At last all was ready, and the plan of the campaign arranged. The army was divided into four divisions. The first, under Colonel Ochterlony, was to attack the westernmost part of the country; the second, under General Gillespie, was to advance against Jytak one of the enemy's

CHAP. XVII. A. D. 1814.

principal forts; the third, under General J. S. Wood, was to proceed farther to the east; and the fourth, under General Marley, was to advance towards Catmandoo, the capital of the kingdom.

Description of Nepaul.

The enemy's country was thus to be invaded in four directions at once. That country was strongly defended by nature. The highest mountains in the world are situated in it; the passes are rocky, steep, and narrow; and the inhabitants fought behind wooden stockades, from which they could easily injure an advancing party, and themselves continue in safety behind their inaccessible defences. A mountain warfare of this nature was very difficult: and the difficulty was, in the present instance, increased by the imperfect knowledge which the assailants possessed regarding the country.

The siege of Kalunga. October 29th.

The second division was the first to commence hostilities. As it advanced, the Goorkhas retreated to a small fort named Nalapani or Kalunga, which was situated on a steep hill, covered with low brushwood. The fort was small, and contained a garrison of only six hundred men. An assault was arranged. The English were divided into two parties, who were to make the attack simultaneously, but the arrangement was accidentally frustrated. The garrison made a sortie, and were repulsed: and General Gillespie, desiring to follow up their retreat into the fort, ordered the men who were with him to advance. But the enemy had placed a gun in such a position as to prevent the English from planting their ladders against the ramparts. Unable, therefore, to scale the walls of the fort, they attempted to burst open the gate; but the fire directed against them was so severe that they were obliged to retreat.

Death of General Gillespie.

Vexed at this disaster, the General, exclaiming that he would take the fort or lose his life in the attempt, put himself at the head of the king's 53rd and a few dismounted dragoons, and led them towards the gate again. But when they came within reach of the enemy's fire, the 53rd held back, and General Gillespie was shot while cheering them on. The party retreated a second time: and the officer who assumed the command of the division after General Gillespie's death, resolved to remain before Kalunga, until more guns could be brought to his assistance. As soon as the field pieces were received, another storming party was led to the assault. The soldiers advanced with the bayonet, their muskets being unloaded, and charged through the breach which had been made; but, on entering the fort, they found the garrison assembled in an enclosure fourteen feet below them, whence arrows, stones, and darts were discharged at them, without their having the power to retaliate. They were finally obliged to retire with considerable loss.

Abandonment of the fort.

The Goorkhas, however, deserted the fort after a short bombardment, and joined another party consisting of three hundred of their countrymen, with whom they were defeated, in the open field, by a small party of sepoys.

CHAP. XVII.

A. D. 1814.

The siege of Jytak.

Dec. 27th.

Another General soon afterwards joined : and the division proceeded to the fort of Jytak, which is situated upon the highest peak of a range of hills, and was protected by several stockades. The garrison of Jytak depended for their supply of water on wells situated outside the fort: and these were defended by a strong stackade, which the General desired to take. For this purpose he despatched two detachments, with directions to march by different routes, but to attack the stockade simultaneously. By some mismanagement, however, one detachment engaged the Goorkhas long beforo the other, and was forced to retire; while the second, after repulsing the Goorkhas who attacked it in large numbers, was obliged to return by order of the General.

The third and fourth divisions are unsuccessful.

The divisions of the army which were acting in the east, were also unsuccessful. Several parties were attacked by the enemy and repulsed ; and the campaign in that quarter was at first any thing but creditable to the English arms.

Triumphs of the first division.

Sad, however, as these first encounters with the hardy mountaineers were, in the greater number of the places attacked, the first division, under Colonel Ochterlony, was victorious. In the west, where it was engaged, Ameer Sing, the most celebrated of the Goorkha chiefs, commanded. The country was divided into three ranges of hills, which were separated from each other by deep valleys, and defended by several strong forts. On the first range was situated the fort of Nalagerh, on the second Ramgerh, on the third

CHAP. XVII.

A. D. 1814.

Maloun, and beyond these fortresses was situated Bilaspore, the capital of a Rajah, who was friendly to the Goorkhas and their cause. All of these places were strengthened by the steepness and ruggedness of the heights upon which they were built. The division reached the first range in the beginning of November. Guns were brought to bear upon the fort of Nalagerh, which the garrison, after a short defence, abandoned, thus enabling the invaders to advance without hindrance to Ramgerh. Finding that this fort could not be safely attacked in front, Colonel Ochterlony moved to the enemy's left; gained a height upon the other side of the range, whence all the defences of the Goorkhas could be distinctly seen; and remained there for some time, employing himself in gaining a through knowledge of the country, until reinforcements should arrive. He had heard at that place of the reverses before Kalunga, and wished to be quite sure of success, before he made any further attack.

Abandonment of Nalagerh. November 5th.

As soon as his division was strengthened, he left a part of it before Ramgerh, and advanced with the remainder to Maloun, which movement threatened to cut off Ameer Sing from all intercourse with his friends, if that chieftain remained in his present position. Ameer Sing, being aware of his danger, withdrew the greater part of his troops to Maloun, where he was closely invested by the English commander. The Rajah of Bilaspore surrendered, and the Goorkha posts near the heights of Maloun were taken.

March to Maloun.

CHAP. XVII.

A. D. 1815.

Attack on the heights of Maloun.

April 15th.

General Ochterlony now resolved to attack those heights. They were protected by two forts, named Surajgerh and Maloun, which were situated upon the extreme right and left of the range, and were connected by a line of stockades. The English were encamped on the other side of a mountain stream directly opposite to these heights, and had taken possession of a small fort, named Ratangerh, upon a detached hill to the right of Maloun. There were also two unoccupied hills between Maloun and Surajgerh. General Ochterlony determined to gain these positions, and thus to cut off all communication between the two forts. The two parties sent to effect this enterprise were successful. The post near Maloun was very important; and Ameer Sing, fully aware of its importance, made a desperate effort to recover it, two days after it had been taken. The Goorkhas fought gallantly. Their chief was there, standing with his son near their standard, and cheering them on to the attack. They rushed upon the bayonets of the English, seized them with their hands, and wildly struck at their opponents over the muskets. Two small guns had been brought up the heights by the English; and, although these field pieces created terrible havoc in their ranks, they returned to renew the struggle again and again. This hard fighting lasted for two hours. Help was at length brought to the English from the nearest detachment. A bayonet charge decided the day: and the Goorkhas retired to Maloun, carrying with them the corpse of the chief who had led them forward to that desperate attack. CHAP. XVII. A. D. 1815.

Surrender of the garrison.

The garrison soon afterwards abandoned the fort and gave themselves up as prisoners of war, for they were unable to persuade their leader to yield. Thus deserted by those who had hitherto fought so nobly for him, Ameer Sing, surrendered the citadel, and was permitted to retire to Catmandoo. The campaign in that quarter was at an end: and the fall of Maloun led to the surrender of Jytak, which the second division had for some time past been blockading.

Conquest of Kumaon.

Meanwhile a small force had been successfully employed in the province of Kumaon. The Goorkhas were defeated in a battle which took place near Almora, the capital; a portion of the town was captured; and, on the following day, the fort was surrendered, and a convention was entered into with the Goorkha chief, by which the whole province was evacuated by the Goorkhas, and left in the undisturbed possession of the English.

The Rajah of Nepaul sues for peace.

The Rajah of Nepaul, now thoroughly terrified by the victories of the English, asked for peace; and his ambassadors accepted the terms upon which the Governor General promised to grant it. The country to the west of the river Kali, about which there had been disputes, was to be restored to the Rajahs to whom it had originally belonged; the plains along the Goorkha frontier were to be ceded; the Rajah of Sikkim

CHAP. XVII. A. D. 1816.

was to receive back all the territory which had been taken from him by the Goorkhas; and a Resident was to be stationed at the court of Catmandoo. The Rajah was, however, persuaded by his counsellors to refuse his signature to the treaty, and to decline the peace which he had previously requested. The war was, therefore, renewed. The country to the west of the Kali had been conquered, and the two divisions of the army which had been engaged in that quarter, had returned to their stations in the low country. The ensuing campaign was, therefore, to take place in the east, in the direction of the capital.

Sir D. Ochterlony turns the Chiria-ghati Pass. Feb. 17th.

The chief command was given to General, now Sir David, Ochterlony, who had been rewarded for his former victories with military knighthood. The General divided his force into four brigades, one of which was to enter Nepaul by a pass upon the right of the main army, another by a ghaut upon the left, and the remaining two were to advance under his immediate command straight towards Makwanpur. The way to that town lay through a steep ghaut, called the Chiria-ghati Pass, across which the Goorkhas had raised three very strong stockades, one behind another. Sir David had, however, discovered a pathway by which he could avoid the difficult route that lay before him. Leaving part of his troops at the foot of the Chiria-ghati Pass, he led the remainder along the steep, narrow, rugged path, himself marching at the head of his soldiers and sharing all their privations.

CHAP. XVII.

A. D. 1816.

The battle of Makwanpur. February 28th

The Goorkhas, as soon as they heard that Sir David Ochterlony had thus out-manœuvred them, abandoned their stockades, and retired to Makwanpur. Thither the General followed them, and encamped before the fortified heights in the neighbourhood of the town. Upon the left of the enemy's position, was a village which the Goorkhas abandoned upon the approach of the English, and of which the latter immediately took possession. But it was an important post: and the enemy soon afterwards attempted with a large force to regain it. A severe battle ensued, which lasted for five hours, and ended in the repulse of the Goorkhas.

Capture of Hariharpur.

Meanwhile a brigade which had been sent under Colonel Kelly to attack Hariharpur, a town situated to the right of the Chiria-ghati Pass, had also defeated the enemy. He had advanced without opposition to the fort, near which a stockade had been constructed between two precipitous rocks. The English took possession of an open space which commanded this stockade, when they were attacked by overwhelming numbers; but they gained the day after a long and severe contest: and the fort was surrendered to them on the following morning.

Conclusion of the Goorkha war. March 12th.

After the engagement near Makwanpur, Sir David made preparations for attacking the town and fort. But the Goorkha government, appalled at the success of this rapid and brilliant campaign, were now willing to agree to the demands of the Go-

CHAP. XVII. A. D. 1816.

vernor General. Peace was made: and, having gained what he required by their submission, Lord Moira restored to the Nepaulese Government a portion of the conquered territory.

Unsettled state of Central India.

It was well that the Goorkha war was, at this time, brought to an end, as all the available forces of the English Government were required for defence against foes in other parts of India. The whole of Central India was in a very unsettled state: there were intrigues at the courts of the Peishwa, Scindia, and other Mahratta chieftains, regarding a general rising against the power of the English; and the Pindarees, and other bands* of robbers, were emboldened to run wild over the interior of the land, and had lately dared to plunder the territories of the Company.

The Pindarees.

The Pindarees were originally mercenaries who had served with the Mahratta army, during the recent wars: but they had been united into several bands under chiefs of their own, since the downfall of the Mahratta power. Their principal leaders at this time were three persons named Cheetoo, Kareem Khan, and Dost Mahomed. Each had a large number of horsemen under him: but the Pindarees did not adhere strictly to one chief, —whoever could secure most plunder, had most followers.

Their mode of robbery and warfare.

During the feast of the Dasra, the leaders met at an appointed spot, and consulted where they could rob and murder with the greatest advantage.

Thousands hastened to their standards: men of every caste and creed, disbanded soldiers, and daring adventurers from the surrounding countries, resorted to them in large numbers. As soon as all was ready, they set out in several parties, which were to meet again, after the conclusion of their forays, to divide the spoil. They rode rapidly from village to village, burning the houses, torturing and robbing the people, and committing the most abominable excess. They were so lightly equipped, that they could, day after day, march fifty or sixty miles. Most of them were armed with spears, and a few had matchlocks. But they scarcely required arms. Their only object was plunder, and they always ran away from any force that might be sent against them. They were so quick, that they could slip through armies and laugh at all defences; and so active, that a regular army could rarely overtake them. These armies of robbers had for several years committed outrages in the Mahratta countries, and in the territories of the neighbouring Rajahs; and they had been favoured by Scindia, the Peishwa, and others, who, although they suffered at their hands, expected to find them useful allies in the event of a war.

Pindaree foray into the Company's territories.

In 1815, however, when the first reverses of the Goorkha war had emboldened the still hostile Mahrattas, the Pindarees under Cheetoo made an incursion into the district of Masulipatam. Early in the following year, a large party of them, encouraged at meeting with little resistance, entered

CHAP. XVII. A.D. 1816.

the Company's territories again; visited Guntoor; passed through Cuddapah; and, although they were only ten days about the work of destruction, left behind them more than three hundred ruined villages.

The English troops attack them. Dec. 26th.

But the English troops were looking out for them. At four or five places small parties of Pindarees had been attacked and destroyed: and, on the 26th of December, the 4th Madras Cavalry, under Major Lushington, came up with a numerous detachment of the robbers, of whom they slew seven or eight hundred. The regiment had marched fifty miles; but, suddenly bursting in upon them, while, unsuspicious of danger, they were dividing their plunder and cooking their rice, the sepoys routed them, notwithstanding the great fatigue of the previous chase, and pursued them for a considerable distance.

The grand armies of Hindostan and the Deckan.

By October 1817, the preparations for crushing these unworthy enemies were completed. In the north a large army was assembled on the frontiers of Hindostan Proper. Five divisions under the command of Sir Thomas Hislop, the Commander-in-chief of Madras, advanced towards the Nerbudda from the Deckan: and brigades were left near Poona, Nagpore, and Hyderabad. There was also a force in Guzerat, which was to be in communication with the army of the Deckan. The whole amounted to about 113,000 men.

Preparations for war.

Central India was thus completely surrounded by armies of imposing strength. There could be no retreat for the Pindarees; no hope of escape for their leaders; and these forces were, at the same time, prepared to act against the Mahrattas and effectually to break their power, should they rise in rebellion. An occasion for war with the latter power was soon afforded: and, while the grand army of Hindostan, under the command of the Governor General himself, and the fifth division of the Deckan army, drove the Pindarees towards the mountains in the west; destroyed parties of those robbers, wherever they were met; and reduced them to a few, feeble bands; the other portions of the army of the Deckan were employed against Mahratta princes, who had defied the might and power of the English.

CHAPTER XVIII.

TWO TREACHEROUS ALLIES.

FROM A. D. 1815 TO A. D. 1817.

Relations with the Peishwa—Intrigues of Trimbakji—Disputes between the Peishwa and the Guicowar—Murder of Gangudhar Shastri—Imprisonment and escape of Trimbakji—He raises insurgent troops—Duplicity of the Peishwa—Decided conduct of the Resident at Poona—Rewards offered for Trimbakji's capture—New treaty with the Peishwa—the Peishwa's plots—Description of Poona—Attack on the Residency—Battle of Kirkee—Arrival of reinforcements—Flight of the Peishwa—Affairs at Nagpore—Appa Sahib made regent—Alliance with the English—Appa Sahib becomes Rajah—Plots against his allies—Description of Nagpore—Battle of Seetabuldee—Captain Fitzgerald's gallant charge, and victory of the English—Negotiations with the Rajah—Arrival of reinforcements—Battle of Nagpore—Siege and surrender of Nagpore—Battle of Jubbulpore—Restoration of Appa Sahib.

SINCE the treaty of Bassein, the Peishwa had been in alliance with the English. English troops were stationed near his capital; an English Resi-

CHAP. XVIII.

A. D. 1815.

dent was at his court; and he was obliged, outwardly at least, to follow English counsels. But he did not admire the restraint which these things implied. He feared his allies: but, at the same time, he hated them.

Intrigues of Trimbakji Dainglia.

Soon after the arrival of Lord Moira, serious differences had arisen between the Peishwa and the Resident. The former had taken into his favour a low-born and disreputable person, named Trimbakji Dainglia who continually urged his master to oppose his unwelcome allies. At Trimbakji's instigation, the Peishwa had been secretly encouraging the Mahratta princes to rise against the English; had taken up the position which former Peishwas had held, as head of the Mahratta confederacy; and had prepared the way for opposition to the English, which, as the following events will shew, was ready to break out as soon as he afforded it any open encouragement.

Disputes between the Peishwa and the Guicowar.

In 1814 disputes had occurred between the Peishwa and the Guicowar, a Mahratta prince, who ruled in Guzerat under the protection of the English Government. In the following year an agent named Gangudhar Shastri was sent by the Guicowar to the Peishwa's court to bring the differences between the two powers to an amicable conclusion. He was at first received in a cold and disrespectful manner; but the Peishwa, in order to disguise his real feelings, afterwards assumed a more cordial tone. The ambassador was invited to visit a celebrated pagoda at Punder-

CHAP. XVIII. A. D. 1816. July 14th.

pore; and, while there, was cruelly murdered by the favourite's order; and it was strongly suspected that the foul deed was committed at the Peishwa's instigation.

Imprisonment and escape of Trimbakji.

Mr. Mountstuart Elphinstone, the Resident, immediately requested that Trimbakji should be surrendered to the English Government. The Peishwa, after some hesitation, consented: and the murderer was taken to Tanna, near Bombay, where he was kept in close confinement. His followers, however, were determined to rescue him. One of them, disguised as a horsekeeper, entered into the service of an English officer, and was employed in the stable, which was situated directly under Trimbakji's prison. As he cleaned his horse, he amused himself by singing snatches of Mahratta songs. This habit was not remarked at the time: but the prisoner's room was one morning found empty, and then it was surmised that the verses which the disguised Mahratta had sung were full of invitations to resistance and to flight.

Intrigues of Trimbakji and the Peishwa.

Trimbakji and the musical horsekeeper fled to the mountains, where the former soon gathered around him a party of daring men, which day by day increased in number; and, although falsehood upon falsehood was told to the Resident upon the subject, he was aided by the favour and the money of the Peishwa. The insurgents were defeated by the English troops, and Trimbakji was again obliged to hide among the hills: but the Resident, foreseeing that there was danger of the Peishwa's rising, insisted on his giving up his favourite again; on his surrendering three of his strongest forts; and on his agreeing to these requests within four and twenty hours. The city was surrounded by English troops to shew that Mr. Elphinstone was in earnest; and these energetic measures so appalled the Peishwa, that he agreed to every thing which the Resident required. A large reward was offered for the apprehension of Trimbakji; his property was seized; and the forts which the Resident had named were surrendered.

CHAP. XVIII.

A. D. 1817.

New treaty with the Peishwa.

June 13th.

The Peishwa's conduct in the recent transactions had been so peculiarly faithless, that the treaty of Bassein was set aside by the Governor General's order, and another treaty concluded, which was designed to counteract his treacherous designs towards his allies, and to dissolve his connexion with the Mahratta confederacy. He was obliged to cede a further amount of territory for the maintenance of the English troops, and to hold communication with other courts, only with the concurrence of the Resident. He signed this new treaty, much against his will, in June 1817.

Continuation of the Peishwa's plots.

These events made him hate his allies still more than he had done before; and he continued his intrigues against them more zealously and more systematically. He assembled a large force at Poona, which, he pretended, was prepared to assist the English against the Pindarees: and he attempted to induce the sepoys who were stationed at that place, to desert their masters. There were only a few troops at Poona but the

CHAP. XVIII. A. D. 1817.

Resident allowed one of the divisions of the grand army, under General Lionel Smith, to leave the neighbourhood, and to march against the Pindarees, at the same time requesting that officer to return, if he failed to hear regularly from Poona.

Description of Poona.

Poona is situated on a small river, upon the opposite bank of which stands the Residency; and two miles lower down the stream, which in that quarter forms a semi-circle, is the small village of Kirkee. To this village the sepoys were removed, and were there kept in readiness for action. Another small force was stationed in the neighbourhood of Kirkee, but at a little distance on the other side of the river. The whole of the English troops amounted to only 2800 men; while the army which the Peishwa had assembled, numbered more than 25,000.

Attack on the Residency.

The hostile forces were soon to be engaged. On the 5th of November, the Peishwa's followers attacked the Residency, and Mr. Elphinstone had only just time to cross the river by a neighbouring ford, before the Mahrattas broke into his dwelling. He recrossed the stream by a bridge, joined the troops at Kirkee, and accompanied them during their attack on the army of the Peishwa.

The battle of Kirkee. Nov. 5th.

As soon as the Resident had joined the troops, the battle began. A fierce charge of Mahratta horse upon the right wing was repulsed. On the left, one of the sepoy regiments was surrounded, thrown into confusion, and nearly broken by the enemy, when the Bombay European Regiment dashed up to its aid. The line was reformed; the division from the opposite side of the river which had fought its way up through masses of cavalry had arrived; and the enemy was effectually prevented from surrounding the troops again. After the engagement the English troops returned to Kirkee. The Mahrattas encamped on the ground which they had previously occupied; but they were afraid to attempt a second attack upon the English encampment.

Arrival of reinforcements.

Meanwhile General Smith, having received no tidings from the Resident, imagined that there was something wrong at Poona, and returned thither with his division. Four days after his arrival, an advance was made on the Mahratta camp: but it was found deserted. The Peishwa, dismayed at the increased strength of the English, had fled during the night. The town of Poona was taken possession of without resistance, for the inhabitants were, in general, favourably disposed towards the English.

Affairs at Nagpore.

Soon after these things, the Rajah of Nagpore, another Mahratta prince, made similar treacherous attacks upon his English allies. The Rajah of Berar whom General Wellesley defeated in 1803, had naturally shown a great dislike to a close and cordial alliance with those who had subdued him. He died in 1815: and, as his son who succeeded him was half an idiot, it was necessary that some one should be appointed Regent of the kingdom. There were many who aspired to that office: but

Appa Sahib appointed Regent.

CHAP. XVIII. A. D. 1817.

a near relation of the Rajah's, named Moodajee Bhoosla or Appa Sahib, was chosen, chiefly owing to the support of the English; and the newly appointed Regent thought that the wisest and safest plan which he could adopt, was to make a firm alliance with those, by whose help he had gained the day against his opponents. He requested permission, therefore, to form an alliance with them: and a treaty was entered into with him, as with the Peishwa, the Nizam, and the Nabob of Oude, by which it was agreed that the Company should defend him from all enemies, and that a certain number of troops should, for this purpose, be stationed at Nagpore, the expenses for maintaining them being paid out of the Rajah's treasury.

Enters into alliance with the English.

Intrigues and plots of Appa Sahib.

The young Rajah soon afterwards died: and Appa Sahib ascended the throne. It then appeared that the new sovereign had asked for alliance with the English to serve his own purposes, and had no desire to retain it, after the object of his ambition had been attained. He entered into correspondence with the other Mahratta chiefs, and especially with the Peishwa, who had now openly risen against their common ally. He received from the Peishwa the title of Commander-in-chief of the Mahrattas, and a gaudy standard belonging to that office; assembled an army, which, he pretended, as the Peishwa had done, was to aid the English against the Pindarees; and, though still professing a wish for peace, prepared to attack the Residency and the English troops. Mr. Jenkins, the Resident, was obliged to apply for assistance, and General Doveton, with a division of the army of the Deckan, was advancing to Nagpore. But, meanwhile, the few men at that place made preparations for resisting the threatened attack, as bravely as those at Poona had done: and soldier and civilian were resolved manfully to oppose their country's enemies, though the latter were in number as twenty to one. CHAP. XVIII. A. D. 1817.

Description of Nagpore.

The Residency was separated from the town of Nagpore by a low range called the Seetabuldee Hills. At the northern extremity of the range was situated a narrow, conical hill; and on the south was another hill larger than the former, but of a lower elevation. The greater part of the infantry was stationed at these two posts, on the former of which two guns were placed. A smaller body of infantry and all the cavalry were drawn up in the grounds belonging to the Residency.

Hostile demonstration of the Arabs.

On the afternoon of the 26th of November, a number of Arabs in the service of the Rajah gathered round the party which was stationed on the heights. The Rajah still pretended to be friendly to the English; but, while two of his ministers were treating with the Resident in his name, the firing of his troops was heard, and plainly shewed his insincerity.

Attack on the Seetabuldee Hills. Nov. 26th and 27th.

During the greater part of the night the darkness was broken by the flashes from the cannon on either side. The Arabs were endeavouring to take the smaller hill, and the sepoys were

CHAP. XVIII.
A. D. 1817.

bravely defending it. At the same time, a Mahratta army advanced from the city to the plain, and in the morning were seen surrounding the Residency and the English who were stationed near it, and who were anxious and interested spectators of the struggle which was still raging on the neighbouring hills. The conflict appeared to be unfavourable to the English. One of the guns on the conical hill was rendered useless. The Arabs rushed up the ascent: overpowered the few sepoys who were posted there; brought some of their own guns to the summit; and opened a furious fire upon the English who still held the other hill.

Captain Fitzgerald's gallant charge.

The Mahrattas in the plain drew nearer and nearer. The day seemed lost, when Captain Fitzgerald, with only three troops of cavalry, charged the advancing line; drove the Mahrattas back; seized their guns; and returned to his position near the Residency, firing the captured cannon as he retired. The bold deed was seen from the hills. With a shout of triumph, the sepoys dashed in among the Arabs with the bayonet. The Arabs, fighting hard, fell back. At the moment of their retreat, a tumbril on the smaller hill, which was still in their possession, exploded, and during the confusion, the sepoys pushed forward, drove the enemy before them, and regained the summit. A small body of cavalry, at that moment, galloped round the heights, and completely dispersed the enemy. A few brave men had gained the victory over a host.

The hypocritical Rajah expressed great sorrow for what had happened, and requested that he might still receive the support and favour of the English. The Resident told him, however, that no terms could be granted him, until his army had left the field. He readily agreed to this proposition: the Mahratta force was withdrawn to a position on the other side of the city, and a short truce was concluded.

CHAP. XVIII.

A. D. 1817.

Negotiations with the Rajah.

But English troops were advancing from every quarter. By the 13th of December the division under General Doveton arrived, and gave the Resident as much support as he required. He could now dictate his own terms. These were, that the Rajah should own he had justly forfeited his crown; that he should disband his army; and, for the present, surrender Nagpore to the English. The Rajah hesitated, made delay after delay, and avoided a plain and explicit statement of his intentions.

Arrival of English troops.

The English army was prepared for battle on the morning of the 15th, and a stated time was fixed, within which a decided answer was demanded. On the 16th the troops marched towards the Mahratta encampment. At the eleventh hour the Rajah rode into the English line, delivered himself up, and promised to surrender his artillery. The army advanced to take possession of the guns, according to the Rajah's orders. The first battery was yielded: but, as the English proceeded, they met with resistance, and the battle of Nagpore began. The English infantry carried the

The battle of Nagpore. Dec. 16th.

CHAP. XVIII. A. D. 1817.

guns before them at the point of the bayonet: while the cavalry and the horse artillery attacked the enemy's left.

Siege and surrender of Nagpore. Dec. 30th.

The Mahrattas in the field being thus dispersed, it only remained to take the city of Nagpore, which was principally defended by Arabs. As the siege artillery, however, had not arrived, a small breach only could be made by the few guns with the force, and an attempt at storming failed. But the Arabs surrendered the city, before another attempt could be made.

The battle of Jubbulpore. Dec. 19th.

Meanwhile a division under General Hardyman had been ordered from Rewah to Nagpore. As he was on his way thither, he encountered an army of Mahrattas at Jubbulpore. They were drawn up in a strong position, with their right on a high and rocky hill, and their left upon a sheet of water and the town. The enemy's horse retreated before the charge of the English: but the infantry, ascending the hill, defended it, for a short time, with vigour and resolution. The English soldiers, however, forced them from their position, and put them to flight. After the battle, General Hardyman advanced towards Nagpore: but he had not proceeded far, when he received a message from the Resident, informing him of the recent battle and surrender of the town, and, as his services were not required there, he returned to Jubbulpore.

When the Governor General heard of the events at Nagpore, he desired that the faithless Rajah

Lenity shewn towards the Rajah.

should be deposed, unless the Resident had already promised to keep him on the throne. Such had been the case; and Appa Sahib, in consequence, held the title of Rajah for a little time longer. His treachery, however, was not yet cured, nor his punishment complete.

CHAPTER XIX.

CONCLUSION OF THE PINDAREE WAR.

FROM A. D. 1817 TO A. D. 1819.

Scindia—Jeswunt Row Holkar succeeded by his son Scindia is intimidated—Majority of Holkar's chieftains declare for war—Murder of Toolsee Bhye—Battle of Mahidpore—Holkar's dominions subdued—Extirpation of the Pindarees—Kareem Khan surrenders—the end of Cheetoo—Pursuit after the Peishwa—Advance of the Peishwa on Poona—Gallant action at Corregaum—the Peishwa's flight continued—Bapur Gokla—Cavalry action at Ashtee—Surrender of the Peishwa—a residence assigned him at Bithoor—Restoration of the Rajah of Sattara—Trimbakji taken prisoner—Capture of Talnere—Execution of the warder—the Rajah of Nagpore—renews his intrigues—is taken prisoner—is sent to Allahabad—escapes—flees to the Mahadeo Hills—Capture of Aseerghur—Appa Sahib flees again—takes refuge in the Punjab—a new Rajah at Nagpore—Conclusion of the war.

WE must now leave, for a time, the affairs of these two treacherous princes, and notice two other Mahratta powers, who had once given great trouble to the English, but whose means of annoyance had been, in a great measure, diminished. Scindia, their old foe, was still alive: but Holkar had died mad, and his territory had past into the hands of his son, Mulhar Row Holkar, and of Toolsee Bhye, one of his concubines, who acted as Regent of the kingdom, during the young Holkar's minority. Scindia had shown signs of hostility to the English: but the threatening array under the Marquis of Hastings kept him from any open acts of enmity. He prepared a force to act with the English; refused to give protection to the scattered Pindarees; and behaved very well towards his allies. There was trouble, however, with many of his chieftains, some of whom refused to surrender their forts upon the presentation of his orders, declaring that they had received from him secret directions of a different nature.

CHAP. XIX.

A. D. 1817.

The conduct of Scindia.

Toolsee Bhye, and part of those who bore rule in Holkar's dominions, were disposed to remain at peace with the English: but the greater number of the chieftains were heartily opposed to such a measure. The war-party prevailed. Toolsee Bhye was murdered; those who had agreed with her were imprisoned; and an army was prepared for the field. The division of the English forces, which was under the immediate command of Sir Thomas Hislop, was stationed near. It was joined by two other divisions at Oojein, and the united army advanced against the enemy at Mahidpore.

Holkar's chieftains declare for war.

A river separated it from the Mahrattas, who were drawn up on the opposite bank,

The battle of Mahidpore. Dec. 21st.

CHAP. XIX. A. D. 1817.

supported by a long and formidable row of guns. A detachment of the enemy which was posted upon the English side of the stream being driven back, the troops crossed the river under cover of the artillery. The bank on the opposite side was high, and they were enabled under the shelter afforded by it, to form into line after crossing. The greater part of the infantry, under Sir John Malcolm, were to attack the enemy's left; and the remainder, with the cavalry, were opposed to his right. As soon as they advanced from the river, an awful fire was opened upon them. But they marched through it without hesitation; fought their way up to the guns; and compelled the enemy to retire. The Mahrattas retreated along the stream in good order, making a second stand near a ford, where they desired to cross the river: but this movement was only made to enable the greater portion of their army to retire, and, when the English came up, they fled, without offering any further resistance.

Subjugation of Holkar's dominions.

This battle put an end to the opposition of the Holkar chieftains. No further engagement took place, the territory of Holkar was effectually subdued, and a treaty was entered into at Mundesore with those who acted for Mulhar Row Holkar, by which large portions of the country were given up to the English, an English force was stationed in his dominions, and all real power passed into their hands.

Extirpation of the Pindarees.

For the present, all the English army, except a division which was pursuing the Peishwa and his troops, were free from the Mahrattas, and the greater part of it could be employed in completing the ruin of the Pindarees. Parties of these robbers were still in arms, under their principal leaders, Kareem Khan and Cheetoo. Some of them had fought with the Mahrattas at Mahidpore; some were at Jawud; and others had fled to the west of the river Chumbal. Several divisions, equipped in light marching order, followed them hither and thither, and put them to flight wherever they were met. The Pindaree leaders, deserted by their followers, wandered about from village to village, and hid wheresoever they could find shelter. At last Kareem Khan and others surrendered themselves, and were sent into the Company's territories, where the former, once the fiercest of the fierce, became a quiet and industrious landholder.

The last days of Cheetoo.

Cheetoo still remained free: but for more than a year he led a wanderer's life. He once fled to the Rajah of Bhopal, through whom he offered to give himself up to the English, if they would bestow upon him an estate in Hindostan. As this request could not be granted, he continued his predatory course; and, when the Rajah of Nagpore plotted against his allies a second time, and fled from his captors, Cheetoo joined him in his flight. But he did not continue with the exiled Rajah long. Appa Sahib one day sought refuge in the fort of Aseerghur. He was admitted within the gates, but Cheetoo was not. The dauntless Pindaree turned away from the unfriendly town; but, as he was riding

CHAP. XIX. A. D. 1817.

through a dark and densely wooded ghaut, in search of another place of shelter, a tiger sprang from a way-side thicket and destroyed him.

Pursuit after the Peishwa.

We must now return to the affairs of the Peishwa, who, as soon as preparations were made for attacking him, had fled from Poona. He was closely followed by the division under General Smith, a small force only being left to defend the capital. He was too quick for his pursuers. Finding that he could not escape towards the south, he returned with the intention of regaining Poona: and in order to strengthen the garrison of that place, a detachment was ordered thither from Seroor, which was situated at the distance of two marches from it. This force consisted of only six hundred sepoys, twenty-six European artillerymen with two guns, and about three hundred irregular cavalry, the whole being placed under the command of Captain Staunton. The little party started from Seroor on the 31st of December.

The battle of Corregaum. Jan. 1st, 1818.

On the following morning, as they reached the heights which overlook Corregaum, they saw before them the whole of the Peishwa's army, numbering about 20,000 horsemen and 8000 foot. About an equal distance from both forces, was situated the village of Corregaum which was built upon the banks of a small river, the houses being separated by low stone walls. Captain Staunton immediately hastened to take possession of this village, and the enemy's infantry, which was chiefly composed of fierce and hardy Arabs, did the same. At first, there was a desperate struggle for the

CHAP. XIX.

A. D. 1818.

whole of the position, the two parties having entered it from opposite quarters at the same time: but numbers prevailed, and the Arabs gained possession of the greater portion of the village, and captured a small fort, upon which they planted two field pieces. They then attempted to drive the English from the other side of the village. The encounter was close and deadly. The Arabs climbed over the enclosure walls, and clambered along the house-tops to encounter their foes. The English met them with the bayonet. The sepoys were half starving. They had nothing to eat, and they had not tasted a drop of water during the day. But they fought for their lives, as they knew that the Arabs would shew them no mercy. The officers led them on nobly, and the surgeons, laying down their instruments, cheered the men forward, and fought side by side with their noble comrades. The hard conflict had begun at noon; and, when the shades of evening fell, it was still continued with unabated vigour. But the Arabs had the advantage. Five out of the eight English officers had been cut down. One of the guns had been taken. The enemy had entered a shed, where many of the wounded lay, and had brutally butchered every one. It was no time for surrender, however, for every man knew that the Arabs would, if he fell into their hands, hack him to pieces, as they had done his wounded comrades. All hope had gone. No! no! while there is life, there is hope. One charge more must be made. Hurrah! It is successful. Captain Staun-

CHAP. XIX.

A. D. 1818.

ton, Lieutenant Jones, and Assistant Surgeon Wylie lead the brave fellows on. They dash into the shed; rush upon the Arabs with the bayonet; and fight with the energy that desperation only gives. Lieutenant Patterson, who is lying on the ground wounded, forgetful of himself and of his suffering, seizes a musket by the muzzle; hastens to his companions' aid; and, striking down every Arab whom his arm can reach, encourages the sepoys forward until he is laid low a second time by a bullet. But the captured gun is retaken, and the Arabs driven back. The fighting continued: but by nine o'clock the enemy was obliged to retreat from the village, and the sepoys were able to procure a little water to refresh themselves after the noble conflict in which they had been engaged.

Capt. Staunton's return to Seroor.

On the following morning the Mahrattas felt no inclination to renew the attack; and in the evening Captain Staunton returned to Seroor, which he entered with colours flying and drums beating, after one of the most gallant actions ever fought by the English in India.

Continuation of the Peishwa's flight.

The Peishwa still continued his wanderings. He was a thorough coward, and always ran away the instant that any danger was apprehended. He was accompanied, however, by a brave officer named Bapur Gokla, who had the command of his army: but Gokla was killed at Ashtee, where the English cavalry overtook the Mahrattas and completely routed them.

CHAP. XIX.

A. D. 1818.

His surrender to Sir John Malcolm. June 3rd.

It would be tedious to follow the Peishwa's course after the death of Gokla. His troops decreased day by day; and, at length, only a small party of Arabs remained with him: but whithersoever he turned, he was met by a division of the English army. At last he retired towards the north, where the force which was under Sir John Malcolm was stationed, and he surrendered to that officer on the 3rd of June, 1818.

Retirement of the Peishwa.

The Governor General confirmed the promises which Sir J. Malcolm had made to the humbled Peishwa, though he did not altogether approve them. He was removed to Bithur, near Cawnpore; an allowance of eight lacks of rupees a year was given to him; and he passed the remainder of his days in the enjoyment of every indulgence and luxury.

Restoration of the Rajah of Sattara.

The office of Peishwa was abolished, and the Rajah of Sattara, who was the lineal descendant of Sevaji and the proper head of the Mahrattas, was restored to his throne, his kingdom being placed under the protection and guidance of the English.

Capture and imprisonment of Trimbakji.

Soon after the Peishwa had surrendered, his favourite, Trimbakji, who was the real promoter of the war, was taken prisoner at Nassuck, where he had hidden himself. He was again placed in confinement at Tanna, whence he had formerly effected his escape, but was afterwards removed to the fort of Chunar, near Benares.

CHAP. XIX.

A. D. 1818.

Return of the English army.

As the principal objects of the campaign had been accomplished, the several divisions of the English had, for some time past, been returning to the Company's territories, a sufficient force being left to contend against those Mahrattas who were still in arms. The division, under the immediate command of Sir Thomas Hislop,* while proceeding from Malwa into the Deckan, was obliged to pass near the fort of Talnere, which overlooked a ford of the river Tapti. The place belonged to Holkar, and Sir Thomas Hislop possessed an order from that prince for its surrender. The commandant, however, would obey neither the order of the English General nor the command of his master; but fired upon the English, as they drew near. Preparations for an attack were immediately made. The storming parties carried the two outer gateways of the fort: but, when they reached the third, a number of the enemy, among whom was the commandant, came out unarmed and were taken prisoners. The other gates were forced open, and, at the last, which led into the interior of the fort, the garrison either desired, or pretended to desire, to surrender. A small wicket door within the gate was opened: but the instant that a few English officers and men stept through it, they were cut down by some Arabs who were crowding round the entrance. The gateway was immediately battered in: and the English soldiers, full of fury at the treachery which they believed had been shewn, rushed in, and put to the sword every armed man within the place.

Capture of Talnere.

February 27th.

CHAP. XIX.

A.D. 1818.

Execution of the commandant.

On the following morning, Sir Thomas Hislop ordered the commandant to be hanged upon the ramparts for his treachery and rebellion. The act was generally condemned both in India and in England: but, whether it was right or wrong, it had the effect of deterring others from similar disobedience.

Treachery and arrest of Appa Sahib. March 15th.

After the surrender of the Peishwa, the principal enemy, still unsubdued, was the Rajah of Nagpore. As soon as he was reseated upon his throne by the kindness and forbearance of the Resident, he began to plot against his protectors. He wrote to the wandering Peishwa for assistance; he entered into correspondence with the Pindarees; and he attempted to incite all the discontented spirits in the Mahratta country against those who had so greatly befriended him. The Resident, having received timely notice of these acts, thought it advisable to take the troublesome Rajah into custody, as he was upon the point of leaving the capital for a strong fort, whither he had sent on his family and treasure. After he had been placed in confinement, it was discovered that he had murdered his predecessor for the sake of obtaining the crown.

Appa Sahib's escape. May 13th.

It was expected, at the time, that the Peishwa would make a desperate effort against Nagpore, and, consequently, all the troops in the neighbourhood were required for its defence. As soon, however, as the likelihood of such an event had past away, Appa Sahib was sent with a strong escort towards Allahabad. But on the

CHAP. XIX. A. D. 1818.

road he contrived to escape by bribing the sepoys, and fled to the Mahadeo Hills which are situated to the north of Nagpore. He found shelter among the wild and savage inhabitants of those mountains, and was assisted by one of their petty Rajahs. He remained in this retreat for some time, doing a great deal of damage to the surrounding country, into which he made incursions with the lawless men whom he had collected around him.

The siege of Aseerghur. April 9th, 1819.

But an English army being ready to attack him, as soon as the season would permit, he fled once more, and, accompanied, as we have seen, by the Pindaree, Cheetoo, sought refuge in the fort of Aseerghur which was commanded by Jeswunt Row Lar, an old friend of the Pindarees. The fort belonged to Scindia, but the commandant would not surrender it according to the order of his master. A few days' siege, however, induced him to alter his resolution, and to place the fort in the hands of the English, who kept it in their possession, as papers were found in it containing ample proof of treachery and underhand dealing on the part of Scindia.

Flight and final refuge of Appa Sahib.

But Appa Sahib was not in Aseerghur. He had continued his flight, as soon as the English appeared near that place. He wandered about from place to place, in the disguise of a fakeer, until he reached the Punjab, where he received a small allowance from Runjeet Singh. He afterwards returned to Hindostan, and the English Government permitted him to reside in the territories of

CHAP. XIX.

A. D. 1819.

the Rajah of Joudpore: but he committed no more mischief, and was guilty of no more treachery.

Changes at Nágpore.

The crown of Nagpore was given to the next heir, whose name was Baji Row. As he was very young, his mother was appointed Regent of the kingdom during his minority: but all the real power was with the English.

Conclusion of the war.

With the siege of Aseerghur hostilities ceased: the Pindaree and Mahratta war was at an end. The Pindarees were extirpated; the Mahrattas were thoroughly conquered; and the might of the English in India had at no time appeared so noble or so strong. Large portions of territory came into their possession, and very soon a change was seen in Central India. Villages which had once been ruined by savage robbers, revived and flourished again; fields which had been trodden down by the march of lawless armies, once more grew fresh and green; and the people who had been in hourly danger of life, were rendered prosperous and happy under the protection of the English Government.

CHAPTER XX.

THE EXPEDITION TO BURMAH.

FROM A. D. 1823 TO A. D. 1826.

Lord Amherst the new Governor General—Disputes with the Burmese—Dissensions about Shapooree—Affairs in Cachar—Declaration of war—Plan of the campaign—Capture of Rangoon. Attacks on stockades—Capture of Kemendine—Position of the English—Repulse of the enemy from the Great Pagoda—Fall of Martaban and other places on the coast—Advance of Maha Bandoola—Total defeat of the Bürmese—Conflagration at Rangoon—Advance into the interior—the water column repulsed at Donabew—Backward movement of the land column—Capture of Donabew—Death of Maha Bandoola—the stay at Prome—Conquest of Arracan—Negotiations—a truce—Defeat of the enemy—Capture of Melloon—Battle of Pagahm—the English draw near Ava—Conclusion of peace—Disturbances at Bhurtpore—Dethronement of the youthful Rajah—Usurpation of Doorjun Saul—Government take the part of the Rajah—Siege and capture of Bhurtpore.

THE Marquis of Hastings left India in January, 1823; and his successor, Lord Amherst, arrived in the following August.

Lord Amherst had not been Governor General long, before it was evident that war was necessary in a quarter towards which the English had not hitherto directed their arms. The Burmese, who had lately conquered the country of Assam, and whose territory had thereby been extended along the eastern frontiers of Bengal, had committed a great many outrages on the Company's subjects in the border lands. CHAP. XX. A.D. 1823. Disputes with the Burmese.

A small guard of sepoys had been stationed upon a sandy, barren island, named Shapooree, which is situated on the boundary between Chittagong and Arracan. Disputes arose about the possession of this island; and, in September 1823, the Burmese landed there, overpowered the weak guard, and drove it from the place. The Governor General remonstrated with the court of Ava regarding these proceedings; but the Burmese looked upon this attempt at negotiation as a sign of fear, and treated it with contempt. The Burmese take Shapooree. Sept. 24th.

In the following January, a large force of Burmese marched into Cachar, drew near the English advanced post at Sylhet, and entrenched themselves behind stockades. The English detachment attacked and routed them: and other attacks were made, one of them unsuccessfully. The Burmese were also guilty of an act of treachery in enticing from their vessel the commander and crew of a schooner called "The Sophia," which had been stationed off Shapooree, and in carrying them off as prisoners. The captives were released after a time; but without a word of apology or regret. Occurrences in Cachar. Jan. 1824.

CHAP. XX.
A. D. 1824.

Declaration of war. March 8th.

War had thus been going on upon the frontier for some time past. It was now declared in form. The Burmese were very eager for war. They had been successful in all their attacks upon the neighbouring states, and they expected the same triumphs over English soldiers.

Plan of the campaign.

The presumption and the boasting of the Burmese monarch were high and proud. But he was soon to be undeceived. A force was in readiness to invade his dominions, and to convince him that his troops could not successfully contend against English discipline and valour. Operations on the frontier were to be principally defensive, while the chief attack was to be made on that part of Burmah which was supposed to be most defenceless; to strike a blow at the enemy's seaports; and to ascend into the heart of the country by the river Irawaddi.

Capture of Rangoon. May 11th.

The invading army was placed under the command of Sir Archibald Campbell. It assembled at Port Cornwallis in the Andaman Islands early in May, and on the 9th of that month a few vessels of war and the transports with the troops reached the mouth of the Rangoon river. On the 11th they anchored off the town. A feeble fire was opened upon them: but the batteries were speedily silenced by the broadsides of the frigate Liffey. The soldiers were then landed, and marched into the town which was found entirely deserted. The Burmese troops had fled, and all the inhabitants had left their homes for the jungles which surround Rangoon.

CHAP. XX.

A. D. 1824.

Capture of stockades. May 26th.

In these jungles the Burmese employed themselves busily in raising stockades, under cover of which they, day by day, approached the English position. They were for a long time concealed by the dense woods: but on the 26th of May they had drawn so near that the English General determined to dislodge them. He advanced with a small party of Europeans, a few sepoys, and two guns. He was obliged to leave the latter behind in charge of the sepoys, and to go forward with the English alone. After a tedious march along a winding pathway, he reached the first stockades at which the enemy remained to fight. In a very few minutes the stockades were carried at the point of the bayonet, and the Burmese were fleeing in every direction for shelter. For a time they fought boldly: but they could not withstand the impetuosity of the English soldiers. On the 10th of June, an attack was made on the Burmese port at Kemendine, a short distance from Rangoon. The assault was perfectly successful. The stockades were carried as gallantly as the others had been, and the enemy put to flight.

Capture of Kemendine. June 10th.

Position of the English army.

There was now a short pause in the war. The Burmese had left their position in the woods around Rangoon, and had not sufficiently recovered from the defeats which they had experienced to attempt another attack. The English were not in a position to advance: the season of the year was unfavourable; sickness was in their camp; they were reduced in number; and they were

CHAP. XX.

A.D. 1824.

obliged to obtain all their supplies from India, as Rangoon was deserted and the surrounding country inundated by the rains.

Attack on the Dagon Pagoda by Thekia Wongee. July 1st.

The Burmese were the first to renew the warfare. A high officer of state, named Thekia Wongee, was sent down to drive the invaders away. He advanced with a large force against the English position, the principal point in which was the Great Dagon Pagoda, an imposing building glittering with gilded turrets. It was situated on a conical hill, commanding the road to Rangoon. The chief effort was made against this post: but the enemy was driven back to the jungles again, by a few discharges from a couple of guns and a bayonet charge of the sepoys.

Capture of stockades. July 8th.

As the Burmese chief had not fulfilled his mission, he was superseded: and Soomba Wongee, the new leader, fearful of attacking, adhered to the old plan of stockades and defence. The English were now the assailants. The troops intended for the assault were divided into two columns, one of which proceeded by water, and the other by land. Both were brilliantly successful. The fire from the enemy's principal stockade was soon silenced by the broadsides of the ships, and a practicable breach effected. The soldiers, being landed, captured two of the stockades, and the third was abandoned by the enemy. The land column had harder work: but it was done well. Seven stockades were taken in half an hour. They were all carried by assault, as the guns had been left behind: and the English soldiers were so eager for the conflict, that, in some instances, they would not wait for their scaling ladders, but mounted into the works upon the shoulders of their fellows. This was the first event which made the Court of Ava doubt of final success.

CHAP. XX.

A. D. 1824.

Capture of Martaban and other towns.

Operations were also undertaken in other places. As the season was unfavourable for an advance, the General determined to reduce the enemy's stations on the sea coast. Syriam and Dalla, two places in the neighbourhood of Rangoon, were captured; Martaban was taken by Colonel Godwin; and Tavoy and Mergui in the Province of Tenasserim were captured by Colonel Miles. An attack, however, on a place called Kyloo was repulsed. The troops were composed of sepoys, without any European soldiers. They were thrown into a panic by the loss of their officers, and were obliged to retreat. A party was afterwards sent to retrieve this misfortune: but the place had been abandoned and the stockades destroyed.

Repulse of the King's Invulnerables. August 30th.

At the end of August, a large force of Burmese, chiefly composed of men who called themselves the King's Invulnerables, and who really imagined themselves proof against bayonets and shot, attacked the Great Pagoda at midnight. A few volleys speedily put them to flight, and convinced them of their vulnerability.

Occurrences in Arracan.

The Burmese commanders had been often changed, and every one conquered. The King of Ava

CHAP. XX.
A. D. 1824.

resolved, therefore, as a last resource, to send for Maha Bandoola, his favourite chief, who had been partially successful in Arracan. A small party of sepoys in that province had been defeated, owing to the misconduct of some of the Company's irregular troops; the Burmese re-entered Cachar; and a few indecisive actions ensued. The removal of Bandoola put an end to all anxiety about the events in that quarter.

Advance of Maha Bandoola. Dec. 1st to 7th.

After a short visit to the capital, Bandoola marched quickly to Rangoon with a large army. He stockaded himself strongly in the forests, and on the 1st of December advanced to attack. The Burmese army came forward in imposing array, with gaudy banners flying, and the gilt umbrellas of the chieftains glittering in the sun. But it suddenly disappeared. The Burmese soldiers had set themselves busily to dig, and had entrenched themselves, two by two, in neat little earth-works. Nothing but heaps of freshly piled earth could be seen in the place, where, a short time before, a flaunting armament had stood. A detachment of English soldiers, however, took them by surprise, and drove them out of their defences. An attack was also made on Kemendine, which was repulsed by the sailors: and fire-rafts were floated, one after another, towards the shipping, but without effect. On the 5th of December, the enemy was attacked, and put to flight; and two days afterwards was routed again, after a brave but ineffectual defence.

CHAP. XX.

A. D. 1824.

Conflagration at Rangoon.

Meanwhile the inhabitants of Rangoon had been induced to return to their dwellings, but, at the same time, a great number of the enemy in disguise had been admitted into the town, which was set on fire by these emissaries of the Burmese. A great deal of damage was done: but the fire was at last extinguished, and the next day a force marched out to punish the enemy. The works which they attacked were strong: the Burmese numbered twenty thousand, and the assailants only fifteen hundred; but, in a quarter of an hour, the former were driven from their formidable entrenchments and put to flight. They fled into the interior of the country, and appeared no more before Rangoon.

Advance into the interior in two columns.

The English force was at this time more healthy than it had been hitherto; the enemy had retreated; and the inhabitants were friendly. Sir Archibald Campbell determined, therefore, to carry out the principal object of the campaign, and to advance into the interior. The army intended for this purpose was divided into two columns; one being directed to proceed up the Irawaddi in boats, accompanied by the boats of the men-of-war; and the other to co-operate with it by land. Sir Archibald Campbell went with the latter. He advanced rapidly, and had proceeded some distance, when he heard that the first column had been unsuccessful in an attack on the defences at Donabew, which is situated about forty miles above Rangoon.

CHAP. XX.

A. D. 1825.

Repulse of the marine column at Donabew. March 8th.

General Cotton, who commanded the water column, had been ordered to dislodge the Burmese from that town, whither they had retreated after their reverses before Rangoon: but the number of the roops was insufficient to take so strong a place as Donabew. The handful of soldiers with him carried the first stockade gallantly: but the second stockade was so strong that the besiegers were compelled to retire. As soon as Sir Archibald Campbell heard of this disaster, he returned, and in a short time appeared before Donabew. The column in the flotilla, which had retired to a place a few miles lower down the river, joined him, as soon as the wind permitted, when Maha Bandoola made a grand sortie upon the re-united force. It was repulsed with coolness and courage: and preparations were made for conducting a formal siege. Directly the batteries were constructed, the firing commenced: but the place fell into the hands of the English without a struggle. Maha Bandoola was killed by a rocket or a shell: and with the death of their leader fell the hopes of the Burmese. They fled precipitately, leaving the town to the English, who found in it supplies for several months.

Occupation ot Donabew. April 2nd.

Occupation of Prome. April 25th.

After the fall of Donabew, the onward march was resumed: and, on the 25th of April, Sir Archibald Campbell reached Prome, which was deserted upon his approach. It was set on fire by the enemy, but the English succeeded in saving a part of it from destruction. As the rainy season was drawing near, they remained there for several months, the army being quartered in comfortable cantonments around the town, to which the inhabitants were induced to return by the conciliating and friendly behaviour of the English troops.

CHAP. XX.

A. D. 1825.

Conquest of Arracan. April 1st.

While these events were taking place, a force was sent into Arracan, with orders to join Sir Archibald Campbell's army, after the reduction of that province had been effected. The capital was taken, although it was well and gallantly defended, and the country conquered: but the climate was found to be unhealthy, and the scheme of crossing the mountains to join the main army impracticable, and the troops were consequently withdrawn.

Negotiations with the Court of Ava.

During Sir Archibald Campbell's stay at Prome, negotiations were opened with the Court of Ava, and a truce which lasted until the 2nd of November, was concluded with the enemy. The Burmese expressed a great desire for peace: but it was perfectly insincere, for they would not agree to the reasonable terms of the English commander. At the end of the truce, therefore, the war was resumed.

Defeat of the Burmese near Prome.

The Burmese had advanced towards Prome, and stockaded themselves in the neighbourhood of that town. Three parties were sent to dislodge them from their stockades: but two of these returned without achieving the desired object. The Burmese drew nearer and nearer, but refrained from attack;

CHAP. XX.
A. D. 1825.

the English General, therefore, again assumed the offensive with a suitable force, and this time with perfect success. Stockade after stockade was rapidly taken. The enemy, scattered hither and thither, fled across the plain to the river, and suffered severe loss from the English horse artillery. These successes were followed up by others. All the enemy's works were taken; and, as the army proceeded, every post was abandoned in succession.

Capture of Melloon.
Jan. 19th, 1826.

Negotiations were again renewed, but they did not stop the advance of the English, who had reached a fortified village named Melloon. Although the Burmese had sued for peace, they would not consent to abandon this post. It was, therefore, assaulted, and carried, as the others had been, in the face of an overwhelming force.

The battle of Pagahm.
February 9th.

The conquering army was met on its march by an American Missionary and a released prisoner, who had been sent by the king to treat for peace. The same terms as before were stated: but the Burmese monarch would not yet agree to them. He made one more effort to drive the victors back. A new leader, who bore the remarkable title of The Prince of Darkness, was appointed to command his army; and, on the 9th of February, the English forces, which were only 2000 in number, again met the Burmese, who, to the amount of 18,000, were arranged in battle array to meet them. The Burmese leader had departed from the usual custom of fighting behind stockades, and had brought all his available forces into the open field. His army was drawn up in a semicircle across the main road, where the ground was so covered with prickly bushes, that it was difficult for an army to manœuvre. The English began the attack by assailing the advanced wings of the hostile force, upon which movement, the Burmese commander threw forward his centre to support the menaced divisions: but all were defeated, and the last hope of the Burmese sovereign failed.

Peace concluded near Ava. February 24th.

The march towards the capital was now unimpeded. The king was filled with alarm, and begged for peace, the negotiations for which were brought to an end, when the English army had arrived at Yandabo, less than fifty miles from Ava. The Burmese agreed to relinquish all claims on the provinces of Assam, Cachar, Jyntea, and Manipore; to cede to the conquerors Arracan and the Tenasserim Provinces; and to pay a crore of rupees in three instalments. Upon the receipt of the second instalment, the English were to leave Rangôon, which they were to retain until the payment was made. The first Burmese war was thus brought to a safe and honourable conclusion.

Affairs a Bhurtpore.

During its progress, military operations had also been carried on in another direction. The Rajah of Bhurtpore, an ally of the English, died in January 1825, leaving a son of tender age, whom Sir David Ochterlony, the Resident in Malwa and

CHAP. XX. A.D. 1825.

Rajpootana, recognized as the lawful successor to the throne. Doorjun Saul, a cousin of the youthful Rajah, however, laid claim to the crown, seized the fortress of Bhurtpore, imprisoned Bulwunt Sing, the rightful Rajah, and murdered his guardian. Sir David Ochterlony immediately assembled a force to oppose the usurper, and ordered it to advance towards Bhurtpore: but the Government, disapproving of these arrangements, commanded the return of all the troops which he had put in motion, and accepted his retirement from the appointment of Resident.

Disturbances in the Bhurtpore territory.

Serious disturbances, however, arose in the country of Bhurtpore. Doorjun Saul's brother with a great part of the population conspired against him, and the whole district was thrown into a state of anarchy and confusion.

English policy with regard to that country.

This state of things could not be permitted to continue, and a considerable force under Lord Combermere, the Commander-in-chief, was sent to attack the fortress of Bhurtpore and uphold the cause of Bulwunt Sing. Doorjun Saul was, however, well supported. Bhurtpore had resisted the attacks of Lord Lake's army twenty years before; the natives imagined that it was still impregnable; the inhabitants of the country were disaffected towards the English; and Doorjun Saul's popularity increased, when it was known that he intended to defend their favourite stronghold.

Siege and capture of Bhurtpore. Jan. 18th, 1826.

On the 10th of December, Lord Combermere appeared before Bhurtpore with an army of more than 20,000 men and a hundred pieces of artillery. Batteries were opened, but it was found that the thick mud walls of the fort would not yield to shot and shell. It was, therefore, resolved to effect a breach by means of mining, and, after two or three failures, an enormous mine was exploded with terrible effect. The explosion caused some loss to the besiegers themselves, but it made a breach through which they were enabled to make an assault. In a few hours the citadel was in their possession; and Doorjun Saul was taken prisoner while he was attempting to escape. This success was opportune. The only fortress that had ever successfully resisted the English arms being taken, the hopes of those who disliked their rule were frustrated; the discontented were overawed; and perfect peace prevailed throughout the length and breadth of the land.

CHAPTER XXI.

WAR IN THE HIGHLANDS OF AFFGHANISTAN.

From A. D. 1828 to A. D. 1842.

Administration of Lord William Bentinck—Conquest of Coorg—Suppression of Suttee—Changes in the Company's Charter—Apprehensions of Russian invasion—Revolutions in Affghanistan—Embassy to Dost Mahomed—Persian invasion of Herat—Siege of Herat—War declared against Dost Mahomed—Tripartite Treaty—Invasion of Affghanistan—Installation of Shah Sujah at Candahar—Capture of Ghazni—Advance to Cabul—Return of the invading army—Return and surrender of Dost Mahomed—Delusive tranquillity in Affghanistan—Desertion and defeat of discontented chiefs—Insurrection at Cabul—Murder of Sir William Macnaghten—Disastrous retreat from Cabul—Arrival of Lord Ellenborough—Gallant defence of Jellalabad—Advance of Generals Pollock and Nott—Release of the English prisoners—Withdrawal of the troops to India.

The next Governor General was Lord William Bentinck, who had some years before been Governor of Madras. His administration was, in general, a peaceful one: but during it the king-

CHAP. XXI.

A. D. 1834.

dom of Coorg, the Rajah of which had behaved in an outrageous manner both to his own subjects and to the Company, was subdued and annexed to the English dominions. Lord William Bentinck will, however, be best remembered by the exertions which he made in the suppression of suttee, the infamous custom by which widows were permitted to burn themselves alive with the dead bodies of their husbands. He made the practice penal.

The conquest of Coorg. April 6th.

Suppression of Suttee. Dec. 4th 1829.

In 1833 great changes were made in the constitution of the East India Company, which had hitherto, while it governed India, held the exclusive right of trading with that country. The latter privilege was taken away; the trade thrown open; and the Company converted into a governing power alone. The charter under which the East India Company governed India, was renewed for twenty years; but, in all other material respects, remained the same as it had been before.

Changes in the Company's Charter. A. D. 1833.

At this time the inhabitants of British India enjoyed peace for several years: but in 1839 it was broken by spirit-stirring events which are still fresh in the memory of Englishmen. We have in a previous page alluded to the fears that were felt regarding the designs of Russia upon the English possessions in the East. At the time of which we are writing they were at their height, and they were not without some foundation. The dimensions of the Russian Empire had wonderfully increased during the preceding fifty years,

Apprehension of Russian invasion.

CHAP. XXI. A. D. 1837.

and had extended towards India, as well as in other directions. Its frontier on the south was, in fact, closer to Lahore than to St. Petersburgh. The conduct of the Russian government and Russian agents likewise indicated, in some measure, what were their intentions on the subject. The latter were employed in sowing dissensions in Affghanistan and Persia, through which countries there is a practicable route to Hindostan. On the other hand, there was little danger to be apprehended, whatever the designs of the Russian government might be, as the route is almost impassable for an army, and the Russians could, at the most, only raise disturbances and arouse fears on the frontiers of British India.

Revolutions in Affghanistan.

The state of Affghanistan was very unsettled. Shah Sujah, who had lately governed there, had been driven from his country and his throne by his brother Mahmud; and had taken refuge in the English territories. Mahmud owed his success to Futteh Khan, one his ministers, whom he afterwards ungratefully and cruelly murdered. The brothers of the deceased minister, of whom Dost Mahomed Khan was the most able, revolted against Mahmud, and seized the greater part of his dominions, which they divided among themselves, leaving him to rule over the district of Herat alone. He died soon afterwards, and his son Kamran succeeded him at Herat.

Embassy to Dost Mahomed.

As Dost Mahomed possessed the principal power in Affghanistan, Lord Auckland, the new Governor General, thought it right to send an am-

CHAP. XXI.
A. D. 1837.

bassador to treat with him, nominally about commercial matters, but in reality abont things of greater importance. It was desirable to render him an ally of the English, and Affghanistan a defensive barrier for India. The ambassador was Captain Alexander Burnes. The mission, however, utterly failed, principally through Russian influence, and Captain Burnes returned to India without achieving the objects for which he had been sent to Affghanistan.

The siege of Herat. Nov. 1837 to Sept. 1838.

The Shah of Persia, who was also influenced by Russian counsels, at this time despatched an army to Herat with the object of taking that important city, which has appropriately been called the key to India. He claimed the whole of Affghanistan, and the fall of Herat would have led to further movements against that country. Herat, however, was well defended. Eldred Pottinger, a young Englishman, was there; and, as English officers have since done at Silistria and Kars, encouraged the garrison to deeds of valour by his energy and heroism. The Persian army was commanded by unskilful leaders, and, after a siege of nine months' duration, it was obliged to fall back completely baffled and defeated.

A orce sent to the Persian Gulf.

The English and Russian ambassadors were in the Persian camp: but the former was treated with great indignity. An English force was consequently sent to the island of Karack in the Persian Gulf, to demand satisfaction for the insult

CHAP. XXI. A.D. 1838. that had been offered to the representative of the British power; and the report of its arrival hastened the retreat of the Persian army from Herat.

The Tripartite Treaty. June 26th

As Dost Mahomed would not agree to his wishes by peaceful means, the Governor General determined to enforce them by war. A treaty was accordingly entered into with Shah Sujah and with Runjeet Sing, the sovereign of Lahore, the objects of which were the invasion of Affghanistan and the restoration of the exiled monarch. An English army, called the army of the Indus, was to advance into the highlands of Cabul by the way of Scinde and Beloochistan. It was to be composed of a force from Bengal; another from Bombay; and a third belonging to Shah Sujah and commanded by English officers. The whole was ultimately placed under the command of Sir John Keane.

Invasion of Affghanistan.

The Bengal column marched first, and it was not joined by the Bombay column until it had reached Candahar. The latter met with opposition from the Ameers of Scinde; but a reserve force put an effectual stop to their resistance by the capture of Kurrachee, an important town upon the coast of Scinde. The advance of both columns was harassing and fatiguing. The way was long; there was little water for man or beast; and continual annoyance was experienced from the fierce robbers, who lurked about the wild hills through which they had to pass. At Candahar, Shah Sujah was solemnly enthroned

Restoration of Shah Sujah. May 8th, 1839.

as King of Affghanistan, in the presence of the English army. CHAP. XXI. A.D. 1839.

The march was continued. Late on the evening of the 21st of July, the army encamped before the citadel of Ghazni, the birth-place of Mahmud, the first Mussulman conqueror of India; and on the 23d the guns opened upon the fortress. A small party courageously approached the walls under cover of the fire, and placed an enormous charge of powder under the Cabul gate, which was blown in by the explosion. The storming column immediately entered the town. A desperate hand to hand encounter ensued: but the town was taken, and the garrison of the citadel surrendered almost without a struggle. Perfect order and quiet were observed by the successful soldiers. The capture of Ghazni. July 23rd.

The English soon afterwards proceeded to the city of Cabul, which passed into their possession peaceably; Dost Mahomed fled with a few followers into the wilds beyond the Oxus; and Shah Sujah was reinstated in his former capital, surrounded by English bayonets, but without the good wishes or the welcome of his subjects. The occupation of Cabul. August 6th.

After the restoration of Shah Sujah, the greater part of the army was withdrawn. A force which was considered large enough to keep the country tranquil, was left at Cabul; and Mr. Macnaghten, who a short time afterwards was made a baronet, was appointed diplomatic agent at the court of the Affghan king. Return of the army.

CHAP. XXI.

A.D. 1839.

State of public feeling in Affghanistan.

The English troops remained two years at Cabul. The temper of the savage tribes in Affghanistan, and their bitter hatred of the people who had given them a king, was shewn on every possible occasion. English officers and soldiers were attacked and cut down, whenever they ventured to any distance from their comrades. Lawless chiefs gathered their followers around them, and offered resistance when there was any probability of success. Parties sent out for supplies were surrounded by crowds of fierce enemies, and were only brought out of the conflicts that ensued with severe loss. But these were only desultory attacks; and the quiet at Cabul itself was so great, that many of the English were joined by their wives and families, who resided with them near the city.

Return of Dost Mahomed.

Dost Mahomed, who had been thrown into prison by the ruler of Bokhara, whither he had fled for refuge, contrived to escape, and returned to make another attempt to drive the invaders from the country. Many of the Affghan chieftains joined him: and a force under Sir Robert Sale was consequently sent to oppose his progress. Dost Mahomed's followers were defeated at a place called Purwan: but the nature of the country prevented the fugitives from being followed, except by a regiment of Bengal Cavalry, which, after it had continued the pursuit for some distance, was attacked by a party of Dost Mahomed's horsemen. Upon the order to charge being given, the English officers galloped towards the enemy,

The battle of Purwan. Nov. 2nd.

fully expecting that their men would follow: but the sepoys' hearts failed them, and they ran away, leaving their officers to fight alone amongst their numerous foes. CHAP. XXI. A. D. 1840.

Surrender of Dost Mahomed. Nov. 3rd.

But Dost Mahomed had been defeated, and hope deserted him. On the following afternoon, as the English Envoy at Cabul was returning from a ride, a single horseman galloped up to him, and, to his astonishment, said that Dost Mahomed had arrived to surrender himself a prisoner. The messenger had scarcely concluded his speech, when Dost Mahomed himself rode up, and, dismounting, presented Sir William Macnaghten with his sword. Every kindness and consideration was shewn to the Affghan chief, who was sent to India, where he was detained in a light and easy captivity.

Revolt of Affghan chiefs.

The following months passed in comparative tranquillity, but at the beginning of October, some chiefs deserted Shah Sujah's Court, and raised the standard of revolt. As they occupied the important pass of Khurd Cabul, a force under Sir Robert Sale, which was on its way to Jellalabad, was sent against them. The insurgents were strongly posted; part of them defended a barrier thrown across the road, and others were scattered on the steep heights around: but the English soldiers drove them back, and cleared the ghaut of its defenders. But resistance was still offered. The force was attacked both by day and night: but at a place called Jugduluk

CHAP. XXI. A.D. 1841.

the enemy was gallantly repulsed; and the soldiers reached Jellalabad, which was instantly surrounded by their foes. The old and crazy walls of that place were put into the best possible state of defence, and Sir Robert Sale determined to hold it to the last. While he was thus employed, he received orders to return to Cabul, where a serious disturbance had arisen: but he declined to do so, as the party under his command was not in a fit condition for the conflicts which such a march would entail. He remained at Jellalabad: and he and his brave soldiers defended the place in a manner worthy of the English name, until brighter days should return.

Insurrections at Cabul. Nov. 2nd.

We return to Cabul, where sad events had happened. The force there was partly stationed in the cantonments which were situated at the distance of three miles, and partly in the Bala Hissar, or the royal palace, which was in close proximity to the town. Some of the English officers lived within the walls of Cabul. On the 2nd of November the whole place was in an uproar. The houses of the English were attacked; Sir Alexander Burnes and other officers were murdered; the Shah's treasury was plundered; the officers' houses were set on fire; and yet, while all these occurrences were taking place, nothing effectual was done to quell the tumult.

Increase of the revolt.

On the morning of the 3rd, some troops which had been stationed at Khurd Cabul, came in, after fighting their way from that place. The Eng-

CHAP. XXI.

A.D. 1841.

lish were now in fact besieged in their cantonments and in the Bala Hissar. A small tower and fort were taken by the Affghans who were pouring in from the adjacent districts, and no effort was made to dislodge them. On the following day an attack was made on a fort in which the principal supplies were kept. An English officer and a few sepoys were in it: but no support was given to them, and they were obliged to retreat. The chief command was held by General Elphinstone, an old and infirm officer, who seemed incapable of action; and General Shelton the second in command, was summoned from the Bala Hissar to assist him.

Attack on Bemauroo.

Nothing was done by either party for several days: but, on the 22nd, the English attacked Bemauroo, a village from which they had hitherto drawn supplies. They were defeated. On the the following day, an attempt was made to retrieve the disaster: but it signally failed. There were mistakes in generalship: but, although some fought nobly, the greater number of the troops behaved in a shameful manner.

Negotiations with Akber Khan.

Negotiations were now opened with Mahomed Akber Khan, a son of Dost Mahomed. His terms were humiliating in the extreme, yet they were listened to. On the 23rd of December, Sir William Macnaghten, who had before treated with Akber Khan, was invited to an audience with that chief; and he went to the retired spot which was named as the place of consultation, accompa-

CHAP. XXI. A. D. 1841.

nied by three officers. While he was talking to the Affghan chief, a number of armed men drew round the party. The English Envoy begged that

Murder of Sir W. Macnaghten. December 23rd.

they might be withdrawn: but his request was refused. Almost directly afterwards, the men rushed forward. A scuffle ensued. Sir William Macnaghten and one of his companions were shot; the former, it is believed, by Akber Khan himself. The others were bound, and carried away prisoners: and the bodies of the murdered men were savagely hacked and mangled. We vividly remember the horror which was felt throughout British India, when these events were known; and the sorrow that all Englishmen experienced, when they saw the flags hoisted half-mast high for their massacred countryman, and heard the toll of his funeral guns.

Renewed negotiations with Akber Khan.

Would that the English in Cabul had joined heart and hand in punishing the deed, or had even, as Major Pottinger proposed, fought their way to brave Sir Robert Sale at Jellalabad: but negotiations were continued, and the force was allowed to retreat from Cabul, on condition of paying largely for the favour, Akber Khan agreeing to ensure their safety on the march. Four officers were surrendered as hostages, and the sick and wounded left behind.

The retreat from Cabul. Jan. 6th, 1842.

On the 6th of January the retreat began. The crowd moved out of the cantonments in a confused, disorderly manner, the fighting men being mingled with the numerous camp followers. The road lay through steep and narrow mountain passes, which were covered with deep, untrodden snow. As the march continued, thousands dropped down on the way side to die of cold and hunger; others fell by the bullets of the Affghans, who crowded around the retreating force, and fired upon it from their places of concealment in the crevices of the mountains; the difficulties of the march increased; the work of destruction was nearly done; weariness, hunger, and cold destroyed those who had escaped from the vengeance of the Affghans. A few tried to force their way to Jellalabad, but only one solitary straggler reached that town. CHAP. XXI. A.D. 1842.

Preparations for retrieving the disasters.

Sir Robert Sale, however, still held out bravely, he and his comrades gaining the well-earned name of "The Illustrious Garrison;" a force was assembling under General Pollock at Peshawur; and General Nott, who had defeated the enemy on the 12th of January near Candahar, held that city.

Arrival of Lord Ellenborough. Feb. 28th.

Early in 1842, Lord Auckland retired from the office of Governor General, and Lord Ellenborough succeeded him. After some hesitation and misgivings, the new Governor General resolved to order an advance into Cabul to retrieve the disasters which had been experienced in that country, and to release the English ladies and officers who were still the prisoners of Akber Khan. Ghazni had been retaken by the Affghans, who had treated the English officers captured in that place with great cruelty; and this barbarity afforded another inducement for exertion.

CHAP. XXI.

A.D. 1842.

The Illustrious Garrison. From Nov. 12th, 1841, to April 16th, 1842.

We must now return to Sir Robert Sale at Jellalabad. His small force had employed themselves diligently in repairing the walls, and securing the place against attacks: but the fruits of their labour were destroyed by an earthquake, and all had to be begun again. Cheerfully, however, they set to work, and soon restored the defences. By the time that all was in readiness for the enemy, Akber Khan approached to blockade the town; and several spirited skirmishes took place with his troops. On the 7th of April, a grand sortie was made on the Affghan camp: all the enemy's guns were taken, the encampment fired, and Akber Khan forced to make a precipitate retreat. This victory was gained by only a handful of troops over a numerous enemy: but it was saddened by the loss of Colonel Dennie, who had distinguished himself by conspicuous gallantry throughout the campaign. Captain, afterwards Sir Henry, Havelock commanded the right attack.

General Pollock's advance to Cabul.

Nine days afterwards, General Pollock reached Jellalabad. He had advanced from Peshawur; stormed the Khyber Pass with perfect success and little loss; and had come to relieve the illustrious garrison. He remained for some months at Jellalabad, before he was permitted to go forward. On the 20th of August, however, he began an advance with all his forces to Cabul. Near Gundamuk he drove the enemy from some forts and a position on the surrounding hills; at Jugduluk, where only a few months before the English had suffered severely in the retreat from Cabul, the Affghans, who crowded round the advancing army, and fired upon it from the heights, were put to flight by a few English soldiers; at Tezeen a harder struggle took place, and was followed by a more decided victory; and, on the 15th of September, an English army, triumphant and inspirited, encamped again at Cabul.

General Nott's advance.

General Nott had likewise advanced from Candahar. On the 30th of August he defeated a force under Shumsoodeen, the Governor of Ghazni; on the 6th of September, Ghazni was abandoned by the enemy; on the 14th and 15th he drove the Affghans, who had assembled in large numbers to oppose him, from the defiles through which he was obliged to pass; and soon afterwards joined General Pollock at the capital.

Release of the prisoners.

As soon as Akber Khan heard of General Pollock's advance, he ordered his prisoners to be removed towards the interior of the country, and threatened to sell them as slaves to the barbarous chiefs of Koordistan. The success of the English had, however, an effect on the mind of the Affghan, to whose charge the captives had been entrusted; and for a large bribe he permitted them to escape. As they were returning to Cabul, they were met by Sir Richmond Shakespear, who was attended by a chosen band of horsemen; and, upon their nearer approach to the capital, they had the happiness to find themselves once more among their own people. A force un-

CHAP. XXI. A. D. 1842.

der Sir Robert Sale, whose wife and daughter were among the captives, had been sent out to welcome and protect them. Amidst the rejoicings, and tears, and congratulations of every one present, from the General to the private soldier, they were conducted to the English camp.

Final triumph and withdrawal of the army. Oct. 12th.

Little more remained to be done. The disgrace had been taken away; the prisoners welcomed back; and the power of the English shewn in victory and moderation. It had been resolved to withdraw all the troops from Affghanistan, so soon as success would permit them to do so without dishonour, as Shah Sujah had been murdered by one of his own chiefs, and an armament was no longer needed for his support. The army, therefore, returned to India, after the towns of Istalif and Charekar had been captured and destroyed: and the savage chiefs of Affghanistan were left to fight their own battles, and to carry on their own feuds, without farther interference on the part of the English.

CHAPTER XXII.

OCCURRENCES IN SCINDE AND GWALIOR.

FROM A. D. 1842 TO A. D. 1844.

The Ameers of Scinde—Ill-feeling against the English Government—Infraction of treaties—a new treaty offered for their acceptance—Attack on the Residency—the battle of Meeanee—Surrender of Hydrabad, the capital of Scinde—the battle of Hydrabad or Dubba—Final subjugation of the Ameers—Conquest and pacification of the country—State of affairs at Gwalior—the Maharajah dies childless—Adoption and installation of a relative—Mama Sahib appointed Regent—Intrigues at the Maharajah's Court—Dada Khasjee Walla appointed in Mama Sahib's stead—the English Resident leaves the Court—State of the Mahratta army—Advance of the English troops—Failure of negotiations—the battle of Maharajpore—the battle of Punniar—Treaty with the Maharajah—Return of Lord Ellenborough to Calcutta—is recalled by the Court of Directors.

THE war in Affghanistan was followed by another war of which it was partly the occasion. We have mentioned the opposition which the Ameers of Scinde offered to the advance of the

CHAP. XXII.
A. D. 1842.

English forces from Bombay, when they were proceeding to Cabul. It was speedily put down at the time: but the march of troops through Scinde left an ill-feeling against the English Government in the minds of the rulers of that country. Their dissatisfaction manifested itself in their corresponding with the enemies of the English, when the reverses at Cabul took place, in their assembling bands of armed followers, and in their breaking engagements to which they had before agreed by treaty. They were, in fact, prepared to take advantage of the disasters in Affghanistan; but the victorious advance of Generals Pollock and Nott deprived them of an opportunity for resistance. There was at this time a force in Scinde, which was ready to act on the offensive, and to the command of which Sir Charles Napier was appointed in October 1842.

Opposition of the Ameers to the English Government.

Scinde is watered by the broad and noble river Indus, and negotiations had, at various times, been carried on between the English Government, and the chiefs or Ameers of the country regarding the navigation of that river. It had been arranged by treaty that no tolls should be levied on English articles of commerce, except such as had been first approved by English officers. This agreement was broken: but, at the same time, there were plausible reasons for the conduct of the Ameers, as well as for their hostile actions. These chieftains were not desirous of the English connexion; an English agent was appointed to reside at the city of Hydrabad in Scinde against their wishes; and a subsidiary force was stationed in their territories. They had in fact been reduced from perfect independence to the same position as the other dependant states of India.

A new treaty offered for their acceptance.

In consequence of the suspicious behaviour of the Ameers, the Governor General prepared a new treaty for their acceptance. The terms of this treaty were hard. A certain amount of territory was to be ceded to the English instead of the tribute then paid to them; the Ameers were to furnish fuel for the English steamers on the Indus; and they were to give up the privilege of coining to the English Government. The Ameers were very unwilling to enter into this agreement: but, after some time, Major Outram, the British Commissioner, persuaded them to affix their seals to it.

Attack on the Commissioner. Feb. 15th.

There was a strong expression of ill-feeling shewn towards the Commissioner, as he retired from his interview with the Ameers; and on the following day his house was attacked. It was surrounded on three sides by the insurgents, the fourth being kept clear by the fire of a small war-steamer which was anchored near the place. For four hours the escort kept their assailants at bay, and then retreated in good order to the English vessel.

The battle of Meeanee. Feb. 17th.

The force under Sir Charles Napier was close at hand. In two days it arrived at Meeanee, near Hydrabad, where the Ameers, who were all up in arms, were awaiting him with a large army

CHAP. XXII. A. D. 1843.

of brave and hardy men. Their position was very formidable. Their main body was drawn up in the dry, sandy bed of the river Fulailee, where they were sheltered at the beginning of the engagement by a steep bank; their left flank was protected by a thick wood which was surrounded by a high wall; and their right by a village and ravine. The enemy occupied both the village and the wood. The English army was not one tenth of the size of that opposed to it; but it was ready to do and dare any thing.

The struggle at the river.

As the English approached, a severe fire was opened upon them from the enemy's guns. It was answered by the artillery of the English, which was stationed on their right; and a few skirmishers were sent forward in that quarter to clear the wood of the enemy: but they were obliged to return without accomplishing their object, and the infantry then advanced to storm the river-bank. They advanced nobly to do the appointed work: but it proved a long and arduous task. A fierce hand-to-hand struggle took place. As soon as the foremost ranks of the enemy were driven back, others crowded forward to take their posts. Defending their heads with thick, broad shields, the Beloochees dashed among their assailants and fought with savage desperation. Expecting no quarter, they gave none: but closed with their opponents, and struggled franticly to the last. Even the bayonet, on that rough and rugged ground, failed to force them back.

For fully three hours the deadly conflict continued: but at last the main body of the enemy gave way, and retired before the glittering array of English bayonets: but the Beloochees retreated, as they had fought, slowly, sullenly, and bravely; more with the air of conquering, than of conquered, men. Their retreat was quickened by a charge of the cavalry which had succeeded in crossing the river near the village on the left. CHAP. XXII. A.D. 1843. The victory.

Next morning six of the Ameers presented their swords to the English General, and two days afterwards Hydrabad, the capital of Scinde, was surrendered. Opposition was not, however, at an end. Enemies were still in the field, and were advancing towards Hydrabad in force. They had reached the village of Dubba which is situated about four miles from that city, and the English army, now largely reinforced, proceeded to attack them. Their position was similar to the one at Meeanee. They were posted on the banks of two deep canals running parallel to each other, with their right on the river Fulailee; and they had considerably strengthened the natural defences of that position. The battle began with a deadly fire from the English artillery, which threw the enemy into some confusion. A charge of cavalry was then made on his left flank, where it was discovered that many of the Beloochees had taken to flight, the horsemen riding nobly across the canal, and scattering the fugitives before them. At the same time the Queen's 22nd stormed the entrenchments and carried them gallantly, reserving their fire un- Surrender of Hydrabad. The battle of Hydrabad. March 24th.

CHAP. XXII. A. D. 1843.

til they arrived within a short distance of their opponents; while the 25th and 21st Regiments Bombay Native Infantry attacked the adjoining entrenchments. The three regiments then advanced together, and, supported by the Horse Artillery, drove the enemy from the village, on his extreme right, where he had rallied in considerable force. After a severe conflict, he fled along the bank of the Fulailee, pursued by a portion of the cavalry. The Beloochees fought almost as valiantly as at Meeanee: and the loss of the victors was severe.

Final subjugation of the Ameers.

The war did not continue much longer. Some of the chiefs were still up in arms, the principal of whom were named Shere Mahomed and Shah Mahomed: but they could not assemble any large amount of troops. The former was defeated by Major Jacob, and forced to flee; and the latter was taken prisoner during an encounter in which his small party of soldiers was quickly put to flight.

The annexation of Scinde.

The country was in the power of the English. It remained in their possession: and Sir Charles Napier was appointed Commissioner on behalf of the English Government. The people, it is said, were rejoiced at the change of masters, as the Ameers had been unjust and ungenerous in their rule. Be that, however, as it may, the inhabitants have been gainers by the change. The state of the province has improved; factions between rival chiefs are at an end; commerce has increased; and one of the most

CHAP. XXII. A.D. 1843.

flourishing ports in the East has arisen during the last few years in the once jealously-guarded and inaccessible territories of Scinde.

Affairs at Gwalior.

The next cause of anxiety to the Governor General was the condition of the independent Mahratta state of Gwalior. Dowlut Row Scindia, the once formidable foe of the English, with whom treaties of alliance had been made by General Wellesley and Lord Hastings, died in 1827 without any offspring. He was succeeded by one of his relatives, who died childless in February 1843.

Installation of a new sovereign.

The widow of the deceased sovereign, who was herself only thirteen years of age, adopted a distant relation of her late husband. He was enthroned as the Maharajah of Gwalior; and as the new king was only eight years old, a nobleman named Mama Sahib was appointed to conduct the affairs of government, as Regent, according to the express wishes of the English Resident.

Intrigues at the Maharajah's Court.

Various intrigues followed. Ambitious men who were eager for power, and the Maharanee herself opposed Mama Sahib in every way; and after he had filled the office of Regent for only three months, he was removed, and was obliged to take refuge in the British territories. A person, called the Dada Khasjee Walla, who in every way opposed the English interests, succeeded him. As the Regent whom the English Government had selected was thus removed, and

CHAP. XXII.

A. D. 1843.

another appointed without consulting the Resident, in direct violation of the treaty with Scindia, that officer was ordered to leave the court at Gwalior, in token of the Governor General's displeasure.

Confusion in Scindia's court and country.

But the intrigues and rivalry at the Mahratta court did not cease. None of the chiefs could trust his neighbour, and, as might naturally have been expected, the country was in a very disturbed state, in consequence of the confusion in the government.

State of the Mahratta army.

The Mahratta army which was very numerous and strong, was ready for plunder or revolt. The Mahratta soldiers were kept together by no bonds of discipline; were scarcely under any control, and, confident in their strength, were anxious and eager for warfare. There were a few Europeans among the officers; but almost all of them were at this time removed, which act alone shewed the power and the spirit of the army.

Advance of the English troops.

The Governor General sternly remonstrated with the Maharanee and her advisers; but, as his warning was unheeded, it became necessary at last, for the safety and tranquillity of the surrounding country, to order the advance of an army which had been assembled a few months before at Cawnpore, and which was placed under the command of Sir Hugh Gough. The Governor General himself accompanied it into the Mahratta territories. As soon as this step was taken, the Dada Khasjee Walla was surrendered to the English: but the English forces could not be recalled, until it was evident that the country was quiet and the government secure. They had approached the river Chumbal: and the Mahratta chiefs repeatedly requested the Governor General not to permit the advance of the army across that river, as the Mahratta troops, who were so entirely without discipline that they could not be restrained, would look upon such a movement as hostile, which would be contrary to the desires of the English, who professed that they had come to restore tranquillity, as friends of the Maharajah. The Governor General, however, appointed a certain day for an interview with that prince, and informed him, that, in the event of his refusing to comply with this request, the English troops would cross the Chumbal. CHAP. XXII. A. D. 1843.

The Maharajah did not arrive on the appointed day, and the army advanced. It was still supposed however that the affair would be amicably arranged, as Bappoo Setowlea, a chief thought to be friendly to the English, had been sent, on the part of the Mahrattas, to negotiate: but he quitted the English camp to join the Mahratta army, and to take command of a portion of it. On the 29th of December, the British troops under the immediate command of Sir Hugh Gough came in sight of the enemy, who were drawn up before the village of Maharajpore. The Mahrattas occupied a very strong position which was defended by a powerful array of cannon. These guns did great damage to the Eng- The battle of Maharajpore. Dec. 29th.

CHAP. XXII.

A. D. 1843.

lish, who drove the enemy from them into the village, where a fierce encounter took place, the Mahrattas tossing their matchlocks away, and fighting hand to hand with their opponents. General Valiant at this time took Maharajpore in reverse to support the troops which were already engaged. Having forced the enemy to retire from the village with the loss of twenty-eight guns, he moved forward, and attacked three formidable entrenchments at a place called Chonda. The Mahrattas fought in a most determined manner; stood to their guns until the very last; and were cut down at their posts, without an attempt to flee. The victory was complete, but it was dearly won; for the loss in men and officers was very great.

The battle of Punniar. Dec. 29th.

Upon the same day another battle was fought at Punniar, by the division of the army under General Grey, which had entered the Gwalior territories by a different route. The Mahrattas, who were posted on the hills surrounding the English army, were chased from height to height; their guns were taken; and they were forced to flee from the field of battle.

Submission of the Maharanee.

The two victories effectually persuaded the Maharanee and her advisers to accede to the Governor General's wishes. It was arranged that the government of Gwalior should be conducted by a council, until the Maharajah became of an age to take charge of it himself; that the advice of the English Resident should be implicitly followed; that the Mahratta army should be reduced to a very small amount; that an English force should be stationed at Gwalior, and be paid out of the revenues of that State; and that all power should be taken out of the hands of the Maharanee, to whom an ample allowance was granted to support her rank and dignity.

Treaty with the young Maharajah.

A treaty containing these terms was agreed to by the Maharajah and the Mahratta noblemen. Having thus restored peace to Gwalior, and, by his prompt conduct, checked the spread of feelings hostile to the English authority, Lord Ellenborough returned to Calcutta. But he did not stay in India long after the warfare had been concluded. The Court of Directors disapproved of his conduct both in Scinde and Gwalior, and were displeased at his supposed delight in war rather than in the quiet pursuits of peace, and they recalled him from the high station of Governor General, without the sanction or approval of the Home Government. Sir Henry Hardinge was appointed his successor.

Recall of Lord Ellenborough.

Lord Ellenborough had, however, restored to India the blessings of peace by successful war; he had upheld the power of the English in rebellious states; and, even if his administration as Governor General were undeserving of grateful remembrance in other respects, it ought never to be forgotten that he vindicated the honour of his country's name in the mountains of Affghanistan, retrieved the disasters suffered there, and restored the English captives to their friends and freedom.

CHAPTER XXIII.

FIRST CONTEST IN THE PUNJAB.

FROM A. D. 1844 TO A. D. 1847.

Arrival of Sir Henry Hardinge—the Sikhs—Death of Runjeet Sing—State of the Punjab—Position of the Sikh government—Power of the army—Invasion of British India—Advance of English troops—the battle of Moodkee—the Sikhs' entrenched camp—the battle of Ferozeshah—a night on the battle-field—the victory—the Sikhs recross the Sutlej—Sir Harry Smith sent to Loodiana—the battle of Aliwal—Preparations for the final struggle—the battle of Sobraon—the English army cross the Sutlej—the advance to Lahore—Goolab Sing negotiates—Interview between the Maharajah and the Governor General—Treaty with the Maharajah—Conclusion of the war—Close of Lord Hardinge's administration.

SIR Henry Hardinge arrived in India with a sincere desire to preserve peace: but he soon found himself engaged in war. New enemies invaded the English possessions, and it was necessary to conquer and expel them.

CHAP. XXIII.

A. D. 1845.

The Sikhs.

These foes were the Sikhs. We have not had occasion to mention this people often in the preceding pages: but, during the progress of the British Empire in India, they had been gradually increasing in power and importance. This sect arose in the sixteenth century, under Nanak, a quiet and peaceable teacher of a mixed Hindu and Mahomedan religion: but they were persecuted by Aurangzib, and, under a leader named Gooroo Govind, they laid aside their primitive character, became a warlike, as well as a religious, power, and gained a large portion of territory during the decline of the Mogul Empire. In the reign of Runjeet Sing, they acquired great strength. Their army was well drilled and disciplined under the guidance of French and Italian officers; the artillery, in particular, was brought into a state of great perfection; and the Sikh soldiers were generally victorious over the enemies against whom they contended. Runjeet Sing, with whom the English Government were in alliance, died in 1839, when the Affghan war was in progress. Since his death the country had been in a state of utter confusion. Anarchy, conspiracies, plots were in the capital. Foul murders were of continual occurrence. And, amidst these scenes of tumult, the army was all-powerful.

Condition of the Sikh government.

In 1845, Dhuleep Sing, a boy of tender age, was the Maharajah of Lahore. His mother, who acted as Regent for him, had, after a revolu-

CHAP. XXIII. A.D. 1845.

tion at the beginning of the year, made her brother the vizier: but he was murdered in a similar revolution, and the power of the office, though not the name, was held by an influential chief named Rajah Goolab Sing. At this time of revolts and turbulence, the Sikh army, eager for warfare, and desirous of employment, determined to invade the British dominious. The Queen-mother and her party encouraged the idea, in order that they might get rid of their unruly subjects. Goolab Sing pretended to favour the army in its desire: but in reality kept himself from any acts of hostility, until he could see the event of such a course.

The Sikh army invades British India.

Invasion of British India by the Sikhs. Dec. 12th.

In consequence of the suspicious movements of the Sikhs, the Governor General sent reinforcements to the frontier, where the English had two stations, named Loodiana and Ferozepore; and proceeded himself to the menaced quarter. On the 12th of December, the Sikhs crossed the Sutlej, entered the British territories "without a shadow of provocation," and proceeded to form an entrenched camp at Ferozeshah, about ten miles from Ferozepore.

The battle of Moodkee. Dec. 18th.

The English troops at Umballa, who were under the command of Sir Hugh Gough, were now ordered to advance as rapidly as possible, to join those at Loodiana. On the 18th of December, they arrived at the village of Moodkee, after a fatiguing march; but they had not had time sufficient to rest themselves, when news was received that the Sikh army was on the way to attack them. Fatigue and hunger were soon forgotten: and the army was marched out in battle order to receive the foe. The ground was flat, but partly covered with low brushwood, behind which the enemy hid his infantry and artillery. The latter opened fire upon the English as they advanced, which was warmly answered. The English cavalry was then sent forward to attack both the flanks of the enemy: and, while he was thrown into confusion by these movements, the infantry advanced, drove the Sikhs from position after position, and captured all their guns. The conflict was continued for some little time by starlight, and at last ended in favour of the English. They had before despised their new enemies: but in this first battle they found that the Sikhs fought with great skill and distinguished valour. The loss on their side was heavy, and among the slain was Sir Robert Sale, the defender of Jellalabad.

CHAP. XXIII.

A. D. 1845.

The battle of Ferozeshah. Dec. 21st.

The Sikhs retreated to their entrenched camp at Ferozeshah. The English, reinforced by the division from Ferozepore, were led, on the 21st, to attack them in their fortifications, which were very formidable, being defended by more than a hundred pieces of cannon. The entrenched camp was in the shape of a parallelogram, against the longest side of which the assault was made. Under fire of their artillery, which was far weaker than that of the Sikhs, the English infantry stormed those fearful batteries, and forced their way into the enemy's camp. A terrific

CHAP. XXIII. A. D. 1845. conflict ensued. The Sikhs were maddened with enthusiasm and religious zeal: and they fought with savage desperation, killing every wounded Englishman, who lay helplessly on the ground: and the horrors of the battle were increased by the explosion of several mines.

Sir J. Littler's division. In the meantime Sir John Littler's division, which was directed against the enemy's left, was not so successful as the others. The carnage among the assailants was awful: and in one quarter, where there was a battery in the shape of a half moon, one of the Queen's regiments suffered so much that it was obliged to retire.

A night on the battle field. In the midst of the rush of the battle and the roar of cannon, the night drew on. The English had been partially successful; they had gained a footing in the Sikh camp: but the enemy was not driven out. Darkness put an end to the contest for a time. The English lay down almost by the side of their opponents. In the gloom, friend and foe were scarcely distinguishable. But, now and then, a shot came from the still untaken guns upon the weary Englishman, who had marched sixteen miles before the fight, and were now suffering from cold and hunger. The Governor General, however, and the Commander-in-Chief were there to encourage the brave men, and to share their sufferings.

The victory. As day dawned, the battle began again. In spite of all their hardships, the dauntless soldiers were full of enthusiasm and energy; their

English 'pluck' was roused, and they were determined to win. Sir Henry Hardinge, who had taken the second place in the command under Sir Hugh Gough, placed himself at the head of the left wing; the Commander-in-chief did the same on the right, and they led the infantry onwards to victory. Every thing gave way before the irresistible charge. They forced the Sikhs back, and captured seventy-eight of their cannon. But as soon as one portion of the Sikh army was conquered, another arose: a reserve of 30,000 men under the Sikh chief, Tej Sing, came forward to oppose the victors, and to re-capture the entrenchments. Again, supported on either side by the cavalry, those heroic foot soldiers charged on. Tej Sing was routed, and the whole of his army forced to cross the Sutlej, and to flee, discomfited and beaten. CHAP. XXIII. A. D. 1845.

Never, perhaps, have English soldiers fought so gloriously as at Ferozeshah: never, most certainly, had they more heroic leaders. The Governor General not only shared the privations of the men on the battle-field, but he showed every kindness in his power to those who had fought with him, and especially to the wounded. Passing from man to man, he cheered them with words of hope; if any were in want of comforts, he supplied them himself; if any were desponding, he shewed them his armless sleeve, and spoke to them of their own dear Home. Gallantry and unselfishness of Sir Henry Hardinge.

The English army remained where it had won this dearly-bought triumph. It could not advance The Sikhs recross the Sutlej.

CHAP. XXIII.

A. D. 1846.

to Lahore, until it could be supplied with more artillery and strengthened by reinforcements. The Sikhs took advantage of delay which they thought arose from indecision, and, crossing the Sutlej, again invaded the British territories. More battles were to be fought. The enemy menaced Loodiana. The Commander-in-chief, therefore, sent Sir Harry Smith with a division to defend that town. Sir Harry Smith met with the Sikhs here and there upon the road: but not in great force. A few skirmishes took place; and the English were not always successful.

The battle of Aliwal.

Jan. 28th.

But these affairs were trifling. Loodiana was relieved; and, with the troops at that place added to his own, Sir Harry Smith marched out to meet the enemy at Aliwal. His troops were scarcely half the number of the Sikhs, who had fifty-six guns and were strongly entrenched behind earthworks. As the English advanced, a severe fire was opened upon them during which Sir Harry Smith ordered them to halt that he might better ascertain the exact position of the enemy. Having learnt that, he moved forward again, and stormed the village of Aliwal, which was the key of the Sikh position. That place was speedily carried; and the enemy were driven across the Sutlej in precipitate flight, leaving their baggage, ammunition, stores, and guns to fall into the hands of the victors. The Sikhs fought boldly. In a charge of the 16th Lancers they met the advancing horsemen with sword and target, and attacked them hand to hand. After

CHAP. XXIII.

A.D. 1846.

the battle, Sir Harry Smith rejoined the main body of the army.

Preparations of the English and the Sikhs.

But great numbers of the enemy were still on the left bank of the Sutlej, where they were employed in strengthening their position at Sobraon, which had more the appearance of a fortress than a camp. Meanwhile heavy ordnance, ammunition, and reinforcements were brought up to the English. At length all was ready for an attack, and an advance towards Lahore.

The battle of Sobraon. Feb. 10th.

Very early in the morning of the 10th of February, the troops were under arms for the assault. A thick mist was over all, but as it began to clear away, the English guns opened fire. For three hours nothing was heard but the roar of the cannon, and the whir of shells and rockets, to which the enemy replied ineffectually. But the cavalry and infantry were not to remain spectators alone; for the fire, although severe, was not sufficient to destroy the fortifications, or to induce the Sikhs to leave them. The English infantry dashed forward to storm the earth-works, when a sanguinary combat ensued. The cannon of the Sikhs inflicted great injury on the assailants, who, in some places, were obliged to retire over and over again, until at length the indomitable courage of the English prevailed, and, marching up to the very muzzles of the guns, they carried them at the point of the bayonet. The cavalry in the meantime, rode by twos and threes through small openings in the entrenchments, and, forming up-

CHAP. XXIII. A. D. 1846.

on the opposite side, charged the Sikh gunners at their posts. The Sikhs fled. Borne down by their opponents, they crowded towards the river, under a heavy fire from the horse artillery. Some fell by the deadly missiles; others were drowned in attempting to cross the stream; and few reached Lahore. The Sikh army that had boasted of invading India, and vanquishing the English, was completely conquered.

Advance to Lahore.

The evening after the battle, part of the English army crossed the Sutlej. In two or three days it arrived at Kussoor, which is not very far distant from Lahore. At that place Goolab Sing, who was sent by the Regent to negotiate, met the Governor General. His first desire was to stop the advance of the English forces: but Sir Henry Hardinge would not listen to this proposition—the humiliation of the Sikhs must be complete, and the English army must dictate terms at the capital. The young Maharajah came to the English camp to have an intreview with the Governor General, who treated him with every kindness and respect: and a few days afterwards he was escorted to his palace by the officers of the English troops, who had advanced to Lahore. The citadel was garrisoned by them, and the town passed tranquilly into their possession.

Treaty with the Maharajah. March 8th.

A treaty was signed on the 8th of March. A large sum of money was paid to the British Government for the expenses of the war: the territory, which forms a triangle between the rivers Beas and Sutlej, was given up to the English;

CHAP. XXIII.

A.D. 1847.

the army was disbanded; all the artillery, which had not been taken in the recent battles, was surrendered; and, as the Lahore government was unable to pay the whole of the large sum of money required, a further portion of territory was given up, which was afterwards presented to Goolab Sing, with whom a separate treaty of alliance was made, in consequence of his neutrality during the war, and his service in bringing the treaty with the Lahore government to a favourable conclusion.

Conquest of the Sikhs.

The Sikhs were thus thoroughly conquered. They had invaded India; they were repulsed, and their own country invaded in return: they had been eager for victory and plunder; they were subdued, and their own territories reduced: they had dreamed of marching to Calcutta, and driving the English from the land; they were beaten in every battle, and their own capital filled with English troops. But their spirit was not yet broken, and it required another war to bring them into perfect submission.

Conclusion of Lord Hardinge's administration.

At the request of some of the Sikh chieftains a force of 10,000 men was left at Lahore, the rest returned to India, and the first war in the Punjab was at an end. The remainder of Lord Hardinge's stay in India was spent in promoting the welfare of the people given to his charge, and in the quietness of peace.

CHAPTER XXIV.

CONQUEST OF THE PUNJAB AND PEGU.

FROM A. D. 1848 TO A. D. 1853.

Commencement of Lord Dalhousie's administration —Moolraj—his treacherous conduct—is removed —Messrs. Agnew and Anderson sent to instal the new governor—Insurrection at Moultan—Murder of the British officers—Shere Sing sent to Moultan—Mr. Edwardes—his admirable conduct —defeats Moolraj's forces—appears before Moultan—General Whish arrives at Moultan—General insurrection in the Punjab—Shere Sing's defection—Siege of Moultan raised—the English army enters the Punjab—the affair at Ramnuggur—the battle of Chillianwalla—the fall of Moultan—Sensation in England—the battle of Gujerat—Annexation of the Punjab—Conduct of the governor of Rangoon—Commodore Lambert's mission—War with Burmah—Capture of Burmese forts—Character of the Burmese war—Advance to Prome—Annexation of Pegu—Lord Dalhousie's policy.

LORD Dalhousie began his administration as Governor General with the prospect of a firm and lasting peace: but he had not been long in India before disturbances arose in the Punjab, which ended in a second struggle with our brave and desperate enemies, the Sikhs. Lalla Moolraj, the governor of Moultan, the capital of a district, which is situated between the rivers Indus and Sutlej, had, for some time past, been intriguing with his fellow-countrymen at Lahore, and inciting them to rise against the English troops, and to expel them from that town, where they had remained at the request of the principal Sikh leaders. It was, therefore, considered necessary to depose him. A chief named Sirdar Khan Sing was appointed governor in his stead; and Mr. Vans Agnew, a Bengal civilian, and Mr. Anderson, of the Bombay army, were deputed to accompany the new governor to Moultan, as the envoys of the English Government. Moolraj appeared to acquiesce in the change, and no disturbance was expected: but the very day after the English officers arrived at the city, they were attacked by a party of Moolraj's followers, and severely wounded. They retired with Sirdar Khan Sing and their escort to the Eedgah, a small fort near the town, from which an ineffectual fire was directed against them. Three days afterwards the Eedgah was attacked. The Goorkha soldiers and the Sikhs with them, were traitors. The gates of the fort were opened to the assailants; the two wounded Englishmen were cruelly murdered, as, with hand clasped in hand, they encouraged each other in their own loved tongue;

Treacherous conduct of Moolraj.

His removal from the Government of Moultan.

Assassination of the English envoys.

CHAP. XXIV. A. D. 1848.

and their bodies were grossly insulted by the savage mob.

Intrigues at Lahore.

This act was not a solitary instance of treachery. It was discovered that conspiracy was also at work among the Sikhs at Lahore, who in vain attempted to allure the sepoys stationed there from their allegiance.

Mr Edwardes's active and energetic proceedings.

As soon as the events at Moultan were known, a force was sent thither under Shere Sing, a Sikh leader, whose faithfulness was considered above question. But there was more effective aid at hand. Mr. Edwardes, a Lieutenant in the Company's army, was stationed at Leiah on the Indus, to assist Moolraj in settling that part of his district, and in collecting the revenue. A detachment of faithful Sikhs was under him, with whom he advanced towards Moultan: and he wrote to the Nabob of the neighbouring district of Bhawulpore, requesting immediate assistance. The Nabob responded to the appeal, and, throughout the war, remained a true, faithful, and useful adherent to the English cause.

Repulse of Moolraj's troops.

But before efficient help could reach them, Mr. Edwardes and his party were attacked by an equal number of the insurgents whom they gallantly repulsed. Hastening forwards, he effected a junction with the troops under Colonel Cortlandt, who commanded the fort of Dhera Ismael Khan, and with the forces of the Nabob of Bhawulpore.

The battle of Suddoosam. June 18th.

On the 18th of June, he again defeated Moolraj at Suddoosam on the Chenab, after a

CHAP. XXIV.

A. D. 1848.

hard and precarious battle of nine hours' duration. He had crossed that river with his infantry, and had separated from Colonel Cortlandt, who came up with two regiments and six guns, in time to give him most desirable aid. Effectually beaten in the open field, Moolraj retired to Moultan, whither Mr. Edwardes advanced with an army, which daily increased in number. That officer had acted with energy, vigour, and skill. He had encouraged those around him to deeds of valour; he had stayed the first violence of the revolt; and he had thus given others time to plan greater things: but he was not able, single handed, to crush the power of Moolraj.

Siege of Moultan.

General Whish, with reinforcements, which raised the amount of the forces before Moultan to about 28,000 men, arrived there in August, and assumed the chief command.

Insurrection in the Punjab, and defection of Shere Sing.

Meanwhile the Sikhs in the Hazara district arose, under a leader named Chuttur Sing; and a spirit of insurrection was generally felt throughout the Punjab. The troops before Moultan were, however, gaining ground. They had driven the enemy from every outwork around the town, which was regularly invested; but, in the midst of their success, they were obliged to raise the siege from an unexpected cause. Shere Sing, who was with the besieging army, and who had been hitherto implicitly trusted, went over to the enemy with five hundred Sikhs.

CHAP. XXIV. A. D. 1848.

Advance of English troops.

The war was henceforward waged on a larger scale. An army, under Lord Gough, the Commander-in-chief of India, who had been made a peer for his services in the last Punjab war, was assembled at Ferozepore. It was immediately ordered forward to oppose the forces of Shere Sing and his father, Chuttur Sing.

Engagement at Ramnuggur. Nov. 22nd.

On the 21st of November, the English drew near the enemy, who was posted, in a strong position, at Ramnuggur on the Chenab. Early on the following morning an attack was made upon the Sikhs by the horse-artillery; and the English cavalry were ordered to engage a large body of their horsemen who had crossed the river. The 14th dragoons and a regiment of native cavalry drove the enemy before them: but they charged too far. They were exposed, in the deep sand of the river-bed, to the full fire of the Sikh guns, and were compelled to retire, after suffering severe loss.

The battle of Chillianwalla. Jan. 13th, 1849.

The hostile forces did not meet again in battle for some time. In the middle of January, however, Lord Gough resolved to move forward, and to act upon the offensive. He drew near the formidable entrenchments of the Sikhs at the end of a fatiguing march, and he desired to defer the engagement until the following day: but the Sikh batteries were nearer than he supposed, and, as their fire inflicted great loss upon the English army, he issued the necessary orders for battle. The ground, with which the English General was unacquainted, was very unfavourable to the movements of a large army. The English troops were, however, engaged with the enemy; there could be no retreat without dishonour; and they fought nobly, notwithstanding the disadvantages of the field. Strong batteries were taken at the point of the bayonet; the Sikhs were driven back; and the English army encamped, after the severe contest, near the battle-ground—victors indeed, but without the fruits of victory. The enemy withdrew unpursued; some of the English guns were taken; and the loss in killed and wounded was enormous. But fearful as the English loss was, the Sikhs suffered still more than they in the battle of Chillianwalla.

The capture of Moultan. Jan. 22nd.

The gloom which this indecisive action spread over British India soon cleared away. On the 21st of January, Moultan fell into the hands of the English. General Whish, being reinforced during December by troops from Bombay, was enabled to renew the siege. On the 31st of that month, a sortie of the garrison was repulsed; on the 2nd of January, the town was taken by storm; and on the 22nd, Moolraj surrendered the citadel. A large body of men was thus released from a long and tedious siege, and was left free to reinforce the army under Lord Gough.

Burial of the English envoys, and trial of their murderer.

After the fall of Moultan, the bodies of Messrs. Agnew and Anderson were reverently exhumed; were borne by their fellow countrymen through the breach which had been made in the battlements; and were buried on the ramparts of the

CHAP. XXIV. A. D. 1849.

fort. Moolraj was put upon his trial for their murder, and, being found guilty, was sentenced to death, a punishment, which was afterwards commuted to imprisonment for life.

The battle of Gujerat. Feb. 21st.

When the tidings of the battle of Chillianwalla were received in England, they caused a painful sensation among all classes of the community; and the Government thought it advisable to appoint Sir Charles Napier to command the army in India, and to prosecute the Punjab war: but, long before he arrived in this country, the war had been brought to a favourable conclusion. On the 21st of February, a decisive action took place at Gujerat, where Shere Sing had taken up a strong position with an army of 60,000 men, fifty-nine guns, and a detachment of Affghan cavalry under a son of Dost Mahomed Khan. Gujerat was almost entirely an artillery battle. The English batteries cannonaded the Sikhs for three hours: and, at the end of that time, the British infantry put the whole of the Sikh force to flight, captured all their cannon, and pursued them until darkness fell. The Affghans fled rapidly from the field, and were followed by Sir Walter Gilbert to the entrance of the Khyber Pass.

Conquest and annexation of the Punjab. March 29th.

This victory was conclusive. All the Sikh chieftains of importance surrendered, and the Sikh army was entirely broken up. The conquest of the Punjab was followed by the annexation of that rich and fertile country. It has since been

CHAP. XXIV.

A. D. 1851.

governed well and vigorously; it has improved in every way; and the administration of the English officers is exceedingly popular among the inhabitants.

Disputes with the Burmese.

While Lord Dalhousie was engaged in carrying out the necessary measures for the government of the Punjab, he received tidings of occurrences at Rangoon, which appeared likely to demand a second war with the Burmese. The governor of that town had unjustly oppressed the commanders of two English vessels, and had shewn himself to be generally hostile to the interest of the English nation at that port. The Governor General, therefore, considered it expedient to send Commodore Lambert in command of a small fleet to desire satisfaction, and, in the event of the governor refusing to afford any explanation of his conduct, to forward a letter to the King of Ava, demanding his recall. The governor of Rangoon treated the English Ambassador with marked contempt. The Commodore consequently communicated with the Court of Ava: and the Burmese monarch immediately removed the offending governor, and appointed another officer in his stead.

Commodore Lambert's mission.

Beginning of hostilities.

The new governor, however, behaved, if possible, in a more insolent manner than his predecessor. Commodore Lambert, on account of this conduct, declared Rangoon and the adjacent Burmese ports to be in a state of blockade; informed the Burmese monarch that he would hold no further communication with the governor; and

CHAP. XXIV. seized a large war-boat, which lay near his ship
A.D. 1851. in the Rangoon river, 'by way of reprisal.' On the following morning, he moved his squadron down the river to carry out the proposed blockade, one of his vessels having the captured war-boat in tow: and, as the ships proceeded, the stockades on the banks of the river, and the Burmese war-boats fired at them. The fire was returned with terrible effect, and effectually silenced. The blockade was commenced, and the Commodore returned to Calcutta to receive further instructions from the Governor General.

War with Burmah.

The King of Ava, upon application being made to him for reparation, refused to afford it, and confirmed the conduct of the governor of Rangoon: and Lord Dalhousie, who had heartily striven to bring the affair to a peaceable conclusion, was obliged to declare war. The favourable season for hostilities had almost passed away, and the rains were near: but the Governor General hastened the preparations for warfare, with the design of striking a severe and sudden blow at the Burmese power. A large fleet, conveying a considerable force under the command of General Godwin, arrived at the mouths of the Rangoon river in the beginning of April 1852. Martaban was taken; Rangoon, after a severe struggle, was carried by assault; Bassein, another important position, was captured; and the English forces thus obtained a firm footing in Pegu before the time for active service passed away: but the Burmese monarch was not induced to desire peace, while the invading troops were still far distant from his capital. CHAP. XXIV. A. D. 1852.

Gallant defence of Pegu.

Pegu, the chief town of the province of that name, was taken in the month of June: but, as it was left with only a slender garrison, the Burmese, a few months later, made a desperate effort to retake it. They were defeated, however, by the persevering gallantry of Major Hill of the Madras Fusiliers, and of the few men under his command, who defended the post committed to their charge against overwhelming numbers, until they were relieved by reinforcements from Rangoon.

Chara cteristics of the war.

In all the engagements which took place the Burmese invariably shewed great cruelty to the wounded and the captives: but the chief enemy with which the English had to contend, was disease. Cholera and fever were more fatal than the weapons of the Burmese.

Conquest and annexation of Pegu. Dec. 20th.

After some delay, General Godwin advanced to Prome, which was placed in the occupation of his troops. The whole of the large country of Pegu was thus possessed by the English forces, and the Governor General thought it advisable to keep it under English protection. A proclamation was consequently issued, by which Pegu was pronounced a part of the British Empire, and it is at present steadily recovering, under its new masters, from the effects of Burmese misrule.

Peace with the Burmese. June 30th, 1853.

The King of Ava had, in the mean time, been dethroned by his brother, who, convinced that

CHAP. XXIV. A. D. 1853.

resistance against the superior power of the invaders was in vain, expressed a desire for peace which was concluded, upon his withdrawing his troops from the frontiers of the newly-acquired territories, and releasing the English captives at Ava.

Lord Dalhousie's policy.

Lord Dalhousie's policy in annexing the Punjab and Pegu to the English dominions has been frequently condemned: but we do not think that he could have acted otherwise without neglecting the interests of his country and the safety of India. It was scarcely desirable that the English possessions in the East should have been extended: but, in neither instance, did the enemies of England afford any option to the English Government. In both quarters war had occurred twice, and constant danger and annoyance might have been expected, if Lord Dalhousie had not made an adequate provision for sustaining the power and honour of the English nation.

CHAPTER XXV.

CONCLUSION OF LORD DALHOUSIE'S ADMINISTRATION.

FROM A. D. 1854 TO A. D. 1857.

Fresh treaty with the Nizam—State of affairs at Nagpore—Death of the Rajah without issue or relations—Nagpore placed in charge of English officers—the Sonthal insurrection—Restoration of tranquillity—the condition of Oude—Disturbances in that country—assembling of English troops—former treaty violated by the Nabob—the annexation of Oude—the province placed in charge of English officers—Departure of Lord Dalhousie—Social improvements during his administration—Changes in the Company's Charter—Arrival of Lord Canning as Governor-General—Growth of English power in India—Benefits of English rule.

DURING the year succeeding the conclusion of the Burmese war new territories were added to

CHAP. XXV. A. D. 1855.

the Company's dominions. In May 1854, a fresh treaty was entered into with the Nizam, in whose country the contingent force had been, for some time past, irregularly paid. In discharge of the debt which had been incurred, four districts to the north and west of Hyderabad, were made over to the management of the English Government. The kingdom of Nagpore likewise, the Rajah of which had died without issue, was, in the same year, annexed to the Company's territories, and is now governed by English officers.

The Sonthal insurrection.

These changes were effected without any disturbance, and for some time perfect peace prevailed throughout India. The quiet was, however, broken, in July 1855, by a startling insurrection in Bengal. The Sonthals, a hill-people in the districts of Bhaugulpore and Rajmahal, who had hitherto been regarded as a harmless, peaceable, and tractable race, irritated, as it is believed, by the oppressions of the money-lenders of Bengal, suddenly broke into rebellion under leaders who pretended to be inspired; descended into the neighbouring plains; plundered and burnt the villages; massacred the unresisting inhabitants; and committed every kind of violence and outrage. There were few troops in the districts they attacked: but, as soon as possible, regiments were sent thither from other quarters. Being unable effectually to operate against the savages on account of the rains, the thick jungle, and the state of the laws, the forces were stationed round the desolated territory to prevent the Sonthals from entering other districts: but, as soon as the hindrances to action were, in a measure, removed, they proceeded, under the command of General Lloyd, against the rebels; engaged them wherever they were to be met; and compelled them to retire to their villages. The disturbed districts were thus restored to order, and the rebellion completely suppressed.

The condition of Oude.

The time of Lord Dalhousie's stay in India was drawing to a close. One of his last acts as Governor General wes the annexation of Oude. Since the treaty made with the Nabob in 1801, that country had been very badly ruled, and, in 1855, it was confessedly the worst-governed native state in India. The Nabob, who was devoted to sensual gratifications, and surrounded by courtiers of the most profligate character, shamefully neglected the affairs of government; the chief posts in the administration were entrusted to worthless favourites; the people were plundered and oppressed; and the ill-paid and ill-disciplined troops supported themselves by rapine, violence, and bloodshed. These evils were aggravated by a religious contest. A party of Mahomedans attacked a pagoda which the Hindus held in peculiar reverence, and were defeated by the Hindu devotees who assembled for ts defence. Enraged at their repulse, they collected in larger numbers, under a fanatical leader named Ameer Ali. It was for some time doubtful what part the Nabob would take in the affair: but he decided upon preventing the outrage which his Mussulman subjects

Disturbances in that country.

CHAP. XXV. A. D. 1856.

contemplated. The fanatics were attacked by the King's troops under English officers; they were defeated and their leader slain.

Assembling of English troops.

As a religious war appeared likely to take place in a country surrounded by the English territories, and as such a warfare would have been, in the highest degree, dangerous to the sepoys, many of whom had relatives in Oude, the Governor General ordered the English troops to assemble on the frontiers. The necessity for their interference, however, happily passed away.

The annexation of Oude. Feb. 9th.

But such a lamentable state of affairs in a dependant kingdom could not be permitted to continue: and the Court of Directors allowed Lord Dalhousie to decide whether Oude should remain in its former position, or be taken under the immediate protection of the English Government. The Governor General resolved upon adopting the latter course. The Nabob was invited to conclude a friendly treaty, whereby the government of the kingdom, which he had shewn himself unfit to rule, should, like the territory of Mysore, be placed in the hands of the English, while ample provision should be made for the support of his own position and dignity. These terms were rejected: and Lord Dalhousie proceeded, without the Nabob's consent, to issue a proclamation, by which Oude was declared a portion of the English possessions. The reasons for his act were given in this document. The English, it was stated, had agreed, by the treaty of 1801, to protect the Nabob of Oude against every foreign and domestic enemy, while that sovereign, on his part, bound himself to establish "such a system of administration, to be carried into effect by his own officers, as should be conducive to the prosperity of his subjects, and calculated to secure the lives and property of the inhabitants." The English had fulfilled their part of the engagement; the Nabob had neglected his: and, therefore, the country, which he had misgoverned, was taken out of his possession.

The system pursued in the Punjab was introduced into Oude. English officers were appointed to the administration of the government, General Outram, who has since been made a Knight Commander of the Bath, being the Chief Commissioner: and the new territory passed into the possession of the Company without any disturbance, or expression of ill-will on the part of the people, for whose benefit the change was made.

Departure of Lord Dalhousie.

The prolonged administration of Lord Dalhousie ceased on the 29th of February 1856, upon which day Lord Canning, who had been for some time appointed as his successor, assumed charge of the Indian Government. Lord Dalhousie's rule was distinguished by various social improvements which will, we trust, contribute greatly to the welfare of the inhabitants of India. Sound and practical education was encouraged; schemes for the instruction of the people were planned; and officers appointed to carry those schemes into effect:

Social improvements.

CHAP. XXV. A. D. 1857.

works for the irrigation of land and the promotion of traffic were multiplied; railroads constructed; and the three principal cities of India connected by electric telegraph.

Changes in the Company's Charter.

Changes were also made in the constitution of the East India Company. In 1853 the Company's Charter was renewed with various alterations, the principal of which were a reduction in the number of the Directors, some of whom are now appointed by the Crown; the formation of a Legislative Council for all India; and the free admission of candidates, who pass the requisite examinations, to the medical and civil services.

Growth of English power in India.

We have thus related the progress of the English Empire in India, from its first struggles for existence under Clive and Lawrence, to the present time, when it extends from Peshawur to Pegu. We have seen it steadily increasing from year to year, until, for wise and good purposes, it has been permitted by the Supreme Ruler, who orders every event in history and in life, to reach its present gigantic limits. This permission has undoubtedly been granted for the benefit of the people of India; and although a great deal still remains to be done for that object, very much has been effected.

Benefits of English rule.

It has been remarked that, if the English were to quit India to-morrow, there would be no memorial nor vestige left of their sojourn in the land. But so it would not be. There have been imprinted broad, deep marks of good, which can never be effaced. Doubtless there are defects in what Englishmen have done for India: but of necessity there are such in all human institutions, and ever will be to the end. For a hundred years there has rarely been any bloodshed in the Company's possessions: and the dominion of the English has been peculiarly distinguished for its gentleness, mildness, and moderation. Englishmen are in the chief places of power: and they are, for the most part, true and trusty men, who bear themselves nobly in the discharge of duty. Justice is free to all, except when kept back by the craft of their own countrymen; suttee, infanticide, and human sacrifices are almost entirely abolished; and, far above all, the good seed of our glorious Faith has been sown, and it will never cease to bud and blossom, so long as India has a name among the nations of the earth.

THE END.

INDEX.

Page.

Abercromby's, General, operations on the Western Coast, 135 ; co-operates with Lord Cornwallis, ... 136
Abington, Major, repulses Hyder's troops on the Western Coast, ... 121
Act, the Regulating, ... 102
Affghanistan, Embassy to, 241 ; revolutions in, 240 ; British invasion of, 242 ; the British forces in, 243 ; disasters in, 247 ; advance of General Pollock into, 250 ; of General Nott, 251 ; conclusion of the war in, ... 252
Affghans, war with the, 242 *seq* : assist the Sikhs, ... 280
Africa, discoveries in, ... 37
Agnew, Mr., assassination of, at Moultan, 275 ; burial of, 279
Agra, Shah Jehan is dethroned at, 28 ; the capture of, 158 ; Lord Lake's army reassembles at, ... 165
Ahmedabad taken by Colonel Goddard, ... 109
Ahmednuggur taken by General Wellesley, ... 155
Ajmir, the Rajah of, attacks Mahmud, ... 15
Akber, birth of, 22 ; his accession to the throne, 24 ; his long and noble reign, 25, 35 ; disapproves of his son's attachment to Nur Jehan, 26 ; East India Company founded in the reign of, ... 42
Akber Khan, son of Dost Mahomed, negotiation with, 247 ; conference of Sir W. Macnaghten with, 247 ; is present at Sir W. Macnaghten's murder, 248 ; renewed negotiation with, 248 ; his consummate treachery, 249 ; his charge of the English prisoners in Cabul 249, is defeated before Jellalabad, ... 250
Albuquerque Alphonso, the Portuguese Viceroy, 40 ; Portuguese conquests under, ... 41
Alexander the Great invades India, ... 13
Alighur captured by General Lake, ... 157
Aliverdy Khan, Nabob of Bengal,... 60

Page.

Aliwal, the battle of. 246
Allahabad, capture of, 90 ; province of, is given to Suja Dowlah of Oude, 104 ; Appa Sahib sent to, ... 221
Almora, the capture of, ... 193
Amboor, gallant defence of, 97 ; battle near, 98 ; taken by Hyder, ... 115
Amboyna, massacre of, ... 42
Ameer Ali, a fanatical leader in Oude, ... 287
Ameer Khan falls upon a detachment of sepoys, 165 ; his foray during the siege of Bhurtpore, 172 ; is defeated by the cavalry, 172 ; invades Berar, and is defeated by the English,... 181
Ameer Sing, the Goorkha chief, 190 ; retreats to Maloun, 191 ; desperate attack of, 192 ; retires to Catmandoo, ... 193
Ameers, the, of Scinde, 253 ; their ill-will to the English, 254 ; break treaties, and create disturbances, 254 ; sign a fresh treaty, 255 ; attack the British Commissioner, 255 ; are defeated at Meeanee, 256 ; and at Hydrabad, 257 ; their final subjugation, ... 258
America, discovery of, ... 38
Amherst, Lord, becomes Governor General, 224 ; engages in war with the Burmese, 226 ; his proceedings with regard to Bhurtpore, ... 236
Amyatt, Mr., murder of, ... 87
Andaman Islands, the Burmese expedition rendezvous at, 226
Anderson, Mr., assassination of, 275 ; burial of, ... 279
Annexation, the, of Scinde, 258 ; of the Punjab, 280 ; of Nagpore, 286 ; of Pegu, 283 ; of Oude, ... 288
Anwar-ud-dien becomes Nabob of the Carnatic, 50 ; his death, ... 50
Appa Sahib is made Regent at Nagpore, 206 ; enters into alliance with the English, 206 ; ascends the throne, 206 ; his intrigues and plots, 206 ; attacks the English at Nagpore, 207 ; negotiations with, 209 ; surrenders, 209 ; is reinstated as Rajah, 211 ; renews his intrigues, 221 ; is placed under restraint, 221 ; is sent to Allahabad, 221 ; his escape and flight, 221, 222 ; takes refuge in Aseerghur, 215, 222 ; flees to the Punjab, 222 ; his final refuge at Jodpore, ... 223
Arabs, contest with, at Nagpore, 207 ; at Corregaum, ... 216

Page.

Archipelago, Indian, The, Dutch commerce in, ... 41
Arcot is taken by Clive, 52 ; gallant defence of, 53, 54 ; is taken by Hyder, 114 ; cavalry from, charge into Vellore, 178
Argaum, the battle of, ... 160
Armogum, English build a factory near, ... 44
Arnee, Clive defeats Rajah Sahib at, ... 54
Arracan, disputes on the frontiers of, 225 ; operations in, 229 ; subjugation of, 233 ; is ceded to the English, ... 235
Aseerghur, Appa Sahib takes refuge in, 215, 222 ; siege of, 222
Ashtee, cavalry action at,... 218
Asoca, king of Magada, ... 9
Asoph-ud-Dowlah becomes Nabob of Oude, 104 ; his death, 143
Assam taken by the Burmese, 225 ; ceded to the English, ... 235
Assaye, the battle of, ... 156
Auckland, Lord, becomes Governor General, 240 ; sends an embassy to Dost Mahomed, 240 ; engages in the Affghan war, 242 ; retires,... 249
Aurangzib, his character, 27 ; rebels against his father, 28 ; his dissimulation, 28 ; proclaims himself Emperor, 29 ; defeats Dara, 28 ; and Shuja, 29 ; his wars with the Mahrattas, 30, 32 ; his zeal for Mahomedanism, 32 ; his death, ... 33
Ava, the English advance to, 233, 234 ; conclusion of peace near, 235 ; king of, dethroned... 283
Azeem-ul-Dowla made Nabob of the Carnatic, ... 151

Baber invades India, 18 ; gains the battle of Paniput, 18 ; his biographical memoirs, 19 ; defeats the Rajputs, 20 ; his death, 21 ; Vasco de Gama visits India during the reign of, ... 39
Bactria, the kingdom of, ... 13
Bahar under the government of Aliverdy Khan, 60 ; given to Meer Jaffier, 68 ; is invaded by Shah Alum, 77 ; passes into the hands of the English, ... 91
Bahoor, French defeated at, ... 56
Baillie, Col., sent to Guntoor, 112 ; returns to join Sir Hector Munro, 112 ; is defeated by Tippoo, ... 113
Baird, General, leads the assault on Seringapatam, ... 146

Page.

Baji Row—*See* Peishwa.
Baji Row made the Rajah of Nagpore, ... 223
Bala Hissar, at Cabul, English in the,... 246
Balkh, or the ancient kingdom of Bactria, under Seleucus, 13
Bandoola, the Burmese General, 230; his operations in Arracan, 230; advance to Rangoon, 230; is defeated, 230, 231; his death during the defence of Donabew, ... 232
Bangalore, the capture of, 135; Lord Cornwallis's army encamped at, ... 136
Bappoo Setowlea, conduct of, in the Gwalior war, ... 261
Barlow, Sir G., becomes Governor General, 174; his peace policy, 174, 175, 177; his good government of Bengal, 177; becomes Governor of Madras, 181; his unpopularity, 182; his disputes with the Commander-in-Chief, 183
Barwell, Mr., one of the first Supreme Councillors, 103; supports Warren Hastings, ... 103
Bassein, the treaty of,... 154
Bassein in Pegu, the capture of, ... 282
Batavia, Dutch capital of Java, founded, 42; force sent from, to Bengal, ... 79
Beah, Lord Lake encamped on the, ... 174
Bednore is taken, 123; re-captured by Tippoo, ... 123
Begums, Affair of the, in Oude, ... 130
Behram, Akber's minister, ... 24
Bemauroo, affair at, ... 247
Bejapore, the government of, attack Sevaji, 31; Aurungzib's war against the Rajah of, ... 32
Beloochistan, Alexander the Great passes through, 13; English army passes through, ... 242
Benares, the Rajah of, under protection of Suja Dowlah, 104; insurrections at, 128, 152; Rajah of, is imprisoned, 128; his escape, 128; rebels, and is defeated, 129; new Rajah at, 129; Lord Cornwallis dies near, ... 290
Benefits of the English rule, ... 272
Bengal, saddening occurrences in, 60; under the government of Aliverdy Khan, 60; given to Meer Jaffier, 68; state of, 85, 90; is given to the English, 91; revenue and judicial changes in, ... 140
Bentinck, Lord W., becomes Governor General, 238; his administration,... 239

Page.

Berar, Rajah of, makes war against the English, 155; is defeated at Argaum, 160; peace with, ... 161
Berar is invaded by Ameer Khan, 181; ceded to the English, ... 286
Bhaugulpore, disturbance in, ... 286
Bhawulpore, Nabob of, faithful conduct of, ... 276
Bhoja, King, ... 10
Bhotwal, English detachment overpowered at, ... 187
Bhurtpore, the Rajah of, treacherous conduct of, 170; his fort of Deeg taken, 171; is besieged at Bhurtpore, 171; peace with, 172; death of, ... 235
Bhurtpore, unsuccessful siege of, 171; disturbances at, 235, 236; capture of, ... 236
Bidjeeghur, flight of Cheyte Sing to, ... 129
Bilaspore, the Rajah of, assists the Goorkhas, 191; surrenders to General Ochterlony, ... 191
Bithur, deposed Peishwa, Baji Row, resides at, ... 219
Black Hole, the, ... 61
Board of Control, ... 131
Bokhara, Dost Mahomed imprisoned in, ... 244
Bombay given to the English, ... 44
Boondee, English abandon alliance of the Rajah of, ... 175
Boundaries of India, ... 1
Bourbon, Labourdonnais, the governor of, 48; conquest of, 184
Brahmins, the, ... 5
Brathwaite, Col., his expedition and defeat, ... 120
Brazil discovered, ... 39
British Parliament legislate for India, ... 102, 131
Brodie, Serjeant, gallant conduct of, at Vellore, ... 178
Bulwunt Sing, Rajah of Bhurtpore, dethroned, 236; reinstated by the English, ... 236
Bundelcund, Cheyte Sing's flight to, ... 129
Burdwan, revenues of, given to the English, ... 84
Burmah, war in, 225; *seq*, ... 282
Burmese, the, disputes with, 185, 225, 281; war with, 226; defeated at Rangoon, 226, 227, 228, 258, 282; surrender Donabew, 222; defeated at Prome, 233; at Pagahm, 234; second war with, 282; defeated at Pegu, 283; peace with, ... 283

Page.

Burnes, Capt. sent as ambassador to Cabul, 241 ; his murder, ... 246
Burns, Colonel, assists in the defence of Delhi, ... 167
Bussy, M. 47 ; his successes in the Deccan, 47 ; is affronted by Lally, 73 ; is taken prisoner at Wandewash, 76 ; returns to India, ... 122
Buxar, the battle of, ... 89

Cabral commands a fleet to India, 39 ; opposes the Zamorin, 39
Cabul, is governed by Camran, 21 ; Embassy to, 181, 240 ; invasion of, 242 ; capture of the town, 243 ; the English at, 244 ; disasters at, 246 ; retreat from, 248 ; General Pollock's advance to, 250 ; General Nott's advance to, 251 ; the English withdrawn from, ... 252
Cachar, operations in, 225, ... 230
Calcutta, given to English, 45 ; Fortifications at, repaired, 60 ; siege and capture of, 61 ; Clive retakes, ... 63
Calicut, the first place visited by Vasco de Gama, 39 ; Alphonso Albuquerque's unsuccessful attack on, ... 41
Calliaud, Captain, relieves Trichinopoly, 72 ; defeats Shah Alum, 82 ; is recalled from Patna,... 86
Calvert, Captain, gallantly defends Amboor, ... 98
Campbell's, Col., gallant defence of Mangalore, ... 123
Campbell, Sir Archibald, commands the army during the first Burmese war, 226 ; takes Rangoon, 226 ; defeats the enemy near Rangoon, 227, 228, 230, 231 ; advances up the Irrawaddi, 231 ; returns to Donabew, 232 ; advances to Prome, 232 ; defeats the Burmese at Melloon, 234 ; and at Pagahm, 234 ; concludes a treaty with the Burmese, ... 235
Camran, Baber's second son, becomes ruler of Cabul, ... 21
Candahar, forms part of Camran's possessions, 21 ; Shah Sujah enthroned at, 242 ; defeat of the Affghans near, 249 ; General Nott advances from, ... 251

Canning, Lord, becomes Governor General,... ... 289
Cape of Good Hope discovered, 37 ; is rounded by Vasco de Gama,... 38
Carangoly taken, ... 75
Carnac, Major, defeats Shah Alum, 84 ; is recalled from Patna, 86 ; defeats Suja Dowlah, ... 90

Page.

Carnatic, the, 3; disputed succession in, 50; taken possession of by the English, 140, ... 151
Cauvery, the, ... 3
Cawnpore, Lord Lake retires to, ... 165
Ceded Districts, the, ... 151
Champion, Colonel, defeats the Rohillas, ... 104
Chanderi, Siege of, ... 20
Chandernagore, one of the French Settlements, 45; the capture of, ... 63
Chandore, the capture of, ... 170
Chandragherry, the Rajah of, gives permission to found Madras, ... 44
Chandragupta, king of Magada, 9, ... 13
Changumma, the battle of, ... 95
Charekar, destruction of, ... 252
Charles the Second cedes Bombay to the Company ... 44
Charter, first granted to the Company, 44; changes in the Company's, 239, ... 290
Cheetoo, the Pindaree chief, 196; makes a foray into the Company's territories, 197; his wanderings and death, 215,216
Cherry, Mr., murder of, ... 152
Cheyte Sing, the Zemindar of, 127; refuses Warren Hastings' demands, 127; his arrest, 128; escape, 128; rebellion, and flight, ... 128
Chillambrum, failure at, ... 115
Chillianwalla, the battle of, ... 279
China, attempted invasion of, by Mahomed Toghlak,... 16
Chingleput taken by Clive, 56; relieved,... 114
Chinsura, one of the Dutch settlements in India, 42,... 79
Chiria-ghati Pass, Sir D. Ochterlony turns the, ... 194
Chittagong, revenues of, given to the English, 84; disputes with the Burmese on the frontiers of, 285, ... 225
Chittoor, Hyder Ali Khan dies at, ... 121
Chola, kingdom of, ... 10
Chunar, Warren Hastings flees to, 129; Trimbakji imprisoned at, ... 219
Chunda Sahib claims the throne of the Carnatic, 50; besieges Trichinopoly, 51; sends his son to Arcot, 52; becomes nominal Nabob, 50; his defeat and murder,... 56

Page.

Chutter Sing, Insurrection of, ... 277

Circars, the Northern, 3; conquest of, 76; given to the English, ... 77

Clavering, Genl., one of the first Supreme Councillors, 103; opposes Hastings, 103, 104; his death, ... 105

Clive, his character, 51, 92; takes Arcot, 52; his gallant defence of Arcot, 53, 54; defeats the enemy at Arnee, 54; and at Covrepauk, 55; goes to Trichinopoly, 55; returns to England, 57; sent to India a second time, 59; assists in the destruction of Gheriah, 59; commands the expedition to Calcutta, 63; defeats Surajah Dowlah, 63; takes Chandrey, 63; engages in the plot against Surajah Dowlah, 64; outwits Omichund, 65; advances against Surajah Dowlah, 66; gains the battle of Plassey, 67; makes Meer Jaffier Nabob, 68; defeats Shah Alum, 78; defeats the Dutch, 79; returns to England, 80; is again sent out, 90; receives the grant of sovereignty for the English, 91; his reforms, 92; his final return to England.. 92

Close, Col., appeases the mutiny at Secunderabad, ... 184

Cochin, Rajah of, assisted by the Portuguese, 40; the Portuguese trade to, ... 40

Coimbatore, Hyder's successes in, 99; capture of, ... 124

Columbus discovers America, ... 38

Combermere, Lord, besieges and captures Bhurtpore, 236, 237

Company, East India, origin of the, 42; coalition of, with the rival company, 43; changes in the Charter of, 31, 239, 290

Condore, the battle of, ... 77

Conflans, M., defeated, ... 77

Conjeveram, the capital of Chola, 10; capture of, by Clive, 54; by Lally, 75; by Hyder, ... 112

Contract, the Tent, ... 182

Control, the Board of,... 131

Coorg, Rajah of, assists the English against Tippoo, 136; subjugation and annexation of, ... 239

Coote commands the army at Madras, 75; gains the battle of Wandewash, 75; defeats the French, 76; sent a second time to Madras, 114; gains the battle of Porto Novo, 115; and the battle of Sholingur, 118; his illness and death, 119: love of the sepoys for, ... 120

Page.

Corah, Suja Dowlah defeated at, 90; given to Suja Dowlah,... 104

Cornwallis, Lord, becomes Governor General, 132; engages in war against Tippoo, 134: visits Madras, and commands the army in person, 135; takes Bangalore, 135; advances to Seringapatam, 135; retreats, 135; at Bangalore, 136; his second advance to Seringapatam, 136; besieges Seringapatam, 136; concludes a peace, 137; takes temporary charge of the Carnatic, 140; his revenue arrangements, 141; retires, 141; returns a second time as Governor General, 173; dies at Ghazipore, 173

Cornwallis, Port, Burmese expedition rendezvous at, ... 226

Corregaum, the action at, ... 216

Cortlandt's, Col., conduct in the Punjab,... 277

Cotton's, Gen., unsuccessful attack on Donabew, .. 232

Court, Supreme, at Calcutta, 103; Nuncomar tried by, ... 104

Covelong, Clive takes,... 57

Covrepauk, Clive defeats Rajah Sahib at,... 55

Cuddalore, Fort St. David built near, 44; the battle near, 115; is taken by Hyder, 119; English besiege, ... 122

Cuddapah attacked by Pindarees, ... 198

Curus, War between the Pandus and, ... 9

Cuttack ceded to the English, ... 161

Dada Khasjee Walla, ... 259

Dagon Pagoda, attack on, 228;... 229

Dalhousie, Lord, administration of, 274; annexes the Punjab, 274; engages in war with the Burmese, 282; annexes Pegu, 284; his policy with regard to the Nizam and Nagpore, 286; annexes Oude, 287; retires, ... 289

Dalla taken, ... 229

Dara, eldest son of Shah Jehan, the character of, 27; becomes Regent during Shah Jehan's illness, 27; is defeated by Morad and Aurangzib, 28; is imprisoned and murdered, ... 30

Darius Hystaspes, invasion of,... 12

Darkness, the Prince of, ... 234

David, Fort St., origin of, 44; siege of, 48; Clive, the Governor of, 59; capture and destruction of, 73; and *Note.*

Page.

Davis, Mr., gallant conduct of, at Benares, ... 153
Deckan, description of the, 2; Holkar's possessions in, subdued,... 170
Deeg, the battle of, 168; siege of, ... 170
Delhi, the capture of, 17; sack of, by Tamerlane, 18; by Nadir Shah, 33; the battle of, 158; is taken, 158; spirited defence of, ... 167
Dennie, Colonel, death of, ... 250
Desert, the Great, 2; mentioned by Herodotus, 12; Mahmud crosses, ... 15
Devicottah, capture and cession of, ... 49
Dhuleep Sing, Maharajah of the Punjab, ... 265
Diaz, Bertholomew, rounds the Cape,... 37
Districts, the Ceded, given to the English, ... 151
Donabew, attack on, and surrender of, 231, ... 232
Doorjun Saul usurps the throne of Bhurtpore, 236; is besieged at Bhurtpore, 236; and captured, ... 237
Dost Mahomed dethrones Mahmud in Affghanistan, 240; Embassy to, 240; refuses the English alliance, 241; war against, 242; retires beyond the Oxus, 243; returns to Affghanistan, 244; is defeated at Purwan, 244; surrenders, ... 245
Dost Mahomed, a Pindaree chief,... 196
Doveton, General, advances to Nagpore, 207; gains the battle of Nagpore, 209; takes the city of Nagpore, 210
Dubba, the battle of, ... 257
Dugarajapatam, English factory at, ... 44
Dupleix, Monsieur, the French Governor, 47; his ambition and schemes of conquest, 47; besieges Fort St. David, 48; assists Chunda Sahib and Mirzapha Jung, 50; his temporary success, 51; his downfall, ... 59
Dutch, commencement of, commerce, 41; possessions in India, 42; collision between the English and, 42; the, expedition defeated, 79, 80; settlements taken, ... 119

Eastern Ghauts, the, ... 3
Edwardes, Mr., his energetic conduct, 276; defeats Moolraj, 257
Egerton, Col., commands a detachment in the first Mahratta war, ... 107

Page.

Elizabeth, Queen, East India Company founded in the reign of,... 42
Ellenborough, Lord, becomes Governor General, 249 ; orders an advance to Affghanistan, 249 ; his policy at Gwalior, 259 ; accompanies the army to Gwalior, 260 ; his arrangements at Gwalior, 262 ; his return to Calcutta, and recall, ... 263
Ellis, Mr., takes the fort at Patna, 87 ; his unselfish conduct, and murder, ... 88
Elphinstone, Mr., quoted, 11 ; the Resident at Poona, 202 ; his energetic conduct, 203 ; his house attacked, 204 ; is present at the battle of Kirkee, ... 204
Elphinstone, Genl., commands at Cabul, ... 247
Emanuel, the king of Portugal, encourages trade to the East, ... 38

Fancourt, Colonel, murdered at Vellore, ... 178
Feroze Shah's good and useful reign, 17,... 35
Ferozeshah, the battle of, ... 267
Fitzgerald, Captain, gallant conduct of, at Nagpore, ... 208
Fletcher, Col. sent to reinforce Col. Baillie, ... 112
Flint, Lieut., gallantly defends Wandewash, ... 114
Forde's, Col., successes in the Northern Circars, 76 ; defeats the Dutch, 79,... 80
Fort St. George, bombardment and capture of, 48 ; siege of, 74
Fort St. David, siege of, 48 ; capture and destruction of, 73
Fox's, Mr., East India Bill, ... 131
France, Isle of, taken, ... 184
Francis, Mr., one of the first Supreme Councillors, 103 ; his enmity towards Hastings, 103, ... 104
Frazer, Genl., assumes command of the British infantry, 167 ; is killed at the battle of Deeg, ... 169
French settlements, 45 ; power in India, downfall of, 77 ; possessions taken, 140 ; intrigues of the, 140 ; assist Tippoo, ... 144
Fulalee, battles on the, 256, ... 257
Fullerton's, Dr., gallant defence of Patna, 82 ; the only one saved in the massacre, ... 88
Fullarton's, Col., energetic proceedings, ... 124
Furruckabad, defeat of Holkar's cavalry at, ... 168

Page.

Futteh Khan assists Mahmud to gain the throne in Affghanistan, 240; is murdered, ... 240

Ganges, the river,... 2
Gangudhar Shastri sent as ambassador from the Guicowar to the Peishwa, 201; murder of, ... 202
Garrison, the Illustrious,... 250
Gawilghur taken, ... 161
Genoa enriched by Indian commerce, ... 37
George, Fort St., origin of, 44; siege of, 48, ... 74
Geriah, the battle of, ... 87
Ghauts, the Eastern and Western, ... 3
Ghazipore, Marquis Cornwallis dies at, ... 173
Ghazni, Mahomed's birth-place, 14; capture of, 243; recaptured by tho Affghans, 249; and by Genl. Nott, 251
Gheriah, the destruction of, ... 59
Ghor, Mahomed of, 15; situation of, ... 16
Gillespie, Genl., relieves Vellore, 178; commands a division in the first Goorkha war, 187; his death at Kalunga, ... 189
Gingee, ineffectual attack on, 56; surrender of,... ... 77
Goa, capture of, by the Portuguese, ... 41
Godavery, the river, ... 3
Godheu, Monsieur, sent out as French commissioner,.. 59
Goddard's, Genl., march to Surat, 108; his success, ... 109
Godwin, Genl., captures Martaban, ... 229
Gokla, an officer of the Peishwa, killed at Ashtee, ... 218
Golconda, Aurangzib's war againt the Rajah of, ... 32
Good Hope, the Cape of, discovered 37; is rounded by Vasco de Gama, ... 38
Goolab Sing, favourable treaty with,... 272
Goorkhas, disputes with, 184; war with, 187; besieged at Kalunga, 188; and at Jytak, 190; defeated at Maloun, 192; at Makwanpur, 195; and at Hariharpur, 195; Peace concluded with,... 196
Gooroo Govind, a Sikh leader, ... 265
Gough, Sir H., commands against the Mahrattas, 260; gains the battle of Maharajpore, 262; commands in the first Punjab war, 266; gains the battles of Moodkee, 266; Ferozeshah, 267; and Sobraon, 271; commands

Page.

in the second Punjab war, 278; fights the battles of Chillianwalla, 278; and Gujerat, 280; is superseded... 280

Governor Generals: The first, 103; Lord Cornwallis, 132; Sir J. Shore, 141; Lord Mornington, 143; Lord Cornwallis, 173; Sir G. Barlow, 173; Lord Minto, 180; Lord Moira, 186; Lord Amherst, 224; Lord W. Bentinck, 238; Lord Auckland, 240; Lord Ellenborough, 249; Sir H. Hardinge, 263; Lord Dalhousie, 274; Lord Canning, ... 289

Greeks, the, invade India, ... 13

Grey, General, gains the battle of Punniar, ... 262

Guicowar, the, an ally of the English in war against Scindia, 161; quarrels with the Peishwa, 201; murder of his ambassador,... 202

Gujerat, the battle of,... 280

Gundamuk, Genl. Pollock defeats the Affghans at, ... 250

Guntoor, Disputes about, 112; attacked by Pindarees, 198

Guzalhatty Pass, Tippoo's attack on a detachment at, ... 134

Guzerat, Krishna, the sovereign of, 9; Mahmud at, 15; Morad in, at the times of his father's illness, 28; the ruler of, quarrels with the Peishwa, ... 201

Gwalior, the storming of, 109; is given to Scindia, 174; confusion in the court and country, 259, 260; war in, 260; Peace restored at, ... 263

Hamilton, Dr. obtains privileges for the English,... ... 45

Hardinge, Sir H., appointed Governor General, 263; arrives in India, 264; is involved in war with the Sikhs, 266; his noble conduct at Ferozeshah, 268, 269; his treaty with Dhuleep Sing, 272; remainder of his stay in India, 273

Hardyman, Genl., gains the battles of Jubbulpore, ... 210

Hariharpur taken, ... 195

Harris, Genl., commands the army againt Tippoo, 145; gains the battle of Malvelly, 145; takes Seringapatam, 146

Hartley, Col., commands against Tippoo on the Western Coast, ... 135

Hastings, Warren, the Governor of Bengal, 102; effects reforms in the government of Bengal, 102; is appointed first Governor General, 103; expels the Rohillas from Oude, 103; disputes with his Council, 103; is accused

Page

of bribery by Nuncomar, 104; his arrangements with regard to the Mahrattas, 106; his conduct of the Mahratta war, 107, 108; his energetic proceedings on the invasion of Hyder, 114; goes to Benares to confer with Cheyte Sing, 127; arrests the Rajah, 128; his imminent danger, 128; escapes to Chunar, 129; his transactions with the Nabob of Oude, 129; affair of the Begums, 130; last days in Bengal, 130; his trial, and character, ... 130

Hastings, the Marquis of, becomes Governor General, 186; engages in war with the Goorkhas, 187; concludes a peace with the Nepaulese, 196; prepares for war with the Pindarees and Mahrattas, 198; differences between, and the Peishwa, 201; joins the grand army, 199; his treaty with Scindia, 213; quits India, 224

Havelock, Henry, Captain, commands right attack at Jellalabad, ... 250

Hay's, Mr., unselfish conduct, and murder at Patna, .. 88

Herat, gallant defence of,... 241

Herodotus mentioned, ... 12

Hislop, Sir T., Commander-in-chief of Madras, commands the army of the Deckan in the Mahratta war, 198; gains the battle of Mahidpoor, 213; executes the killadar of Talnere,... 220

Hobart, Lord, Governor of Madras,... 142

Hole, the Black,... 61

Hill's, Major, gallant defence of Pegu, ... 283

Himalayas, the, ... 2

Hindus, the, early civilisation of, 4; their institutions 5; their character, ... 7

Holkar, Jesuant Row, a Mahratta chief, 154; his insolence, 164; war with, 164; his flight, 164; harasses Col. Monson's retreat, 164; besieges Delhi, 167; is defeated with his cavalry, 168; his infantry defeated, 169, 170; is assisted by the Rajah of Bhurtpore, 170; joins Scindia, 173; flees to the Punjab, 174; Peace with, 174; dies mad, ... 213

Holkar, Mulhar Row, succeeds Jeswunt Row, 213; reduction of his dominions, ... 214

Holwell, Mr., one of the sufferers in the Black Hole,... 61

Page.

Honore taken, ... 122
Hooghly taken, ... 63

Humayun becomes Emperor, 21; is dethroned by Shir Shah, 21; restoration of, 22; death of, ... 23
Humberstone, Col., defeats Tippoo at Paniani, ... 121

Hyder Ali, 94; seizes the throne of Mysore, 94; alliance against, 94; bribes the Mahrattas and the Nizam, 95; is defeated at Changumma, 95; and Trinomallee, 96; and baffled at Amboor, 98; his successes against Col. Wood, 99; peace with, 100; invades the Carnatic, 111; his successes, 112, 113, 115; is defeated at Porto Novo, 115; and at Sholingur, 118; his death, ... 121
Hyderabad, struggle for the throne at, 49; Lord Minto appoints a minister at, ... 181
Hydrabad in Scinde, occupation of, 257; the battle of, 257
Hyphasis, the, the limit of Alexander's conquests, ... 13

Ibraham Lodi, the reign of, 18; is defeated by Baber, 19; is slain at Paniput, ... 19
Illustrious Garrison, the, ... 250

Indore subdued by Col. Murray, ... 170
Indus, the river, 2; Army of the, 242; disputes about the navigation of the, ... 254

Invincibles of the Deckan, ... 158
Invulnerables, Burmese, ... 229
Irawaddi, principal river in Burmah, 226; the English proceed up, 231, ... 232
Isle of France, Labourdonnais, the Governor of, 48; conquest of, ... 184
Istalif destroyed, ... 253

Jacob, Major, defeats Shere Mahomed, ... 258
Jaulnah captured by Col. Wallace, ... 170
Java, the Dutch settle in, 42; conquest of,... 184
Jehangir succeeds to the throne of Delhi, 25; marries Nur Jehan, 26; rebellions during his latter years,... ... 26
Jellalabad, Sir R. Sale forces his way to, 245; gallant defence of, ... 250
Jenkins, Mr., the Resident at Nagpore, 206; treats with

Page.

the Rajah, 207, 209; reinstates the Rajah, 211; takes him prisoner, ... 221
Jeswunt Row Holkar—*See* Holkar.
Jeswunt Row Lar besieged at Aseerghur, ... 222
Jeswunt Sing is defeated by Aurangzib, 28; his treachery against Aurangzib, ... 29
Jodpore, Appa Sahib permitted to reside at, ... 223
Jones, Lieutenant, his gallant conduct at Corregaum,... 218
Jubbulpore, the battle of, ... 210
Jugduluk, Affghans repulsed at, 245, ... 250
Jumna, the, made the boundary of the English possessions, 175
Jypore, the Rajah of, is plundered by Holkar, 164; is deserted by the English, ... 175
Jyntea, arrangements regarding, ... 235
Jytak, the siege of, 190; the surrender of, ... 193

Kali, country west of the, conquered 194
Kalunga, the siege of, ... 188
Kamaon subdued, ... 193
Kamran, the ruler of Herat, ... 240
Karack, British force sent to,... 241
Kareem Khan, a Pindaree chief, 196; surrender of, ... 215
Kars, Defence of, mentioned,... 241
Keane, Sir John, commands the army of the Indus, 242; takes Ghazni, 243; and Cabul, ... 243
Kelly, Col., takes Hariharpur, ... 195
Kemendine taken, 227; the Burmese attack, ... 230
Khilji Dynasty, the, ... 16
Khurd Cabul, the pass of, cleared by Sir R. Sale, 245; Force from, reaches Cabul, ... 246
Khyber Pass, forced by General Pollock,... 250
Kirkee, the battle of, ... 204
Kishna, the river, ... 3
Knox's, Capt., march from Moorshedabad to Patna, 82; Defeats the Emperor's army, ... 83
Kota, the Rajah of, refuses admittance to Col. Monson, ... 166
Kshatriyas, the, ... 5
Kumaon, the conquest of, ... 193
Krishna, a prince of Guzerat, ... 9
Kurrachee, the port of,... 242

Page.

Kussoor, negotiations at, ... 272
Kutb-ud-dien, the reign of, ... 16
Kyloo, disaster at,... 229

Labourdonnais takes Madras, ... 48
Lahar, capture of,... 109
Lahore, near the southern frontier of Russia, 240 ; anarchy at, 265 ; English advance to, 272 ; treaty at, 272 ; English remain at, 272 ; intrigues at, ... 276
Lake, General, commands an army against Scindia, 154 ; takes Alighur, 157 ; gains the battles of Delhi, 158 ; and Laswaree, 158 ; advances against Holkar, 164 ; retires to Cawnpore, 165 ; reassembles his army, 167 pursues Holkar, and defeats him, 168 ; besieges Deeg, 170 ; and Bhurtpore, 171 ; pursues Holkar, 173 ; enters into treaty with him, 174 ; remonstrates against the peace policy, ... 175
Lally, Count de, arrives from France, 73 ; his character, 73 ; captures Fort St. David, 73 ; plunders Tanjore, 74 ; lays siege to Madras, 74 ; is defeated at Wandewash, 75 ; and at Pondicherry, 76 ; his return to France, 77 ; and trial and death, ... 77
Lambert, Commodore, is sent on a mission to Rangoon, 281
Laswaree, the battle of, ... 158
Lawrence, Major, attacks the French at Trichinopoly, 55 ; repulsed at Gingee, 56 ; his victory at Bahoor, 56 ; defends Fort St. George, ... 74
Leslie, Colonel, loiters on his march from Bengal to Poona, 108
Liffey, the, silences the batteries at Rangoon,... ... 226
Lines, the Travancore, ... 133
Littler, Sir J., commands a division at Ferozeshah, ... 262
Lloyd, General, commands against the Sonthals, ... 287
Loodiana, menaced by the Sikhs, 270 ; and relieved by Sir H. Smith, ... 270
Lucan, Lieut., destruction of, and his irregular cavalry, ... 165
Lucknow, taken, ... 90
Lushington, Major, attacks the Pindarees, ... 198

Macdowall, General, at the head of a faction at Madras, 183
Machery, the Rajah of, arrangements with, ... 175

Page.

Macnaghten, Sir William, diplomatic agent at Shah Sujah's Court, 243; receives the surrender of Dost Mahomed, 245; negotiates with Akber Khan, 247; his murder,... 248

Madras, origin of, 44; the siege of, 48, 74; Tippoo's foray at, 97; extreme danger of, 111; mutiny at,... 182

Madura the capital of Pandya, 10; an English force sent to, ... 72

Magada, kingdom of,... 9

Mahadeo Hills, Appa Sahib flees to, ... 222

Maharajpore, the battle of, ... 261

Mahé, a French settlement on the Western Coast, ... 45

Mahidpore, the battle of, ... 213

Mahmud of Ghazni invades India, 14; his last expedition, 14; besieges Somnat, 14; his stay in Guzerat, and return to Ghazni,... 15

Mahmud, dethrones his brother, and is dethroned himself, 240

Mahomed Ali, son of Anwar-ud-dien, is assisted by the English, 50; flees to Trichinopoly, 50; is there besieged, 51; is generally owned Nabob of the Carnatic, 54; is supported by the English, 72; ally of English against Hyder, 95; unsatisfactory conduct of, 140; fresh treaty with, 140; his death, ... 142

Mahomed Ghori, the reign of, ... 15

Mahomed Toghlak, the reign of, 16; his mad acts and capricious conduct,... ... ... 16, 17

Mahrattas, the rise of, 30, 34; allied with the English against Hyder, 95; war with, 106; attack the Nizam, 142; second war with, 155; are defeated at Assaye, 156; at Delhi, 158; at Laswaree, 159; and Argaum, 160; renewal of war with, 164; under Holkar, harass Colonel Monson, 166; besiege Delhi, 167; are defeated at Furruckabad, 168; and Deeg, 168; peace with, 174; renewal of war with, 204; are defeated at Kirkee, 204; at Nagpore, 209, 210; at Jubbulpore, 210; at Mahidpore, 213; and Corregaum, 216; peace with, 223; war with, 260; are defeated at Maharajpore, 262; and Punniar,... 262

Makwanpur, the battle of, ... 195

Malay Peninsula, Malacca in, captured by the Portuguese, 41

Page.

Malcolm, Sir J., on the peace policy, 175 ; commands a division at Mahidpore, 214 ; receives the Peishwa's surrender, ... 218
Malacca, capture of, by the Portuguese, ... 41
Maloun, attack on the heights of, 192 ; surrender of, ... 193
Malvelly, Tippoo defeated at, ... 145
Malwa, Vikramarka's kingdom, 10 ; is subdued, 170 ; Sir David Ochterlony, Resident in,... 235
Mama Sahib appointed Regent at Gwalior, 259 ; his dismissal, ... 259
Mangalore, gallant defence of, 123 ; treaty of, ... 125
Manipore, arrangements regarding, ... 235
Marley, Genl., commands a division in the Goorkha war,... 188
Martaban taken, 229, ... 282
Masulipatam, siege and capture of, 77 ; given to the English, 77 ; mutiny at, 183 ; desolated by the Pindarees, 197
Mathews, Genl., sent to command on the Western Coast, 122 ; takes Bednore, 123 ; his fatality, 123 ; is defeated and imprisoned, ... 123
Medows, Genl., commands against Tippoo, ... 134
Meeanee, the battle of, ... 256
Meeran murders Suraja Dowlah, 70 ; opposes Shah Alum, 82 ; his death, ... 83
Meer Cossim relieves Meer Jaffier from difficulties, 83 ; is made Nabob of Bengal, 84 ; his preparations for war, 85 ; his treatment of Ramnarrain, 86 ; engages in war with the English, 87 ; is beaten at Geriah, 87 ; commits the massacre of Patna, 88 ; flees to Oude, 89 ; and is beaten by Major Munro,... 89
Meer Jaffier conspires against Suraja Dowlah, 64 ; his vacillating conduct, 66 ; is made Nabob, 68 ; his treaty with the English, 69 ; plots against the English, 78 ; financial difficulties, 83 ; is deposed, 84 ; is again restored, 87
Melloon taken, ... 234
Menu, code of,... 5
Mergui taken, ... 229
Mewar, Rajah of, attacks Baber, ... 20
Midnapore given to the English, ... 84
Miles, Col., subdues the Tenasserim Provinces, ... 229

Page.

Minto, Lord, becomes Governor General, 180; abandons the peace policy, 181; sends embassies to foreign courts, 181; visits Madras, 184; takes Java, Bourbon and the Isle of France, 184; returns to England, ... 185

Mirzapha Jung lays claim to the throne at Hyderabad, 50; is killed in battle, ... 50

Mohabat Khan rebels against and imprisons Jehangir, 26

Moira, Lord—*See* Hastings, Marquis of.

Mokundra Pass, Col. Monson's retreat to the, ... 166

Monghir, Meer Cossim's capital, 85; is taken, ... 88

Monson, Col., one of the first Supreme Councillors, 103; opposes Warren Hastings, 103, 104; his death, ... 105

Monson, Col., pursues Holkar, 164; his advance, 165; his disastrous retreat, 166; commands at the battle of Deeg,... 169

Moodajee Bhoosla.—*See* Appa Sahib.

Moodkee, the battle of, ... 266

Moolraj, treachery of, 275; is deposed, 275; revolts, 276; is defeated by Mr. Edwards, 276; is besieged at Moultan, 277; surrenders, 277; and imprisoned for life, 280

Moorshedabad, Installation of Meer Jaffier at, 68; Mutiny at, 83; deposition of Meer Jaffier at, 84; Meer Cossim abandons, ... 85

Morad, a son of Shah Jehan, Character, 27; joins Aurungzib in rebellion, 28; defeats Dara, 28; is imprisoned, 29

Morari Row, a Mahratta chief, assists Clive, ... 53

Mornington, Lord—*See* Wellesley, Marquis.

Moultan, insurrection at, 277; siege and fall of, ... 279

Mulhar Row Holkar—*See* Holkar.

Mundesore, treaty of, ... 214

Munro, Major, commands the army in the north, 89; subdues an alarming mutiny, 89; defeats Suja Dowlah, 89, 90; commands the army on Hyder's invasion, 112; his retreat, 114; takes Negapatam, ... 119

Munro, Colonel, upholds the Ryotwary system of Revenue, 141

Munro, Colonel J., writes the Tent Contract Report, 182; is arrested, and released,... 183

Murray, Colonel, advances toward Oojein, 164; retreats, 165; advances again and is successful, ... 170

Page.

Mysore, Rajah of, assists Mahomed Ali, 55 ; claims Trichinopoly, 72 ; is seized by Hyder Ali, 94 ; invasion of, 95, 122, 135, 145 ; Rajah restored to the throne of, 148

Nadir Shah Invasion of, ... 33
Nagpore, capital of the Mahratta commander-in-chief, 34 ; affairs at, 205 ; Appa Sahib made Regent at, 206 ; description of, 207 ; attack on the English at, 207 ; the battle of, 209 ; the siege and surrender of, 210 ; renewal of at, 210 ; new Rajan made, 223 ; annexation of, ... 286
Nalagerh, siege and abandonment of, ... 191
Nalapani, siege of, ... 188
Nanak, the Sikh teacher, ... 265
Napier, Sir C., commands in Scinde, 254 : gains the battle of Meeanee, 256 ; and of Hyderabad, 257 ; appointed Commissioner in Scinde, 258 ; appointed Commander-in-chief, ... 280
Napoleon in communication with Tippoo,... 144
Nassuck, Trimbakji caught at,... 219
Nazir Jung, claimant of the throne at Hyderabad, ... 50
Negapatam, a Dutch settlement in India, 42 ; capture of, 119
Neilgherries, the, ... 3
Nellore, English factory at Dugarajapatam in the district of, 44 ; unsuccessful attack on,... 72
Nepaulese, disputes with the, ... 184
Nepaul, invasion of, 187, 188 ; description of, 188 ; second invasion of,... 198
Nerbudda, the river, ... 3
Nizam-ool-Mulk, becomes independent, 34 ; contest about the title of, 46 ; arrangements made with the, 151 ; gives up the Ceded Districts, 151 ; cedes Berar, ... 286
Nizam Ali, an ally of the English, 94 ; invades Mysore, 95 ; his treachery, and defection, 95 ; defeated at Trinomallee, 96 ; rejoins the English, 97 ; makes war against Tippoo,... 144
Norford, Capt., his gallant behavionr at Deeg, ... 169
Northern Circars, the, 3 ; operations in, 76, 77 ; given to the English, except Guntoor, ... 86
Nott, Genl., occupies Candahar, 249 ; advances to Cabul, 251

Page.

Nuncomar, Rajah, accuses Warren Hastings, 104 ; his trial and execution, ... 105
Nundidroog taken, 136 ; mutiny at, ... 180
Nur Jehan, the beautiful and ambitious Empress of Jehangir, ... 26

Ochterlony, Col., gallantly defends Delhi, 167 ; commands a division in the Gookha campaign, 187 ; his successes, 190, 191 ; attacks Maloun, 192 ; and captures it, 193 ; commands during the second campaign, 194 ; turns the Chiria-ghati Pass, 194 ; gains the battle of Makwanpur, 195 ; is the Resident at Delhi, 235 ; espouses the cause of the young Rajah of Bhurtpore, 236 ; and resigns, ... 236
Omdut-ul-Omra, becomes Nabob of the Carnatic, 142 ; his death, ... 151
Omichund, nearly defeats the plot against Suraja Dowlah, 65, his avarice, 65 ; is outwitted by Clive, 65, 69 ; his melancholy death, ... 69
Oojein, the city of Vikramarka's capital, 10 ; Col. Murray sent against, 164 ; is taken,... 170
Orissa, under the Government of Aliverdy Khan, 60 ; given to Meer Jaffier, 68 ; passes into possession of the English, 91
Ormuz, capture of, by the Portuguese, ... 41
Oude, 8 ; becomes independent, 34 ; Rohillas driven from, 103 ; arrangements with the Nabob of, 129 ; affair of the Begums of, 130 ; disputed succession at, 143 ; treaty with the Nabob of, 153 ; condition of, 287 ; religious war in, 287 ; annexation of,... 288
Outram, Major, is attacked by the Ameers of Scinde, 256 ; made a K. C. B., and appointed Chief Commissioner of Oude, ... 289

Pagahm, the battle of, ... 234
Palghaut, advance to, 121 ; capture of, ... 124
Pandus, the, ... 9
Pandya, kingdom of, ... 10
Paniani, Tippoo defeated at, ... 121
Paniput, the first battle of, ... 18
Parliament, the British, legislates for India, 102, ... 131

Page.

Patna, sieges of, 78, 82, 87 ; the massacre of, 88 ; battle near, 83, ... 89
Patterson's, Lieut., gallant conduct at Corregaum, ... 218
Pearse's, Col., admirable march from Bengal to Madras, 118
Pegu, gallant defence of the town of, ... 283
Pegu, the conquest and annexation of, ... 283
Peishwa, or prime minister of the Mahrattas, office of, 34 ; disputes about, 105 ; is abolished, ... 219
Peishwa, treachery of Baji Row, the, 196, 201 ; is restored to throne, 154 ; his continuance of Trimbakji, 201 ; disputes with the Guicowar, 201 ; is overawed by the Resident, 203 ; signs a new treaty, 203 ; continues his intrigues, 204 ; attacks the Residency, 204 ; is defeated at Kirkee, 204 ; flees from Poona, 205 ; his flight, 216 ; surrenders, 219 ; receives a pension, ... 219
Pennar, the river, ... 3
Perron, M., deserts Scindia's service, ... 157
Persia, Humayun flees to, 22 ; embassy to the Shah of, 182 ; Russian counsels in, ... 240
Persians invade India, 12, 33 ; besiege Herat, ... 241
Persian Gulf, Ormuz in the, captured by the Portuguese, 41 ; an English force sent to, ... 241
Petersburgh, St., the Russian capital, far from southern frontier of Russia, ... 240
Pigot's, Mr, gallant defence of Fort St. George, ... 74
Pindarees, the, 185 ; 187 ; 188 ; 197 ; make a foray in the Company's territories, 196 ; are attacked, 198 ; and extirpated, ... 223
Pittapore, battle near, ... 77
Pitt's, Mr., East India Bill, ... 131
Plassey, the battle of, ... 67
Pollilore, actions at, 113, ... 118
Pollock, General, at Peshawur, 249 ; relieves Sir R. Sale at Jellalabad, 250 ; defeats the Affghans, and advances to Cabul, ... 251
Pondicherry, the French capital in India, 45, 47 ; siege of, 48 : and capture of,... 76
Poona, the capital of the Peishwa, 34 ; French officers at, 107 ; advance to, and retreat from, 107 ; saved by General Wellesley, 154 ; treachery of the Peishwa at, 201 ;

Page.

description of, 204; attack on the English at, 204; battle near, 204, 216; is taken, ... 205
Poornia, the Naib of, assists the Emperor, 83; is defeated by the English, ... 83
Poorundher, the treaty of,... 106
Popham, Captain, takes Lahar and Gwalior, ... 109
Porto Novo plundered by Hyder, 112; the battle of, ... 115
Portuguese, the, ... 38
Porus opposes Alexander, ... 13
Pottinger's, Lieut., gallant conduct at Herat,... ... 241
Prome, advance to, ... 232
Punjab, the geographical position of, 2; Alexander invades, 13; forms a part of Camran's dominions, 21; becomes independent, 34; Holkar flees to, 174; Appa Sahib flees to, 222; affairs in, 265; first war in, 266; conquest of, 273; second war in, 276; conquest and annexation of, ... 280
Pulicat, one of the Dutch possessions in India, 42; Detachment marches by, 117; capture of, ... 119
Punderpore, Gangudher Shastri murdered at,... ...201, 202
Punniar, the battle of, ... 262
Purwan, the battle of, ... 244

Ragoba claims the office of Peishwa, 106; is supported by the English, 107; surrender, ... 108
Rajah Sahib besieges Arcot, 53; is defeated by Clive, 54, 55
Rajmahal, insurrection in, ... 286
Rajputs, the, 19; are persecuted by Aurangzib, ... 32
Rama, ... 8
Ramgerh taken, ... 191
Ramnarrain, defends Patna, 78; is defeated by the Emperor, 82; ill-treated and murdered by Meer Cossim, 86
Ramnuggur, the action at,... 278
Rangoon, capture of, 226; position of the English at, 227; Bandoola's attack on, repulsed, 230; is set on fire, 281; retreat of Burmese from, 231; occurrences at, 281; second capture of, ... 282
Ratangerh, near Maloun, occupied by the English, ... 191
Read, Col., initiates the ryotwary system of revenue, ... 141
Regulating Act, ... 102

Page
Revenue systems, ... 140
Rohillas expelled from Oude, ... 103
Runjeet Sing, contracts an alliance with the English, 242
his death, ... 265
Russian invasion, fears of, 181, 239 ; intrigues, ... 241
Ryotwary system, ... 141

Saadut Ali made Nabob of Oude,... 143
Sadras, capture of, ... 119
Salabut Jung is made Nizam, 50 ; is dethroned by his brother, Nizam Ali, ... 94
Sabbye, treaty of, ... 110
Sale, Sir Robert, proceeds against Dost Mahomed, 244 ; forces his way to Jellalabad, 245, 246 ; his gallant defence of Jellalabad, 249, 250 ; meets the rescued prisoners, 252 ; his death at Moodkee, ... 267
Salivahana, ... 11
Salsette, disputes about, 105 ; is given to the English, ... 106
Sandracottus, king of Magada, 9, ... 13
Sanga, the Rajah of Mewar, opposes Baber, ... 20
Sattara, the Rajah of, restored, ... 219
Scinde, geographical position of, 2 ; Alexander the Great passes through, 13 ; English army passes through, 242 ; the Ameers of, 254 ; disturbances in, 255 ; war in, 256 ; annexation of, ... 258
Scindia, a powerful Mahratta chief, makes war on Holkar, 154 ; war with, 155 ; is defeated at Assaye, 156 ; Delhi, 158 ; and Laswaree, 159 ; truce with, 160 ; is defeated at Argaum, 160 ; peace with, 161 ; assists Holkar, 173 ; peace with, 174 ; intrigues against the English, 196 ; is overawed by the English in the Mahratta war, 213 ; alliance with the English, 213 ; his underhand dealing, 222 ; his death, ... 259
Secunderabad, mutinous proceedings at, 180, 184 ; French officers at, disarmed, ... 144
Seedasere, Tippoo defeated at,... 145
Seetaduldee Hills, gallant defence of the, ... 207
Seleucus, one of Alexander's successors, 9, ... 13
Selim Prince—*See* Jehangir.

Page.

Sepoy corps, formation of,... 49
Seringapatam, Lord Cornwallis's advance to, 135 ; retreat from, 135 ; first siege of, 137 ; last siege of, 146 ; kept by the English, 148 ; description of, 148 ; mutiny at, 183
Seringham, the French besieged at, ... 56
Seroor, party sent from, to Poona, 216 ; Staunton's triumphant return to, ... 218
Shah Alum invades Bengal, 77, 81 ; becomes Emperor, 81 ; is defeated by Col. Calliaud, 82, 83 ; and by Major Carnac, 84 ; makes war on the English, 89 ; his defeat and surrender, 89 ; gives a grant of Sovereignty to the English, 91 ; released from the Mahrattas, ... 158
Shah Jehan accedes to the throne of Delh, 26 ; his dangerous illness, 27 ; rebellion of his sons, 27 ; is imprisoned by Aurangzib, 29 ; his death, ... 30
Shah Mahomed, an Ameer of Scinde, defeated, ... 258
Shah Sujah is dethroned and exiled, 240 ; Lord Auckland espouses his cause, 242 ; is reinstated, 242 ; returns to Cabul, 243 ; Affghan chiefs revolt against, 245 ; is murdered,... 252
Shakespear, Sir Richmond, meets the English prisoners in Cabul, ... 251
Shapooree, disputes about,... 225
Shelton, General, assumes the command at Cabul ... 247
Shere Mahomed, an Ameer of Scinde, defeated, ... 258
Shere Sing sent to Moultan, 277 ; his defection, 277 ; is defeated at Gujerat, ... 280
Shir Shah dethrones Humayun, 21 ; his short, but useful reign, 22, ...35
Sholingur, the battle of, ... 118
Shore, Sir John, becomes Governor General, 141 ; his peace policy, 141 ; his arrangement at Oude,... 143
Shuja, a son of Shah Jehan, character of, 27 ; his rebellion and defeat, 27 ; is defeated by Aurangzib, 29 ; is treacherously betrayed and put to death, ... 29
Sikhs, rise of the, 34 ; refuse assistance to Holkar, 174 ; invade British India, 265, 266 ; are defeated at Moodkee, 267 ; Ferozeshah, 267 ; Aliwal, 270 ; and Sobraon, 271 ; conquest of, 273 ; second war with, 276 ; are de-

Page.

feated at Cillianwalla, 279 ; and Gujerat, 280 ; are entirely subdued, ... 280
Sikri, the battle of, ... 20
Silistria, the defence of, mentioned, ... 241
Sirdar Khan Sing appointed governor of Moultan, ... 275
Slave Kings, the, ... 16
Smith, Col., commands the army against Hyder, 95 ; his retreat, 95 ; defeats Hyder at Changumma, 95 ; at Trinomallee, 96 ; and Amboor, 98 ; invades Mysore, 99 ; is superseded, 99 ; resumes command, ... 100
Smith, General Lionel, commands a division of the Deckan army, 204 ; advances to reinforce the troops at Poona, 205 ; pursues the Peishwa,... 216
Smith, Sir H., gains the battle of Aliwal,... 270
Sobraon, the battle of,... 271
Soliman, Dara's son, defeats Shuja, ... 27
Somnat besieged, ... 14
Sonthal insurrection, the, ... 286
Soomba Wongee, the Burmese commander, is defeated near Rangoon, ... 228
Sophia, the crew of, captured by Burmese, ... 225
Spice Islands, the Dutch commerce with the,... ... 41
Staunton's, Captain, victory at Corregaum, 216 ; triumphant return to Seroor,... 218
Stevenson, Col., commands the Nizam's force against Scindia, ... 155
Stuart's, General, inaction, 121 ; besieges Cuddalore, ... 122
Stuart, General, defeats Tippoo at Seedasere, 145 ; joins the main army, ... 146
Suddoosam, the battle of,... 276
Sudras, the, ... 5
Suja Dowla, Nabob of Oude, invades Bengal, 77, 81 ; is made Grand Vizier of the Empire, 82 ; makes war on the English, 89 ; is defeated, 89, 90 ; surrenders, 90 ; is assisted by Warren Hastings in expelling the Rohillas, 103 ; his death,... 104
Sumroo, commands Meer Cossim's army, 87 ; perpetrates the massacre of Patna, ... 88
Surajah Dowlah, accession and character of, 60 ; attacks Calcutta, 61 ; his indifference to the horrors of the

Page.

Black Hole, 62 ; is defeated by Clive, 63 ; his inconsistent conduct, 64 ; the plots against him, 64, 65 ; is defeated at Plassey, 67 ; his flight, capture, and murder,... 70
Surajgerh, attack on, a fort near Maloun, ... 192
Surat, French attempt to found a settlement at, 45 ; Col., Goddard's admirable march to,... 108
Sutlej, the limit of Alexander's conquest, 13 ; the Sikhs cross the, 266 ; are driven across, 269 ; recross, 269 ; are finally driven across, ... 272
Suttee, rendered penal, ... 239
Sylhet, attack by the Burmese on, ... 225
Syriam, capture of, ... 229

Talnere, the capture of, 220 ; the Killadar of, executed, 221
Tamerlane, invasion of, 16 ; Nadir Shah's incursion similar to, ... 33
Tanjore, petty war in, 48 ; invaded by Lally, 74 ; invaded by Hyder, ... 115
Tanna, Trimbakji's escape from, ... 219
Tapti, the river, 3 ; Fort Talnere on the, captured, ... 220
Tavoy, capture of, ... 229
Tegnapatam, Fort St. David built at, ... 44
Tellicherry gallantly defended, ... 121
Tenasserim Provinces subdued, 229 , ceded to the English, 235
Tent Contract, the,... 182
Tegeen, Affghans defeated at, ... 251
Thekia Wongee, the Burmese commander, defeated, ... 228
Thiagur taken, 77 ; is taken by Hyder, ... 115
Tinnevelly, a portion of the kingdom of Pandya, 10 ; an English detachment sent to, ... 72
Timur, the invasion of, ... 17
Tippoo, his foray to Madras, 97 ; is present at Col. Baillie's defeat, 113 ; at Col. Brathwaite's, 120 ; goes to the Western Coast, 121 ; accedes to the throne, 122 ; returns to the Western Coast, 123 ; takes Bednore, 123 ; besieges Mangalore, 123 ; peace with, 125 ; prepares for war, 132 ; his savage warfare on the Western Coast, 132 ; his attack on the Travancore Lines, 133 ; invades Travancore, 134 ; engages in war with the English, 134 ;

Page.

his fears for Seringapatam, 135 ; is besieged in Seringapatam, 136 ; sues for peace, 137 ; prepares for his last war, 144 ; is defeated, 145 ; is besieged in Seringapatam, 146 ; his death, 147 ; his sons at Vellore, ... 179

Toghlak, the House of,... 16
Tonk Rampura taken, ... 164
Toolsye Bhye, one of Jeswunt Row Holkar's concubines, is in favour of the English alliance, 213 ; murder of,... 213
Travancore, Tippoo's attack on, 132 ; his invasion of, ... 134

Trichinopoly besieged by the French, 51 ; relieved by the English, 55, 56 ; taken possession of by the English, 56 ; is claimed by the Rajah of Mysore, 72 ; besieged by the French, and relieved by Capt. Calliaud, ... 72
Trimbakji Dainglia, his elevation and intrigues, 201 ; murders the Guicowar's ambassador, 202 ; is imprisoned, 202 ; escapes, 202 ; and continues his intrigues, 202 ; reward offered for his apprehension, 203 ; is caught a second time and imprisoned, ... 219
Trinomalee, the battle of, ... 96
Tripartite Treaty, the, ... 242

Upton, Col., sent to negotiate with the Mahrattas, ... 106

Valiant, General, takes the village of Maharajpore, ... 262
Vansittart, Mr., becomes Governor of Bengal, 84 ; dethrones Meer Jaffier, and makes Meer Cossim Nabob, 84 ; abandons Ramnarrain to Meer Cossim, ... 86
Vasco de Gama's first voyage to India, 38 ; lands at Calicut, 39 ; proceeds to India a second time, ... 40
Veishyas, the, ... 5

Vellore is besieged by Hyder, 114 ; relieved by Sir E. Coote, 119 ; army assembled at, 144 ; the mutiny at,... 177
Venice enriched by Indian commerce,... 37

Vikramarka, king of Malwa, 10 ; said to have been conquered by Salivahana, ... 11
Vindhya mountains, ... 2
Vizier Ali succeeds to the throne of Oude, and is deposed, 143 ; creates a disturbance at Benares, 152 ; and murders the Resident, ... 152

Page.

Wallace, Col., takes Chandore and Jaulnah, ... 170

Wallajabad, mutinous proceedings at, ... 180

Wandewash is taken by Coote, 75 ; relief of, 75 ; the battle of, 75 ; brave defence of, 114 ; is relieved by Coote, ...114, 119

Warren Hastings—*See* Hastings.

Watson, Admiral, commands the fleet sent to Calcutta, 63 ; refuses to sign the papers for deceiving Omichund, ... 65

Watts, Mr., the English resident at Moorshedabad, ... 64, 65

Wellesley, Col., commands the Nizam's troops against Tippoo, 144 ; takes charge of Seringapatam after the assault, 148 ; is made Commissioner of Mysore, 148 ; proceeds against Scindia, 154 ; gains the battles of Assaye, 156 ; and Argaum, 160 ; takes Gawilghur, ... 161

Wellesley, Marquis, becomes Governor General, 143 ; his policy, 143 ; makes war on Tippoo, 144 ; his arrangements with regard to Mysore, 145 ; with the Nizam, 155 ; the Nabob of the Carnatic, 151 ; with regard to Zemaun Shah's invasion, 152 ; with the Nabob of Oude, 153 ; and the Peishwa, 154 ; makes war on Scindia, 155 ; aud on Holkar, ... 168

Wellington, the Duke of—*See* Wellesley, Col.

Western Ghauts, the, ... 3

Whish, Genl., conducts the siege of Moultan, 277 ; takes Moultan, ... 279

William, Fort, origin of, 45 ; repaired, 60 ; siege and capture of, ... 61

Wood, Col., captures some of Hyder's fortresses, 99 ; supersedes Col. Smith, ... 99

Wood, Genl. G. S., commands a division in the Goorkha war, ... 188

Wylie's, Dr., gallant conduct at Corregaum, ... 218

Yandabo, peace with the Burmese concluded at, ... 235

Zamorin, the ruler of Calicut, 39 ; his contests with the Portuguese, ... 39, 40, 41

Zemaun Shah, threatened invasion of,... 152

Zemindary system of Revenue, ... 140

BY THE SAME AUTHOR.

I.

A GEOGRAPHY:

CONTAINING

A CONCISE ACCOUNT

OF THE

VARIOUS COUNTRIES OF THE EARTH,

WITH A

MORE DETAILED DESCRIPTION OF INDIA.

II.

A HISTORY OF ENGLAND:

PRINCIPALLY INTENDED FOR THE

INHABITANTS OF INDIA.

Price Fourteen Annas.